Pathways to Privatization in Education

Contemporary Studies in Social and Policy Issues in Education: The David C. Anchin Series

(formerly Social and Policy Issues in Education:
The David C. Anchin Series)

Kathryn M. Borman, Series Editor

Assessment, Testing, and Evaluation in Teacher Education
edited by Suzanne W. Soled, 1995

Children Who Challenge the System
edited by Anne M. Bauer and Ellen M. Lynch, 1993

Contemporary Issues in U.S. Education
edited by Kathryn M. Borman, Piyushi Swami, and Lonnie D. Wagstaff, 1991

Critical Education for Work: Multidisciplinary Approaches
edited by Richard D. Lakes, 1994

Early Childhood Education: Policy Issues for the 1990s
edited by Dolores Stegelin, 1992

*Effective Schooling for Disadvantaged Students:
School-based Strategies for Diverse Student Populations*
edited by Howard Johnston and Kathryn M. Borman, 1992

Home Schooling: Political, Historical, and Pedagogical Perspectives
edited by Jan Van Galen and Mary Anne Pitman, 1991

*Implementing Educational Reform: Sociological Perspectives
on Educational Policy*
edited by Kathryn M. Borman, Peter W. Cookson, Jr.,
Alan R. Sadovnik, and Joan Z. Spade, 1996

Informing Faculty Development for Teacher Educators
edited by Kenneth R. Howey and Nancy L. Zimpher, 1994

In preparation:

Pathways to Privatization in Education

by

Joseph Murphy
Scott W. Gilmer
Richard Weise
Ann Page

Vanderbilt University

Ablex Publishing Corporation
Greenwich, Connecticut
London, England

Printed in the United States of America

Library of Congress Cataloging-in-Publication Data

Pathways to privitization in education / by Joseph Murphy ... [et al.].
      p. cm. — (Contemporary studies in social and policy issues in education)
      Includes bibliographical references (p.) and index.
      ISBN 1-56750-363-2 (cloth). — ISBN 1-56750-364-0 (pbk.)
      1. Privitization in education—United States. 2. Educational vouchers—United States. 3. Home schooling—United States.
      I. Murphy, Joseph, 1949-   . II. Series
LB2806.36.P38 1997
379.3'2'0973—dc21   97–30771
                                                                          CIP

Ablex Publishing Corporation   Published in the U.K. and Europe by:
P.O. Box 5297   JAI Press Ltd.
55 Old Post Road #2   38 Tavistock Street
Greenwich, CT 06831   Covent Garden
                                                      London WC2E 7PB
                                                      England

To the sunshine girl from Codicil Cove

Contents

One of the means by which democracies continually redefine themselves is through debates regarding the purpose and operation of the education system. (Guthrie, 1996a, p. 2)

The privatization of the schools would symbolize a final retreat from the already faded ideal of bringing the disparate children of a community under a common roof (Starr, 1987, p. 135).

Privatization of educational opportunities ... will exacerbate the division of the wealthy and the poor in the United States. (Clark, 1996, p. 5)

Opponents of privatization say that such experiments show no tangible successes—and little promise. But even more ardently, these education experts take issue with the principles of privatization. (Avenoso, 1995, p. 79)

The present system of "socialized education" has failed, and some kind of new departure, either "capitalist" or "syndicalist," is needed. (Jencks, 1966, p. 27)

Nowhere is the problem of monopoly more serious and competition more needed than in education (Savas, 1987, p. 252). Put simply, the nation desperately needs new ways to conduct the business of educating the young. Entrepreneurial activity must be at the top of any reformer's list (Doyle, 1994b, p. 51).

I believe that the only way to make a major improvement in our educational system is through privatization to the point at which a substantial fraction of all educational services are rendered to individuals by private enterprises. Nothing else will destroy or even greatly weaken the power of the current educational establishment—a necessary precondition for radical improvement in our educational system. And nothing else will provide the public schools with the competition that will force them to improve in order to hold their clientele. (Friedman, 1995, p. 70)

Privatization can serve a useful purpose. It also carries some dangers. The effort should be to secure the former while avoiding the latter. (Kolderie, 1991, p. 260)

The appropriateness and success of using a particular privatization option is *highly situational.* Success depends on many factors that are individual to the particular public agency, in the particular location and at the particular time. (Hatry, 1991, p. 262)

In education, we suffer from a lack of good evidence on the effects of privatization. (Gormley, 1991b, p. 308)

The question is, therefore, whether the values—human, intellectual and spiritual—which are promoted by the two sides, can be brought into compatibility. If they can, then the effort should be made urgently, before yet more damage is done to all our educational institutions and relationships. If it cannot, again it is better we know soon, so that we can pick our side. (Tomlinson, 1986, p. 214)

1

Understanding Privatization

In the general debate over the private provision of public services, schools and education have been central topics. (Levin, 1987, p. 628)

Engaged in the ongoing process of educational improvement, education policymakers and school administrators increasingly are considering the private sector as a resource to obtain expertise and cost-effective services. ("Sobis network to manage public school," 1995, p. 1)

For a variety of reasons which we discuss in detail throughout this volume, market-oriented improvement efforts are becoming increasingly visible on the educational reform landscape. In particular, privatization strategies, such as vouchers and contracting out, are receiving considerable attention at all levels of educational governance and administration. Our objective in this volume is to help the educational community develop a deeper understanding of the privatization movement in general and the major pathways to privatization in particular. To accomplish that task, we devote this introductory chapter to an analysis of the concept of privatization writ large. Subsequent chapters explore the five approaches to privatization that have the greatest applicability to education: vouchers, self-help (home schooling), contracting out, and deregulation.

This introductory chapter[1] begins with an explanation of why privatization is such an important issue and a "hugely controversial" (Applebome, 1994a, p. 83) topic. The balance of the chapter is then devoted to forging a deeper understanding of privatization. We undertake that assignment in three ways. First, we examine the various forms that privatization takes and the multitude of objectives it is designed to achieve. Second, we analyze the forces that are pushing privatization to the center of efforts to reform the public sector. And third, we review the intellectual foundations that support privatization.

AN IMPORTANT AND CONTENTIOUS TOPIC

Today privatization has become one of the most interesting, provocative, and controversial subjects in public education. (Hunter, 1995a, p. 137)

Privatization is, to put it mildly, a "hot topic" in the economic, political, and managerial realms of public service provision and is much in "popular fashion" (Applebome, 1994b, p. 86)—"much in discussion and highly controversial" (Kolderie, 1991, p. 250). The ideology of privatization has, according to Hardin (1989), descended on the debate about public service "like a low-flying fog" (p. 4): "All across the country, state and local officials—liberals and conservatives alike—are jumping aboard the privatization bandwagon" (Worsnop, 1992, p. 979). In particular, there is growing interest in the application of privatization to the social services (Savas, 1987). We agree with the President's Commission on Privatization (1988) that it "may well be seen by future historians as one of the most important developments in American political and economic life of the late 20th century" (p. 251). In short, it is an important topic. We believe that there are two fundamental reasons why this is the case.

First, starting with the larger societal context, the literature supports the conclusion that we are engaged in a fundamental debate about and a reengineering of the appropriate social, political, and economic foundations of the nation. The moorings that have supported us for the past century are likely to give way—many would say are giving way—to new (or revisited) social, economic, and political perspectives. In many ways, the liberal democratic state is being dismantled, and the foundations for a new era are being poured. From this angle, Reagan and Thatcher were not simply figures in a cyclical production but rather harbingers of a "fundamental political and economic rethinking that today is reassessing the roles of government and the private sector in the modern welfare state" (President's Commission on Privatization, 1988, p. xii). It can be argued that privatization is one of the most significant and most tangible products of this new political-social-economic algorithm. It also provides a remarkable window by which to view the reweaving of the fabric that holds us together as a nation.

Turning directly to education leads us to the second explanation for the importance of privatization. The school reform movement of the last decade in many ways marks the struggle to move from one educational era to another—from an industrial to a post-industrial system of schooling. That fight or quest is defined by basic changes in the three operational dimensions of schools—the technical core level, the managerial and governance level, and the institutional level. At the technical core level, the change is from behaviorally grounded to social constructivist anchored views of learning and teaching. At the managerial level, the shift is from hierarchically grounded to community anchored perspectives on organizations. And at the institutional level, the evolution is from views of schooling grounded in conceptions of public monopolies to market-sensitive conceptions of education. Privatization and privatization-flavored initiatives largely define this marketization theme. In short, privatization is at both the core of the new political-economic axis supporting society and a foundational element in the reform of education.

As one becomes enmeshed in the privatization literature, it does not take much time to conclude that "views about privatization's virtues and pitfalls...vary widely" (Hirsch, 1991, p. 123). "The anecdotes are endless, and each has its own seemingly unequivocal conclusion. Privatization of public services is either the greatest innovation in government management since Benjamin Franklin's first American fire company or an insidious means of destroying the public work force" (Darr, 1991, p. 60). "Whether you want to prove that public ownership is good and private ownership is bad, or vice versa, there is a constant and abundant supply of triumphs and scandals to bolster your case" (Martin, 1993, p. 7). On the one hand, we hear from proponents who maintain that privatization is the cure to the acute economic and political problems that confront many nations, states, and localities. Inspecting the same phenomenon, skeptics reach a completely different conclusion. At a minimum, they maintain that "public ownership...is not the uniform disaster that the privatization movement makes it out to be" (Starr, 1991, p. 30). More forcefully, they argue that "privatization is class-based violence" (Fine, 1993, p. 38). Not surprisingly, they view privatization with a more jaundiced eye than do proponents. Thus we have a movement that "in the eyes of some is the cure for an anemic, inefficient economy; in the eyes of others, privatization is bad medicine that hurts workers, interferes with real accountability to consumers, and prevents women and other minorities from climbing up the social ladder" (Hirsch, 1991, p. 123).

It is important to remember that these disparate reviewers do not come to the analysis unencumbered with deep-seated beliefs and values about the phenomenon under scrutiny (Guthrie, 1996a). In addition, they often employ different yardsticks to measure the salutary or harmful effects of privatization. Even when they use similar criteria, the weights they apply to these standards often vary. Equally important, the complexity of privatization encourages analysts to break off manageable pieces of the puzzle for inspection. Reviewers studying these discrete parts can fall prey to what Starr (1987) labels "heroically selective attention" (p. 128). Thus "advocates of more or less privatization frequently talk past one another because they are talking about different phenomena" (Van Horn, 1991, p. 261). Finally, because privatization involves "gainers and losers" (Bell & Cloke, 1990, p. 24), how one, or one's reference group, is affected may shape the frames used in analysis.

Privatization means different things to different people (Florestano, 1991), and it can unfold in a variety of settings. It represents a complex cultural, political, legal, and economic equation (Bell & Cloke, 1990). It has political, technical, strategic, and ideological dimensions. It comes in a myriad of forms, from asset sales to vouchers. Privatization is proposed as a strategy to meet an almost limitless set of objectives, from shrinking the overall size of government to enhancing the technical efficiency of specific public sector services. For some it is an end in itself; for others it is the means to other valued outcomes (Savas, 1987). "Nothing [about the process of privatization] is either certain or clear-cut" (Darr, 1991, p. 60).

One of the most troubling aspects of privatization is the extent to which the "discussion of government activities runs instantaneously into a barrier of very strongly held ideas" (Tullock, 1988, p. 70)—ideas that "confound dispassionate public discussion" (Shannon, 1995, p. 75). In particular, "arguments [for or against it] are often advanced by special interest groups" (Hirsch, 1991, p. 65). Another is the extent to which analysts have cloaked themselves in the mantle of ideology. The debate has been "fundamentally ideological" (Ismael & Vaillancourt, 1988, p. vii), undertaken by "acolytes" (Hardin, 1989, p. 5) on the left and right imbued with an "ideological fervor" (De Hoog, 1984, p. 15), "hurling political slogans back and forth" (Van Horn, 1991, p. 261). As a result, while both sides address relevant issues, they often "do so in a highly lopsided manner and possibly incorrectly" (Hirsch, 1991, p. 65).

Equally troubling, and of critical importance as we examine implications for education, is the fact that "the political and organizational contexts of contracting out have been largely ignored in the empirical research" (De Hoog, 1984, p. 11). Despite acknowledgments that the "resolution of the assignment problem is site specific" (Ross, 1988, p. xiv)—that "the feasibility of privatization should be determined on a site specific basis" (Goldman & Mokuvos, 1991, p. 26; see also Lieberman, 1989)—unanchored cross-locality (Hemming & Mansoor, 1988) and cross-sector claims are commonplace in the literature. As we ponder the application of privatization concepts to education, it is important to remember that no universal assertions are possible (Donahue, 1989) and that lessons from one sector of activity must be applied with caution to other public services: "What works in one place or in one circumstance doesn't necessarily work somewhere else" (Darr, 1991, p. 60).

Much of what we have described above casts a long shadow over assessments of privatization initiatives. Many of the studies are "based on small and unsystematic sets of observations and on relatively primitive methodologies" (Donahue, 1989, p. 133). This work "invite[s] ideological rivals to brandish equally dubious statistical studies demonstrating the opposite point" (p. 133). This trading of stories (Martin, 1993) or "argument by anecdote and…selective statistics" (Donahue, 1989, p. 133), while common, is not particularly helpful.

Even when higher quality studies are available, the assessment of privatization remains problematic. Evaluations often play out outside "the grand ideology and narrow electoral calculations [that] form an inescapable backdrop against which privatisation must be assessed" (Bell & Cloke, 1990, p. 8; see also Bailey, 1987). Concomitantly, while it is desirable that "*inquiry* into privatization ... be multidisciplinary in nature ... much of the privatization debate has focused on cost containment—the province of economics" (Gormley, 1991a, p. 4): "Debates about the merits of privatization usually focus exclusively on the question of efficiency: is it cheaper to deliver a public service through a private vendor as opposed to a government agency?" (Van Horn, 1991, p. 262). Other relevant criteria for evaluating privatization—such as effectiveness, equity, and accountability—are often ignored (Ross, 1988). Thus the larger and more relevant macro-level criterion of "social efficiency" (Hirsch, 1991, p. 6) is subordinated to the issue of technical efficiency. Even when multiple criteria are brought to bear on privatization decisions, since "they are not all measured in the same units" (Ross, 1988, p. 19), analysts have a difficult time aggregating assessment findings. Finally, even when all goes well, empirical comparisons in this area "are messy, tentative and hedged about with conditions" (Donahue, 1989, p. 57). All of this analysis supports our claim that privatization is a contentious topic.

DEFINING PRIVATIZATION

Another complicating factor in a possible shift toward privatization is that ... there is no universal agreement on its meaning. (Russo, Sandidge, Shapiro, & Harris, 1995, p. 129)

One useful way to develop a deeper understanding of privatization is to define the concept. The most straightforward and informative way to engage this task is to examine the objectives that privatization is intended to meet and the various forms that it takes.

Objectives

To really see the concept of privatization, one must examine the goals of this policy framework. It is at this level—as well as during implementation—that much of the complexity of privatization becomes evident. Privatization is, according to its supporters, a policy tool designed to reach an enormous array of goals. As Donahue (1989) relates, "the word can signify something as broad as shrinking the welfare state while promoting self-help and volunteerism, or something as narrow as substituting a team of private workers for an all-but-identical team of civil servants to carry out a particular task" (pp. 5–6). The major goals of privatization are of two types: macro- and micro-level objectives.

Macro-Level Objectives

Macro-level goals refer to changes that are designed to affect the larger political and economic structures of the nation, to redefine the algorithm by which markets and governments address fundamental questions about the allocation and provision of goods and services.

Some authors perceive of privatization as a vehicle to help "restore government to its fundamental purpose to steer, not to man the oars" (Savas, 1987, p. 290). Others who view "privatization as part of a wider neo-liberal policy package" (Martin, 1993, p. 99) maintain that a key objective, for better or worse, is to reconstruct the "liberal democratic state" (Starr, 1991, p. 25), to redefine the operational "set of assumptions about the capacities of democratic government and the appropriate sphere of common obligation" (p. 25). Privatization here is viewed, in particular, as a vehicle to overcome the "dependency culture" (Martin, 1993, p. 48) associated with a social order dominated by government activity. Another aim is to depoliticize service operations (Hanke & Dowdle, 1987). As Pirie (1988) argues, "the actual transfer to the private sector…can take the service into the purely economic world and out of the political world…freeing it from the political forces which acted upon it in the state sector" (pp. 52-53) and overcoming "structural weaknesses inherent in the nature of public sector supply" (p. 20).

Perhaps the central purpose and most highly touted objective of privatization is "reduction in the size of the public sector" (Pack, 1991, p. 284), "reducing public spending and taxation as proportions of gross domestic product" (Hardin, 1989, p. 20). The goal is to "downsize or rightsize government" (Worsnop, 1992, p. 984). Based on the belief that government is too large and too intrusive (Savas, 1982) and that "government's decisions are political and thus are inherently less trustworthy than free-market decisions" (p. 5), the focus is on "rolling back either the rate of growth or the absolute amount of state activity in the social service delivery system" (Ismael, 1988, p. 1).

Two highly related objectives deal with raising additional revenue (Hanke & Dowdle, 1987; Savas, 1982) and reducing the size of government debt (Hardin, 1989; J. R. Miller & Tufts, 1991).

A further objective is to enhance the overall health of the economy: "If reducing the size of the public sector is the dominant theme in the work of privatization advocates, enhancing the efficiency of the economy as a whole and the public sector in particular is their *leitmotif*" (Pack, 1991, p. 287). The sub aims are: to enhance "efficiency and responsiveness" (Bell & Cloke, 1990, p. 7); to promote "savings, investment, productivity, and growth" (Starr, 1987, p. 126); "to increase the use of scarce resources" (J. R. Miller & Tufts, 1991,

p. 100); to ensure that customers are "served more effectively" (Hanke & Dowdle, 1987, p. 115); and to promote cost effectiveness by "help[ing] get prices right" (Starr, 1991, p. 32). Related to the issue of cost effectiveness is still another objective of privatization—"to reduce the power of public sector trade unions" (Hardin, 1989, p. 30) and thereby to exercise "control of wage rates" (Bell & Cloke, 1990, p. 7).

Finally, privatization is often portrayed as a tactic for promoting "choice in public services" (Savas, 1987, p. 5): "The key word is *choice*. Advocates claim that privatization will enlarge the range of choice for individuals while serving the same essential functions as do traditional programs" (Starr, 1987, p. 131). According to Gormley (1991b) and other analysts, "privatization enable[s] individual consumers to pursue their private choices more freely" (p. 309). These same analysts further posit that "greater freedom of choice will generally lead to a more just distribution of benefits" (Starr, 1987, p. 131), serve the interest of equity, and promote democracy (Bell & Cloke, 1990; Thayer, 1987).

Micro-Level Objectives

Macro-level goals are designed to affect the larger economic and political infrastructure of society. The micro-level goals of privatization focus on improvements in a particular government function or set of functions. The major objective here is enhanced efficiency, most often expressed in terms of reduced costs. Other related outcomes sought through moving functions from the public realm to the private sphere include: better quality, defined in terms of effectiveness and reliability; greater flexibility and reduced taxpayer risk; additional consumer choice; more effective accountability; and enhanced citizen participation. We return to these claims as they apply to education in each of the subsequent chapters.

Types

Privatization not only is intended to meet quite diverse objectives but also comes in a variety of forms—forms which "vary widely … in terms of relevance to public education" (Lieberman, 1989, p. 8). It is a "highly complex process which unpacks into a plethora of individual initiatives" (Bell & Cloke, 1990, p. 9). Similarly, a variety of criteria are employed to classify privatization techniques, including, most commonly: (1) the extent of privatization—"from the most complete to the least complete" (Butler, 1991, p. 18); (2) the domain of activity involved—usually financing and production; and (3) the place in the delivery of the service where privatization takes root—policy, administration, or provision.

It is useful here to introduce the distinction between the allocation/financing of goods and services and the production/delivery/distribution of those goods and services: "Allocation involves decisions about whether a given good or service should be offered, and if so, who should receive it, how much of it, and at what price. The term *distribution* is commonly used...to mean the activity carried out by the sellers to get the good or service to the consumer" (Hirsch, 1991, p. 25).

According to Savas (1987), this "distinction between providing or arranging a service and producing it is profound. It is at the heart of the entire concept of privatization and puts the role of government in perspective" (p. 61). Thus in defining privatization:

> We cannot talk simply about a public sector and a private sector. Only a *four*-part concept of the sectors—combining providing and producing, government and non-government—will let us have a useful discussion about the roles of public and private and about the strategy of privatization. (Kolderie, 1991, p. 251)

In Figure 1.1, we provide a typology of the significant forms of privatization. The objective of privatization is to replace activities in quadrant 1 (government

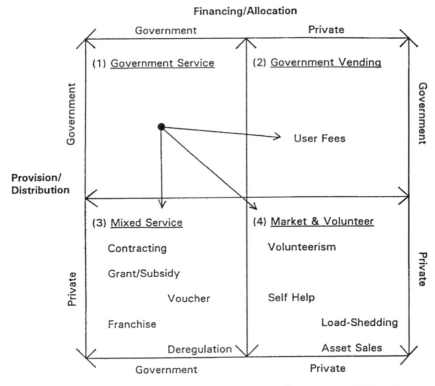

FIGURE 1.1. A typology of privatization initiatives—by extent and domain.

Note: From Murphy (1996). Copyright 1996. Reprinted by permission of Corwin Press.

...gs (Clarkson,

...g at the local level include the withdrawal from the
...trash collection business by the City of Knoxville, Tennessee (M.
R. Fitzgerald, Lyons, & Cory, 1990) and the abandonment of municipal solid-
waste collection services in Wichita, Kansas (P. E. Fixler, 1991). Examples of
load-shedding in education include the elimination of transportation services,
advanced language classes, and co-curricular activities.

Asset Sales

Another method of privatization is asset divestiture, where the public sector sells an asset, such as government land holdings, to the private sector to
generate revenue and/or to spur private sector development (Dudek &
Company, 1989, p. 7). What is really being proposed in these "privatizations"
is the liquidation of assets for their cash value (Bailey, 1991, p. 235).

Activities in this area are often bundled together under the heading of dena-
tionalization. While "asset divestiture is probably the most controversial"
(Seader, 1991, p. 33) of the privatization arrangements, as well as the most popular in much of the world (Dudek & Company, 1989; Hardin, 1989), it is the
least active form in the United States (Seader, 1991), "primarily because many
of the functions now being privatized in other countries have traditionally been
in the private sector in this country" (Butler, 1991, p. 18). In education, the sale
of an unused school facility to a corporation or volunteer agency would be an
example of an asset sale.

Volunteerism

Privatization through volunteerism refers to situations in which govern-
ment-like services are financed and delivered privately but without the use
of traditional market mechanisms. "As a privatization strategy, the use of volunteers generally refers to the recruitment of individuals to work for government without remuneration, thereby reducing the degree of

tax-supported involvement by government in the provision of public services" (Clarkson, 1989, p. 148). Examples of volunteerism in education are legion and include everything from room parents to unpaid volunteer instructors.

Self-help

Self-help, "the most basic delivery mode of all" (Savas, 1987, p. 81), has a good deal in common with voluntary forms of privatization. A critical difference is that with self-help strategies those who provide the services are the direct beneficiaries (Clarkson, 1989). R. Fitzgerald (1988), Gormley (1991a), and Savas (1987) all narrate examples of self-help initiatives in which functions generally provided by the public sector, such as managing public housing projects and caring for public facilities and lands, have been shifted to neighborhood development organizations. In education, self-help includes more moderate activities such as parents taking their children to school, as well as more radical ideas such as home schooling.

User fees

User fees represent a fifth type of privatization. Also known as "charging" (Bell & Cloke, 1990, p. 9), this strategy, which is housed in quadrant 2 in Figure 1.1, involves "the imposition of user fees to privately finance public services" (P. E. Fixler, 1991, p. 39). "User fees are designed to foster financing of public services by the direct beneficiaries" (Clarkson, 1989, p. 149) rather than by the taxpayers in general (President's Commission on Privatization, 1988). One purpose of user fees is to raise funds. However, the primary objective of "linking spending programs directly to taxes levied for that purpose" (Savas, 1987, p. 248) is to "satisfy people's demands more cost effectively" (p. 249) by "reveal[ing] the true cost of the service" (p. 248). User fees in education are rare, but examples can be found in the levying of charges for co-curricular activities and certain science laboratory classes.

Contracting

Contracting and the other privatization strategies in quadrant 3 of Figure 1.1 "by shifting only the locus of service production…privatize the means of policy implementation but not the functional sphere of government action" (Starr, 1987, p. 125). Privatization in quadrant 3 means "retaining collective financing but delegating delivery to the private sector" (Donahue, 1989, p. 215): "The public sector remains the financer, but not the producer" (Pack, 1991, p. 296). Most of the privatization that is occurring and being advocated in the United States is captured by the strategies listed in quadrant 3.

Contracting is the "best known" (Clarkson, 1989, p. 169), the "most extensive" (Pack, 1991, p. 304), the "most convenient" (Gormley, 1991b, p. 312), the "most popular" (De Hoog, 1984, p. 5), and the "most commonly promoted"

...and Walters (1987) have identified two basic forms of franchises—those in which "the expenses for the installation of major civil works are borne by the local community" (p. 111) and those in which "a private company is entrusted with construction of the facility as well as its operation" (p. 110), what Scully and Cole (1991) call a full service franchise. It is important to note that, because franchising "can only be employed for services received by the identifiable individuals since the provider must charge consumers directly" (Peters, 1991, p. 55), this privatization strategy has not been used extensively. Exclusive contracts to provide class rings or caps and gowns to prospective high school graduates are examples of franchises in education.

Vouchers

"Another form of privatization is the voucher, whereby certain consumers are authorized to purchase earmarked goods or services from the private market. The government specifies who is eligible to purchase the services and who is eligible to provide them" (Gormley, 1991a, p. 4). "The use of vouchers keeps financing in the public sector" (Pack, 1991, p. 283), while "distributing purchasing power to eligible consumers" (President's Commission on Privatization, 1988, p. 2). A system of vouchers is "designed to encourage the consumption of particular goods by a particular class of consumers" (Savas, 1987, p. 78). Under a voucher program, anyone "issued a voucher can use it as a form of currency or script to purchase supplies, goods, or services in the open market" (Savas, 1985, p. 19).

Although well-known examples of voucher systems are in place in the United States—such as the food stamp program and the GI Bill—and other uses—such as for K–12 education and housing—have long been suggested (Savas, 1985), vouchers are an infrequently used privatization strategy (Clarkson, 1989; Peters, 1991). The recent Milwaukee initiative to provide funds to low-income parents to send their children to schools of their choice is an example of a voucher program in education.

Subsidies

"The use of grants and subsidies is another method for fostering the privatization of public services. Under this approach, government provides financial or in-kind contributions to private organizations or individuals to encourage them to provide a service" (Clarkson, 1989, p. 146). "Subsidies" refers to the "general strategy of changing the demand for public-sector goods by altering the incentive structure and thus creating self-interest coalitions" (Butler, 1987, p. 12). The goal is "to make the private sector more responsive to public goals through a manipulation of incentives thought to govern market behavior" (Hula, 1990b, p. 7). Or, stated more concretely, the objective of subsidies is "to encourage private organizations to provide a service" (Peters, 1991, p. 55) "at reduced costs to users" (Clarkson, 1989, p. 170). A variety of measures find a home under this broad construct, including: direct cash payments; in-kind contributions; use of materials, equipment, land, and facilities; low-cost loans; and tax abatement and other taxing powers such as modified depreciation rules (Clarkson, 1989; Hula, 1990b; Savas, 1987). A tax program that encourages corporations to donate materials, supplies, and equipment to schools is a good example of privatization via a subsidy.

Deregulation

Unlike many other countries, the United States has not nationalized much of its industry. Alternatively, we have relied extensively on widespread government regulation of private sector industries. Thus, "the widespread deregulation movement in the United Sates has been a home-grown version of what in other nations has taken the form of outright divestiture of government properties" (President's Commission on Privatization, 1988, p. 229). At the heart of the deregulation movement is an attempt to privatize "many so-called public services...through the free market" (Savas, 1985, p. 21). As with subsidies, the goal is to foster the private provision of activities historically housed in the public sector (Fixler, P. E., & Poole, 1991). The recent debate at the state level in Pennsylvania to change code language to allow districts to purchase teaching and management services from outside sources is a good example of deregulation in education (McLaughlin, 1995).

PRESSURES FOR PRIVATIZATION

In the past few years, however, a loss of confidence in public enterprises in general, and in state education in particular, has led people in many countries to question

... that illuminate the rising tide of discontent with public pro-vision of goods and services and those that help define an alterative philos-ophy about the proper role of government in society. On the first issue—discontent—we examine a declining confidence in the public sector and fiscal stress. On the second issue—an alternative philosophy—we review the changing political culture and the changing economic climate of the nation.

Discontent With the Public Sector

Declining Confidence

According to many analysts, a "powerful alliance of ideological and com-mercial interests" (Martin, 1993, p. 2) has turned its guns on the issue of gov-ernment provision of services: "The U.S. is now deeply into a period of sustained criticism of public institutions, including public education" (Elmore, 1996, p. 28). Critics maintain that government in the United States is troubled and is becoming more so. They point to polls revealing widespread dissatis-faction with government, polls that indicate that: only three in 10 citizens believe that government is operated for the benefit of all citizens (Savas, 1987); one in two citizens believes that the federal government has become so large and so influential that it represents a real and immediate danger to the rights and freedoms of citizens (Urschel, 1995); only one in three voters expresses trust in government—down from four in five in the late 1950s (Savas, 1982). Other chroniclers of this unrest speak of a mounting sense of skepticism—"skepticism about public enterprises" (R. Fitzgerald, 1988, p. 22) in general and "skepticism as to the ability of government to implement social goals" (Hula, 1990a, p. xiii) in particular. They believe that a "philosophy borne of suspicion for big government may underlie this [privatization] revolution in America" (R. Fitzgerald, 1988, p. 20).

Still other reviewers discern a "deeper ... and much more dangerous"

(Savas, 1982, p. 1) cynicism toward (Hula, 1990b), distaste for (Donahue, 1989), or "distrust of government and government officials among Americans" (De Hoog, 1984, p. 1). These analysts portray "the electorate's disappointment in activist government" (Hirsch, 1991, p. 1) and the rise and spread of an antigovernment philosophy in the 1970s and 1980s, a time during which the "government plumbed new depths of disfavor" (Donahue, 1989, p. 3). They describe a "fundamental concern that government simply 'doesn't work.' Planning is seen as inadequate, bureaucracy as inefficient and outcomes highly problematic" (Hula, 1990a, p. xiii). They go on to argue that the consent of the governed is being withdrawn to a significant degree (Savas, 1982). In its softest incarnation, this cynicism leads "politicians and citizens alike to argue that government is no longer the solution to everything" (Florestano, 1991, p. 291) and to question the usefulness of much government-initiated activity (Hula, 1990b). At worst, it has nurtured the belief "that government is destined to fail at whatever it does" (Starr, 1991, p. 34). In short, anchored in reaction to government growth and intrusiveness, fundamental reanalyses of the rationale for government activity, stories and data about the performance of the public sector, increasingly vociferous attacks on bureaucracy, and spreading dissatisfaction with the wealth transfer aspects of government, public confidence in government is on the decline.

Perhaps nowhere is this declining confidence in the public sector more visible than in the attacks leveled against public education during the years since the publication of the reform reports of the early to mid 1980s (see Murphy, 1990, and Murphy & Beck, 1995, for reviews). "Citizens apparently believe public schools are not good and the situation is getting worse" (Guthrie, 1996b, p. 8). Rightly or wrongly[2] there is a widespread feeling that "the country's public schools...are very sick" (Gerstner, cited in Harp, 1996b, p. 22)—that they are failing society and its youth (Hakim, Seidenstat, & Bowman, 1994). The sentiments expressed by David Kearnes, former CED of Xerox, are representative of many assessments of the health of the nation's schools:

> Public education consumes nearly 7% of our gross national product. Its expenditures have doubled or tripled in every postwar decade, even when enrollments declined. I can't think of any other single sector of American society that has absorbed more money by serving fewer people with steadily declining service. (Kearnes, 1988, p. 566)

In the midst of this perceived educational crisis—and growing concern that we seem to be making little progress in effectively responding to the crisis (Thomas, Moran, & Resnick, n.d.; Walsh, 1993c): "If the declining quality of public education continues, it is not wholly for lack of reform efforts" (Beers & Ellig, 1994, p. 19). The very viability of public education is being called into

..., one of the key factors contributing to the popularity of privatization has been "the growing cost-revenue squeeze on government" (F. L. Fixler & Poole, 1987, pp. 176-177): "In the late 1970s and throughout the 1980s ... officials became squeezed between escalating demands of constituents—coupled with rising claims by public employees' unions—and the reality of fixed or declining budgets" (Donahue, 1989, p. 131). Indeed, the period when privatization was breaking over the political landscape corresponds exactly to the era when states and cities were "experienc[ing] all at once almost every conceivable fiscal nightmare" (S. Moore, 1987, p. 70) and a severe "deterioration in fiscal conditions" (Dudek & Company, 1989, p. 9), including their own vulnerability to bankruptcy (Ross, 1988). Such problems included: political, judicial, and constitutional restrictions on their ability to raise funds; taxpayer revolts; restrictions in federal and state aid; double-digit inflation; a sobering economic recession; heightened demands for public services; increased interest in using the public sector to support political goals; and rising demands by public employees (Darr, 1991; Donahue, 1989; Dudek & Company, 1989; S. Moore, 1987; Peters, 1991; Renner, 1989). With this new era of fiscal strain, "the more predictable days of local government" (Kemp, 1991, p. 1) disappeared and pragmatism and expediency (De Alessi, 1987; Donahue, 1989) moved to center stage as government officials attempted "to extricate themselves from the bind of limited resources and the constant or increasing demand for services" (Kolderie & Hauer, 1991, p. 87).

One side of the equation of fiscal pressure highlights the demand for services and the costs of those activities. Indeed, Van Horn (1991) has shown that "the inability to meet rising demands for services, rather than the fear of budget cutbacks or the desire for efficiency, has goaded several large and rapidly growing departments into using private contractors" (p. 268). A number of dynamics are at work here. Public expectations of government services are heightened during periods of economic hardship such as the recessions of the 1970s and 1980s (Kemp, 1991). It is also during such periods that union resistance to trimming the government workforce tends to be most strident. At the same time, states and municipalities are being hit by expanding requirements for services from Congress and from the executive branch of the federal government—especially regarding environmental issues (Seader, 1991)—as well as from federal and state courts (e.g., demands to eliminate prison overcrowding) even as federal revenues are declining. Finally, "growing financial responsibilities" (Hirsch, 1991, p. 15) are being fed by a "combination of client advocates, the media, and the political process [that] work powerfully to turn needs into rights, rights into entitlements, entitlements into programs, and programs into budgets" (Kolderie, 1991, p. 259).

The revenue side of the cost-revenue squeeze—the lack of funds or shrinking budget side—is comprised of two issues: decreased tax revenues and "less generous and less reliable federal aid than in the past" (Worsnop, 1992, p. 979). As a number of scholars have concluded, "reduced transfers of funds from the federal government…and growing hostility to increased taxes" (Hanke, 1985, p. 3) have "worked powerfully to constrain the resources that come into the economy and the amount available for public service provision" (Kolderie, 1991, p. 259).

A particularly troublesome dimension of the fiscal squeeze being experienced by state and local governments—and one that intersects with both cost and revenue strands—is the "infrastructure crisis" (Gomez-Ibanez, Meyer, & Luberoff, 1990, p. 172), or "the mounting problem of 'crumbling' infrastructure" (Worsnop, 1992, p. 992). According to most observers, "local governments are facing a common dilemma—an enormous need for infrastructure facilities without the financial wherewithal to fund their construction" (Goldman & Mokuvos, 1991, p. 25). The demand for these capital projects, both for repair of existing structures and the production of new ones, is continuing to mount (Hudgins & Utt, 1992). While the demands for more and better infrastructure, as well as for capital to fuel development of that infrastructure (Seader, 1991), are increasing, the ability (or willingness) of municipalities to pay for new facilities is failing to keep pace. As a result, because they "limit or avoid large capital expenditures" (Roehm, Castellano, & Karns, 1991, p. 280), "creative financing techniques available through privatization are…becom[ing] an increasingly attractive option" (Dudek & Company, 1989, p. 8) for the "environmental, social and economic development needs [of] municipalities without the monetary means to finance infrastructure facilities" (Goldman & Mokuvos, 1991, p. 28).

Along with the rising tide of discontent with public sector activities, fiscal pressures have provided a wake-up call to public agencies, many of whom "are having to reconsider once again how they pursue their fundamental purposes" (M. R. Fitzgerald, Lyons, & Cory, 1990, p. 70), including "searching for new ways of delivering services" (Peters, 1991, p. 53). As various analysts have noted, "when governments face severe fiscal stress, that is, when the cost of government activities is rising but the public's resistance to higher taxes is also rising, public officials seek any promising solution to their quandary" (Savas, 1987, p. 4)—"any alternative delivery mechanism that might allow government to

achieve more with less money" (Van Horn, 1991, p. 263'
looking for "new funding methods for traditional ser
1991, p. 32), turning to the market—or "private provi'
services" (Wilson, 1990, p. 59)—for help.

Changing Fabric of the Nation

Changing Political Context

"The political and economic concepts that have traditionally given legitimacy to government actions have come under growing criticism" (President's
Commission on Privatization, 1988, p. 229). What can we safely say about the
changing political environment? The short answer is that dominant ideologies
change over time and we appear to be in the midst of one of these fundamental shifts. Indeed, a number of analysts argue that the resurgence of "conser-
vatism, libertarianism (or classical liberalism), and free-market ideas" (P. E.
Fixler, 1991, p. 44)—what Tomlinson (1986) labels "the social market theories of
the 'new right'" (p. 212)— signals the potential dismantling of the liberal democratic state that has grown up over the last 75 years (Donahue, 1989; Jacobs,
1993; Starr, 1991).

The political context is defined in large part by "a general political movement toward the right" (Brazer, 1981, p. 21) and the fact that "Americans have
turned to conservatives for the answers to the most important problems facing
the U.S." (Pines, 1985, p. v). The fusion of a political agenda increasingly dominated by "conservative politics" (Martin, 1993, p. 46) and an "economic the-
ology...undergoing a return to fundamentalism" (Thayer, 1987, p. 165) has
given birth to the doctrine of neo-liberalism (Seldon, 1987) and to "the ideological and profit-oriented agenda of the New Right" (Martin, 1993, p. 182)—
"the conservative view of government as an economic black hole" (Starr, 1987,
p. 126). In the process, "an ideology which has long lurked in the darkest shad-
ows of right-wing thinking [has been] transfer[red] into an apparatus at the very
centre of the policy process" (Bell & Cloke, 1990, p. 4).

At the core of the shifting political context then are a particular set of values and political goals and a specific "concept of the relationship between the
individual and the state" (Martin, 1993, p. 48). Economic growth and individual choice are the movement's predominant goals and the market, which is
seen as "consistently and wholly benign" (p. 47), is touted as the best vehicle
to secure those objectives. Not surprisingly, the "language of 'choice' and
'empowerment'" (p. 188) is central to the new political context. Alternative
approaches to government intervention and bureaucratic structures, it is
argued, must "buttress individual liberties" (De Alessi, 1987, p. 24)—they must
minimize interference with individual freedom and the market (Martin, 1993).
Thus fueled by citizen discontent with activist government and fiscal stress,
newly formed conservative winds are pushing society away from the agenda

of the Progressive era and toward a "reconstructing [of] the liberal democratic state" (Starr, 1991, p. 25).

Changing Economic Context

As Donahue (1989) reminds us, "Two political legacies of the 1980s will color and constrain the economic policies of the 1990s. [One] is the virtually worldwide cooling toward collectivism. [Another] is a renewed cultural enthusiasm for private enterprise" (p. 3). As we have already begun to describe, the evolving economic and political context is defined in some ways by an emerging populist view against large government and collective public endeavors. On the one hand, we have seen a weakening of the Progressive vision and a lessening of the influence of Progressive philosophy—a widespread "reaction against the theories and results of Progressive thought" (President's Commission on Privatization, 1988, p. 230), focusing particularly upon the appropriateness of public provision of goods and services that are highly redistributive in nature. Critics argue that "government is too big, too powerful, too intrusive in people's lives and therefore is a danger to democracy" (Savas, 1987, p. 5). This critique of large government is grounded in an analysis of interest group government and "the excess of current interest group politics" (President's Commission on Privatization, 1988, p. 233)—of "distant and unresponsive organs of government" (Savas, 1987, p. 7); "meddling by ministers and civil servants" (Bell & Cloke, 1990, p. 14); groups who are "able to use the political system to secure and maintain benefits at the general expense" (Pirie, 1988, p. 58); and programs that "have too often operated mainly to enlarge the income, status, and power of the industry of bureaucratic and professional service producers, whether governmental or private" (Kolderie, 1991, p. 259). The backlash against government is also driven by the "deficit-induced imperative to limit government spending" (Donahue, 1989, p. 3).

Finally, consistent with an increasingly popular libertarian philosophy, there is an ongoing reassessment of the appropriate size of government in general and particular units of government specifically (Tullock, 1988) and an emerging "belief that small is beautiful when applied to domestic government" (R. Fitzgerald, 1988, p. 21) and a rekindling of belief in the appropriateness of self-help and local initiative, especially of "traditional local institutions" (Savas, 1987, p. 10). These winds are blowing us in the direction of decentralization, a "rebuilding America from the bottom up—and the trend away from reliance on political institutions in favor of individual self-help initiatives" (R. Fitzgerald, 1988, p. 16).

Critique of large government represents the negative case for the dismantling of the liberal democratic state. It is balanced on the positive side by the growing belief that "free market economics provide the path to prosperous equilibrium" (Thayer, 1987, p. 168)—by "the political pendulum swing toward market-oriented solutions" (Seader, 1991, p. 32). Supported by the intellectual pillars of market theory and by the public choice literature, the economic context of the nation is being rewoven in important ways. There is a "new spirit of enterprise in the air" (Hardin, 1989, p. 16)—a renewed interest in "private market values" (Bailey, 1987, p. 141) and in the "virtues of private property" (Hirsch, 1991, p. 2) and a "promarket trend" (President's Commission on Privatization, 1988, p. 237) in the larger society.

While analysts are quick to point out the fallacy of this emerging belief in the infallibility of private business (Baber, 1987; Riley, 1996) and to remind us that "idealization of the market's invisible hand has served to conceal the grubbier ones directing it" (Martin, 1993, p. 6), there is much reason to assert that the currently emerging economic context of the nation is anchored firmly on "belief in the superiority of free market forms of social organization over the forms of social organization of the Keynesian welfare state society" (Ian Taylor, cited in Martin, 1993, p. 48). This expanding reliance on the market moves individuals in the direction of "exercis[ing] choice as consumers rather than as citizens" (Starr, 1991, p. 27).

The expansion of pro-market sentiment is powered to some extent by the picture painted by some of "a bloated, parasitic public sector blocking the bustle and growth of a more free flowing private economy" (Starr, 1987, p. 124). Two beliefs are central to this line of reasoning: (1) that "the structural organization of the public sector itself" (Pirie, 1988, p. 34) is flawed and (2) that political decisions "are inherently less trustworthy than free-market decisions" (Savas, 1987, p. 5). Starting from here, we find many analysts are adopting an increasingly skeptical stance on the usefulness of government intervention (Tullock, 1988, 1994a, 1994b). Their revisiting the case for public action (P. E. Fixler, 1991) "has caused mainstream economists in recent years to narrow significantly the circumstances thought to require government intervention to correct market failings" (President's Commission on Privatization, 1988, p. 237; see Beers & Ellig, 1994). Accompanying this reconsideration of the case for public action has been a reanalysis of the supposed problems of markets and a recognition that because "market forces can find ways round or through vested interests" (Seldon, 1987, p. 133) that "the regulation which the market imposes in economic activity is superior to any regulation which rulers can devise and operate by law" (Pirie, 1988, p. 10)—a feeling that since "the level of efficiency of government action is apt to be low, and the possibility of damage through erratic, ill-informed decisions is great, government action should be resorted to only when the social cost emanating from the market is quite great" (Tullock, 1988, p. 103).

In education, as elsewhere in the public sector, pro-market sentiment is also being fueled by the shift from an industrial to a service economy. According to this logic, "with the development of a service economy [comes] the need for new markets, as well as the need to break the state's monopoly on the delivery of human services so that private enterprises [can] expand. Enter 'deinstitutionalization,'" (Lewis, 1993, p. 84), "deregulation and privatization" (Caldwell, 1990, p. 17), and, according to some, "thinly disguised profit schemes masquerading as 'help'" (Achilles & DuVall, 1994, p. 9). According to this line of analysis, privatization is, in some ways, a type of new colonialism (Hardin, 1989)—an opportunity for the private sector to move into, and possibly gain control of, the 285 billion-dollar-a-year K–12 education enterprise (Cooper & Doyle, 1996) at the very time that traditional industrial growth opportunities are closing (Murphy, 1993).

INTELLECTUAL FOUNDATIONS

A third strategy that is helpful in reaching a deeper understanding of privatization is to analyze the theoretical foundations that support privatization initiatives. As Pack (1991) reminds us, the intellectual scaffolding for privatization is comprised of two key elements most fully developed in a body of scholarship known as the public choice literature—"a competitive model to demonstrate the efficiency of private production, and a public choice government failure model wherein the public sector does too much and does it inefficiently" (p. 287). In our analysis, we therefore group theoretical arguments from public choice scholars into two clusters: the advantages of competitive markets and the dynamics of nonmarket decision making.

The Advantages of Competitive Markets

"Orthodox economic theory of markets" (Buchanan & Tullock, 1962, p. 17) and accompanying perspectives on monopolistic behavior, with their dual engines of competition and profit incentives, provide the economic touchstone of privatization advocates (Beers & Ellig, 1994; Hakim, Seidenstat, & Bowman, 1994). Indeed, it is safe to say that competition is the "nuclear centre of the whole privatization argument" (Hardin, 1989, p. 11). That is, "the more important factor in determining performance may be competition rather than the type of ownership *per se*" (Vickers & Yarrow, 1988, p. 41).

> The real issue is not so much public versus private; it is monopoly versus competition. Far too many government services—federal, state, and local—are provided as monopolies when they need not be, and it is very difficult to tame monopolies and make them work in the public interest. So the introduction of competition is appropriate whether the competition comes about from the use of vouchers, competitive bidding for service contracts, franchising, or voluntary efforts. It is the introduction of competition that makes the difference. (Savas, 1985, p. 23)

Thus the market theory broadside on public sector services focuses on the monopolistic nature of that activity: "the underlying, structural problem of government monopoly…is the dominant factor responsible for malperformance of government services" (Savas, 1987, p. 251); "the monopolistic nature of local-service delivery is the greatest impediment to government effectiveness" (Bailey, 1991, p. 233)—specifically in education "that the political monopoly in the American education industry is the source of the problem" (Beers & Ellig, 1994, p. 34). Reviewers maintain that public monopolies "induce inefficiencies" (Hilke, 1992, p. 134) and "result in the provision of goods and services substantially lower in quality and higher in cost than those provided in the presence of competition" (Wilson, 1990, p. 65). In education, for example, one often hears the assertion that "the currently almost monopolistic stance of public schools allows for inefficient use of resources" (Hakim, Seidenstat, & Bowan, 1994, p. 11).

According to a number of analysts—especially public choice theorists—these conditions occur because "management policy in government exhibits few of the pressures produced by competition of the profit motive" (R. Fitzgerald, 1988, pp. 17–18), either for organizations in the way they conduct business or for individuals in the way they acquire information with which to make choices (Tullock, 1988, 1994a). Most troublesome, according to public choice theorists, is the fact that public monopolies "attenuat[e] incentives to minimize costs among managers of government agencies" (Hilke, 1992, p. 134). Because of the absence of competition and profit incentives—the dual engines of markets—public organizations "tend to absorb resources on internal preference scales" (Bailey, 1987, p. 141). This, so our public choice colleagues tell us, fosters "a redirection of production factors towards political rather than economic ends" (Pirie, 1988, p. 5) and the evolution of a producer-oriented system "serving the values and meeting the needs of those who direct it and work within it" (p. 7). "For this reason, no matter how noble the intentions of public employees, no matter how skilled or energetic their efforts, they usually find themselves unable to transcend their bureaucratic restraints to achieve policy goals in a timely, cost-effective manner" (R. Fitzgerald, 1988, p. 18). What this means is that "the internal organization is subject to subversion by the bureaucratic process" (Hirsch, 1991, p. 60). The bottom line effect, according to Tullock (1988), is that "the government is apt to impose social costs rather than to eliminate them" (p. 93).

The logical conclusion of this line of reasoning is that markets are to be preferred to government activity—"competition works much better than monopoly [and] a profit incentive is a stronger incentive than any bureaucratic management incentive" (Poole, 1985, p. 37). Competition produces "incentives for improvements in performance" (Hilke, 1992, p. 20) and "tends to motivate organizations to lower prices and sometimes to improve quality" (Brown, 1991, p. 273). "Output which [can] be described as desirable from the standpoint of almost everyone's preference function" (Tullock, 1994b, p. 66) results, and overall economic efficiency is enhanced (Hakim, Seidenstat, & Bowman, 1994).

The Disadvantages of Nonmarket Decision Making

Privatization initiatives are also heavily buttressed by analysts who argue that nonmarket (political) decision making promotes situations in which the interests, needs, and desires of consumers and taxpayers are subjugated to the interests of actors in the political arena. These analysts often portray the public arena as little more than "a political marketplace where politicians, public employees, and competing groups of beneficiaries seek their narrow interests at the expense of the general welfare" (Starr, 1987, p. 127).

Politicians

To begin with, public choice analysts maintain that "the behavior of both the executive and the legislature can best be interpreted as the result of maximizing their own personal interests" (Niskanen, 1971, p. 137)—"that decisions are taken with a view of maximizing the probability of electoral success" (Vickers & Yarrow, 1988, p. 30). Thus politicians are said to employ a type of economic algorithm that closely links position-taking and election calculations (Stiglitz, 1986): "politicians, instead of doing what they thought was in the public interest, would do things which might help them get re-elected, or in some cases, might raise their income" (Tullock, 1994b, p. 65). In short, "politicians act in ways that will advance their careers" (Tullock, 1965, p. 29).

The logical deduction here, public choice scholars maintain, is that politicians use tax dollars to enhance their own utility by nurturing the support of the other two players in the public choice triangle—public employees and beneficiaries of governmental programs (Bennett & DiLorenzo, 1987; Niskanen, 1971, 1994). Politicians engage in this tax-funded politics in two main ways: (1) through the creation of programs and the maintenance of existing programs (Pirie, 1988; Tullock, 1965) and (2) through "payoffs to workers in publicly owned firms" (Vickers & Yarrow, 1988, p. 31) in terms of wages, benefits, and job security (Bennett & Johnson, 1980; Savas, 1982). Niskanen (1994) argues that most of this tax-funded self-promotion centers on the portion of a bureau's discretionary budget that the legislature reclaims for its own use through bargaining with the bureau's managers. In effect, Niskanen argues that the political share of a bureau's surplus (or discretionary budget) provides a system of spoils that allows politicians to "reward their supporters and finance their re-election" (p. 278).

Bureaucrats

At the heart of the public choice scholarship that provides the theoretical foundation for the privatization movement is a reassessment of the interests of public employees, especially managerial employees well known to us all as government bureaucrats. Central to this reinterpretation is a dismantling or "undermining of the naive faith in the benevolence of governmental bureaucracy"

(Buchanan, 1987, p. 206). According to Niskanen (1971), "the beginning of wisdom is the recognition that bureaucrats are people who are, at least, not entirely motivated by the general welfare or the interests of the state" (p. 36). Rather than accepting the assumption that managers of public agencies are "passive agents [who] merely administer and carry out programs" (Bennett & DiLorenzo, 1987, p. 16) with the sole intent of maximizing public interest, public choice analysts advance the belief that these "civil servants often [make] decisions in the interest of their own power or income" (Tullock, 1994b, p. 65): Bureaucrats are much like other people, "people who are less interested in the ostensible objectives of the organization than in their own personal well being" (Tullock, 1965, p. 21)—a well being that is often expressed in terms of "salary, perquisites, rank, prestige, [and] opportunities for promotion" (Bennett & DiLorenzo, 1987, p. 17).

In economic terms, this means "that government employees, like other economic agents, respond to the opportunities for gain provided by the structure of property rights embedded in the institutions used to control their choices" (De Alessi, 1987, p. 24) and that bureaus act as "a type of special interest group" (Hilke, 1992, p. 13). At the most basic level, this results in the notion of the bureaucrat as a public service maximizer giving way to the conception of a manager who attempts to maximize his or her own utility function—a utility function that contains a variety of variables: "salary, perquisites of the office, public reputation, power, patronage, [and] output of the bureau" (Niskanen, 1971, p. 38). "The two most commonly cited variables that are likely to affect utility in this case are the size of the relevant government department or subdepartment and rents accruing to the officials" (Vickers & Yarrow, 1988, p. 32).

Since, such an analysis continues, improving one's utility function is directly dependent on the resources available to the bureau, budget maximization becomes the operant goal of bureau managers (Niskanen, 1971). Or, more precisely, the objective is to maximize the bureau's discretionary budget (the difference between the total budget and the minimum cost of producing expected outcomes) (Niskanen, 1994). Consequently, managers have a strong incentive to engage in "bureaucratic imperialism" (Tullock, 1965, p. 134) or "empire building" (Dudek & Company, 1989, p. 49). "If such a system is applied throughout a whole organization...the higher officials will actually encourage their inferiors to build up the size of the whole hierarchy since their own position, as well as that of their inferiors, will depend on the number of subordinates" (Tullock, 1965, p. 135).

The point to emphasize here is that budget maximization and empire building impose real costs on citizens in terms of public control and overall efficiency of the economy (Bennett & Johnson, 1980). According to public choice scholars, the switch from maximizing the public interest to maximizing the discretionary budget means that bureaus have the potential to become "producer-oriented" (Pirie, 1988, p. 26), to capture the agency and to direct its energies toward meeting the needs of government employees (Hardin, 1989; Vickers & Yarrow, 1988). The result is goal displacement (Downs, 1967; Tullock, 1965):

"Some public sector activities clearly are serving the interest of their own work-force more than the interests of their customers" (Pirie, 1988, p. 26).

The dynamic of provider capture is supported by a number of related con-ditions. To begin with, bureaus often dominate the relationship with their polit-ical sponsors. As Niskanen (1971) reports, "although the nominal relationship of a bureau and its sponsor is that of a bilateral monopoly, the relative incen-tives and available information, under most conditions, give the bureau the overwhelmingly dominant monopoly power" (p. 30). And even when this is not the case, bureaus still maintain a major role in the bargaining relationship (Niskanen, 1994). Both conditions indicate

> that the political forces which operate within and through the state sector of the economy are more powerful than the forces which government can bring to bear upon it. In the struggle for control, it is more often the government which loses and the institutions of the public sector which win. (Pirie, 1988, p. 49)

Second, even a "bureaucrat who may be personally motivated to maximize the budget of his bureau is usually driven by conditions both internal and external to the bureau to do just that" (Niskanen, 1971, p. 39). In these cases, budget maximization may be less a "property of rational behavior" (p. 41) than a need to survive in office by meeting the needs—"effective demands" (Niskanen, 1994, p. 272)—of others, especially the bureau's sponsor and employees (Niskanen, 1971, 1994).

Whatever the causes, because (1) "people are more prodigal with the wealth of others than with their own" (Hanke, 1985, p. 6), (2) "public employees have no direct interest in the commercial outcome" (p. 6) of the enterprise, and (3) "the supply of government services by bureaus generates a net surplus that is shared with members of the government" (Niskanen, 1994, p. 278), public choice theory posits that bureaus are characterized by significant inefficiencies (Hilke, 1992; Niskanen, 1971, 1994; Pack, 1991). A cardinal conclusion of pub-lic choice scholarship is that "the budget of a bureau is too large, the out-put...may be too low, and the production of this output is uniformly inefficient" (Niskanen, 1994, p. 274), or, more succinctly, "inefficiency in production is the normal condition" (p. 274).

Employees

It is important to note that in the public choice literature the motivation and behavior of government employees are viewed as paralleling the interests and actions of their managers: "The employees' interests in larger budgets are obvi-ous and similar to that of the bureaucrat: greater opportunities for promotion, more job security, etc." (Niskanen, 1971, p. 40). Therefore, because "they ben-efit from continued operation of the public agencies that employ them ... [they] thus have a vested interest in maintaining public agencies even when they might not be efficient" (Hirsch, 1991, p. 72). More to the point, it is generally in their interests to have an expanding public sector.

One avenue of public choice discourse suggests that because public employees are, next to transfer payment recipients, "the most direct beneficiaries of government spending" (Savas, 1987, p. 26), they are likely to use the power of the ballot box to promote the objective of government growth (Tullock, 1994a): "Government employees have a vested interest in the growth of government and, because of this interest, are very active politically. Relative to the general public, they vote in greater proportion and have a correspondingly disproportionate impact on political decisions" (Bennett & Johnson, 1980, p. 372). A second plank in the public choice framework holds that public sector unions in particular are key instruments in the growth of bureaus and the concomitant subordination of consumer interests to the objectives of the employees themselves. Ramsey (1987) concludes that, when the economic influence of unions is combined with political muscle, public-sector unions have considerable "ability to tax the rest of society" (p. 97). A final slice of the public choice literature focusing on public employees asserts that employee self-interest is nurtured in what might, presented in the best light, be thought of as a symbiotic relationship with the bureau's sponsor—the intersection where "the self interest of the politician [and] a well-organized union cadre" (p. 97) converge to maximize the utility of both groups: "The political power of public employees and their unions is not restricted to their voting strength. Political campaign contributors and campaign workers are a potent influence on office seekers. The situation lends itself to collusion whereby officeholders can award substantial pay raises to employees with the unspoken understanding that some of the bread cast upon those particular waters will return as contributions" (Savas, 1987, p. 26). As described above, the well-being of politicians and government employees often comes at the expense of the general citizenry, especially in inefficiencies visible in inappropriate production schedules and unearned rents enjoyed by public servants (Hilke, 1992; Hirsch, 1991; Niskanen, 1971, 1994).

Beneficiaries

If politicians occupy one point on the public choice triangle and employees (bureaucrats and their subordinates) hold down a second, the third is populated by two related groups that also benefit heavily from government sector expenditures—producers and recipients of specific public services. On the issue of service providers as beneficiaries, Bennett and DiLorenzo (1987) and De Hoog (1984) demonstrate that both politicians and bureaucrats mobilize considerable support for themselves by forging strong relationships with private-sector producers. Concomitantly, "service providers...can become powerful advocates for government spending" (Butler, 1987, p. 6): "Within the business sector, groups develop that see their interests joined to those of the political bureaucracy" (Meltzer & Scott, 1978, p. 116).

At the same time, recipients of public services often act as interest groups that "seek to socialize the costs of services that disproportionately benefit them" (P. E. Fixler, 1991, p. 44). At the core of this line of reasoning is the proposition that, because "groups who, one way or another, get the government to provide services for them normally do not pay the full cost,...they take advantage of the possibility of imposing part of the cost on other people" (Tullock, 1994b, p. 67). Or, stated less charitably, "interest groups compete in the voting marketplace to redistribute for themselves income plundered through taxation of others" (R. Fitzgerald, 1988, p. 9)—"well-entrenched private interests...succeed in benefiting at the public expense" (Pack, 1991, p. 290).

The public choice literature posits three conditions that make possible these "opportunities for exploitation of the majority by well-organized minorities" (Ross, 1988, p. 14)—what De Alessi (1987) refers to as "wealth redistribution" (p. 29). The first condition is the separation of the beneficiaries from the funders of public services (Ross, 1988). The second is the fact that while benefits for any particular interest group "are visible and individual...the costs are diffuse and shared by all" (Savas, 1987, p. 20). The third is the presence of a political process which provides a robust vehicle for recipient interest groups to socialize the costs of the benefits accruing to them (Butler, 1987; Meltzer & Scott, 1978; Niskanen, 1994). As is the case with politicians and government employees, producer and recipient interest group self-interest generally results in the situation in which "the amount of service generated is not optimal" (Tullock, 1994b, p. 67), real external costs are imposed (Buchanan & Tullock, 1962), and inefficiencies abound (Niskanen, 1971, 1994; Stiglitz, 1986).

CONCLUSION

In this introductory chapter, we provided background to inform the debate about the privatization of schooling. We began by explaining why privatization in education is such an important and contentious topic—touching on both its fit with the changing economic, social, and political context of society and its centrality in the current reform struggle in education. We then catalogued the various forms of privatization and examined the general set of objectives to which these policy initiatives are linked. We also analyzed the forces that are propelling privatization measures to the forefront of the debate about redefining the public domain. Finally, we briefly reviewed the theoretical scaffolding supporting privatization policies.

The balance of the volume is devoted to examining privatization in education. We undertake that assignment by providing a detailed analysis of the five privatization strategies that have the greatest applicability to schooling—contracting out, vouchers, deregulation, home schooling, and volunteerism. We turn first to the most prevalent form of privatization in education—contracting out.

2

Contracting Out:
The Descriptive Story

Within the past few years a number of innovative contracting arrangements have been embraced by school administrators. New approaches now have private-sector enterprises providing all or part of the operational and instructional services in a classroom, a school, or a group of schools. (Beales & O'Leary, 1993, p. 18)

School board members across the country are deliberating the benefits and drawbacks of contracts with private companies. (National School Boards Association [NSBA], 1995, p. 1)

I n the next two chapters, we examine the most popular form of privatization in education—contracting out. In section one of this chapter, we expand on the description of contracting provided in Chapter 1. The final three sections describe contracting activity in education to date. We begin with a discussion of contracting initiatives in the area of educational support services. We then analyze contracting out in the area of curriculum and instruction, both in the performance contracting era (1969–1972) and in the current era of privatization (1990→). In Chapter 3, we will confront the question of whether or not contracting is a good tool for education or, more precisely, under what circumstances it may be helpful.

UNPACKING CONTRACTING OUT

"Privatization" by contract is an operational notion of privatization—in which a traditional responsibility of government is maintained but conducted by a private firm—and yet the état power of government is responsible for both the policy and the financial success of the "private" actor. (R. W. Bailey, 1987, p. 140)

Contracting out of public services is defined as the contractual utilization of nongovernmental entities to provide or help to provide public services. "Nongovernmental entities" can be companies, partnerships, individuals, nonprofit organizations, and/or independent contractors, whether for-profit or nonprofit. The test is whether the persons providing the service are school district employees. If they are and are also acting in that capacity, their services are not contracted out. (Lieberman, 1989, p. 7)

At a macro level, the attractiveness of privatization arises from a number of factors. To begin with, given the limited nationalization of industry in this country, the use of the more radical privatization measures popular in other countries, such as asset sales and load-shedding, are restricted (Pack, 1991). The popularity of contracting also "stems in part from the existence of legislative guidelines for the procurement of goods and the management of contracts, and from the degree of control that a governing body may retain over a service" (Clarkson, 1989, p. 169). Finally, while most Americans are eager to secure greater efficiency in the production of goods and services in the public sector, considerably fewer are willing to overturn the welfare state completely (Gormley, 1991a). Stated alternatively, for most government services, the issue of allocative efficiency is subordinated to the issue of technical efficiency (Pack, 1991). Contracting out is particularly useful in this context because it maintains a central role for the government in helping to define and finance services for its citizens while it holds out the possibility that those services can be produced more efficiently.

At the micro level, contracting out is popular because "it does not require basic changes in the governance structure or the statutory framework of public education" (Lieberman, 1989, p. 115). It is also seen as a moderate alternative to the more radical strategies of vouchers and deregulation (Whitty, 1984). Finally, there is a growing belief that contracting out will reduce costs and promote efficiency in public schools (NSBA, 1995).

As with all strategies in quadrant 3 of Figure 1.1, contracting out rests on the assumption that "few theoretical differences exist between public and private sector goods and services in how they can be supplied" (De Hoog, 1984, p. 5). It also draws strength from claims that "production is not the government's strong suit" (Savas, 1987, p. 288)—that "privatization by prudent contracting permits government to continue providing a service but to limit itself to the roles that best suit it: articulating the demand, acting as purchasing agent, monitoring the contractor's performance, and paying the bill" (p. 288). Through this arrangement, a variety of desirable outcomes—cost savings, flexibility, responsiveness—are expected.

The topic of "the variations of contracting for services also deserves some attention" (Kolderie & Hauer, 1991, p. 87). There can be significant variation in the number and types of contractors employed (Clarkson, 1989). Government agencies can contract with an assortment of producers, including private firms, nonprofit organizations, voluntary or neighborhood groups, or their own in-house departments (Savas, 1987; Worsnop, 1992): "Anyone willing to share the financial risk of education could be a party to a performance contract, such as teachers or teacher unions, nonprofit corporations and foundations, universities and professors, government agencies or civic groups" (Mecklenburger, 1972, p. 41). Production can also be split among these different sectors (Dudek & Company, 1989; Worsnop, 1992). Type-of-producer patterns often characterize the privatization of different areas of government operations. For example, for-profit private firms tend to be associated with utility services, while in health and human services, contracts with nonprofit organizations and neighborhood groups are most prevalent (Clarkson, 1989). There are also variations in the level of the production cycle, with "contracting...used most often for the procurement of intermediate goods" (Pack, 1991, p. 283), but with increasing frequency for inputs and final services as well.

Variations also exist because different domains of production—policy, administration, and service provision (Ismael, 1988)—can be highlighted in contracting. Or, to use Hirsch's (1991) terminology, different patterns of "vertical disintegration" (p. 27) can be realized. According to Hirsch, vertical disintegration occurs when a government agency that previously maintained control over all domains contracts out one or more of these activities to a non-public agency. This "vertical disintegration can take place in different parts of the vertical supply chain" (p. 27). For example, policy oversight and provision of a given service area may be retained in the public sphere, while management may be contracted to a private firm (President's Commission on Privatization, 1988):

> There are instances when government enters into a contract with a private management company to manage a public enterprise. For example, some municipalities contract out to private firms the managing of a municipal bus service or other types of urban transportation. Government then owns all the physical assets, the employees are public employees, and the government collects the fare from commuters—but the management service is provided by a private firm. (Hirsch, 1991, p. 32)

Alternatively, policy oversight and administration can be retained in the public sphere while the government unit contracts with a non-public agency to assume responsibility for production.

Another reason for variations in contracting is the considerable diversity in the ways government agencies treat service delivery. They "can purchase a service, or they can break the service down into its different components and buy certain elements of it: pieces of the work itself, support services for the work, the supervision of the work or of their support services, or the equipment and facilities needed for the work" (Kolderie & Hauer, 1991, p. 87). For example, public agencies in areas such as corrections and education might choose to contract out some or all of the support functions (e.g., transportation, maintenance, housekeeping), or they might choose to hand over to private producers the core service itself (i.e., custodial care in corrections and teaching in education).

Finally, considerable variance in two other aspects of contracting—contractor selection and type of contract developed—merits acknowledgement. The most common methods used to select a contractor at the local government level are as follows: lowest bid among qualified companies (57.5%); other (23.9%); lowest bid (12.3%); and best reputation (6.3%). The types of contracts that local agencies employ with contractors are: firm fixed price (43.4%); fixed price with incentives (25.9%); fixed price with escalation (14.6%); cost plus incentive fee (2.2%); fixed price with incentive (1.6%); and cost plus fixed fee (1.6%) (Roehm, Castellano, & Karns, 1991; see also Mecklenburger, 1972).

CONTRACTING OUT SUPPORT SERVICES

There is a long history of privatization in public education. Most of these involvements are in noninstructional areas. (Hunter, 1995a, p. 143)

Services that are not associated with the primary mission of public schools, often called support services, have traditionally been the chief candidates for privatization. School board members and superintendents report that they frequently seek help from the private sector for services like student transportation, food services, and facilities maintenance. (NSBA, 1995, p. 2)

What can we safely say about the contracting out of educational support services? To begin with, these services are significant, accounting for about 42 percent of total public school expenditures (Beales & O'Leary, 1993) and totaling some $100 billion. We know that "school districts have a long history with contracting out for noninstructional activities" (Lamdin, 1996, p. 2)—or what Brown (1995) refers to as the "hard services" (p. 115) of schooling—and that most of the contracting out in education has centered on these support functions (Lieberman, 1989; NSBA, 1995). We also know that school districts have contracted out a wide range of these services, everything from accounting to utilities management (see Table 2.1; also Beales & O'Leary, 1993; NSBA, 1995). There is also evidence that contracting out for support services is less contentious and more acceptable than are similar initiatives in the instructional realm (Brown, 1995; Doyle, 1994b). Furthermore, summary reports reveal that,

TABLE 2.1.
Noninstructional Services That Are Contracted Out by Public School Districts

Accounting/auditing services	Insurance services
Advertisements/public notices	Legal services
Architectural services	Medical/nursing services
Building cleaning	Moving services
Building maintenance	Paving services
Building security	Parking lots or garages
Construction	Procurement of goods
Data processing	Public relations services
Energy management	Pupil transportation
Evaluation services	School security
Executive searches	Solid waste collection or disposal
Fleet or vehicle maintenance	Utilities
Food service	Vehicle towing or storage

Note: From Hunter (1995a). Reprinted with permission of Corwin Press.

despite the relatively longstanding tradition of contracting out support services, there is also considerable room for expansion of such services. No support area is more than one-third in the hands of private firms, and schools use contractors much less frequently than do other organizations (Beales & O'Leary, 1993). Finally, there is a growing belief "that more educational support services will be contracted out to private entities in the future" (Lyons, 1995, p. 156).

While schools use private companies to provide an increasing assortment of support functions, the areas that are most likely to be contracted out are transportation, food services, and building maintenance (Beales & O'Leary, 1993; Lyons, 1995). According to recent studies, the moving of youngsters to and from school "represents an enormous transportation system, with $8.3 billion spent in 1990" (Beales & O'Leary, 1993, p. 5). Currently, roughly 30 percent of the public school transportation system is provided by the private sector (Beales & O'Leary, 1993; NSBA, 1995). In the area of food services, private management of school cafeterias is on the upswing. According to Beales and O'Leary (1993), in 1987 only four percent of school districts contracted for food services. By 1993, that figure had increased to 11 percent. The 1995 NSBA survey suggests that this figure may have increased even more dramatically over the last two years, with upward to 30 percent of the cafeteria function of schooling now provided by private firms. Four companies have been especially active in the for-profit, public school food-service market: Aramark, Inc., Marriott, Canteen, and Service America (Hunter, 1995a). As of 1993, the cleaning, repair, and maintenance of the nation's 83,000 K–12 public school buildings cost taxpayers approximately $9 billion annually. Roughly 10 percent of this work was being let to private contractors.

CONTRACTING OUT EDUCATIONAL SERVICES: THE PERFORMANCE CONTRACTING ERA (1969-1972)

> The history of private management of public schools is rooted in the history of performance contracting. (Richards, Shore, & Sawicky, 1996, p. 18)

> Although performance contracts of one sort or another have been widely used in government procurement for a number of years, it was not until the Texarkana experience of 1969 that this technique was applied to the procurement of educational services. (Gramlich & Koshel, 1975, p. 52)

> Since its inception in 1969, thousands of words describing performance contracting have appeared in the mass media and in the education press. But most educators still don't have an accurate picture of what has happened. (Mecklenburger, 1972, p. 1)

While "the idea of using economic incentives in education is actually very old" (Gramlich & Koshel, 1975, p. 5), dating back to performance contracting in mid-to-late nineteenth-century England (Blaschke, 1972), contracting for educational services in the United States was virtually unheard of until the famous Texarkana experiment in 1969. Then, during a brief period in the early 1970s, it inspired a series of interesting and informative—if often ill-fated—experiments, only to be returned to the warehouse of policy initiatives until resurfacing again some twenty years later in the early 1990s. In the two sections that follow, we review the trials in contracting out during: the performance contracting era (1969–1972) and the privatization era (1990→). In reviewing the performance contracting era, we focus on the Texarkana, OEO, and Banneker experiments.

The Texarkana Project

Fueled by many of the same forces energizing the current interest in privatization (see Chapter 1), especially assessments of the poor quality of education, heightened demands for accountability, and a nearly unbridled faith in the power of private market mechanisms, policymakers and educators brought contracting to the educational forefront for one brief and explosive moment in the early 1970s. As Mecklenburger (1972) notes, "The original promoters of the idea [performance contracting] in education were U.S. Office of Education (USOE) officials, private firms in the education business and a few educators" (p. 2). The first experiment took place in Texarkana[3] when three districts— working with Charles Blaschke, who was the nation's leading expert on performance contracting in education, and with the support of federal compensatory aid (from ESEA Title VIII funds)—joined forces to employ a private contractor "to use performance contracting to discourage students from dropping out" (Blaschke, 1972, p. 12). Mecklenburger (1972) sets the scene as follows:

> Texarkana, with its low achievement, high dropout rate, desegregation deadline and tight budget, provided an opportunity to demonstrate that schools could purchase low-cost, low-risk attempts to solve their problems.
>
> From school superintendents' point of view, Blaschke's proposal would ease a crisis, provide extra money and jobs, lower the dropout rate, enhance their reputation and bring new techniques and expertise to the schools. Also, Blaschke adds, a successful program would enable school officials to demonstrate that certification, tenure and other regulations restrain school systems from solving their own problems. It was a something-for-everyone proposal which had wide public appeal in Texarkana. (p. 10)

A number of aspects of the Texarkana contracting design are noteworthy, almost all of which became central planks in the infrastructure that has been forged to support compensatory and special education activities in the United States over the last quarter century. To begin with, the contractor, Dorsett Educational Systems, was a "manufacturer of teaching machines" (Mecklenburger, 1972, p. 11) and "relied heavily…on audiovisual aids" (Gramlich & Koshel, 1975, p. 6) in its effort to enhance learning.

> Dorsett made heavy use of its teaching machine to present instructional materials. This machine coordinates a film presentation with a sound recording. It responds by voice to students' correct and incorrect answers. However, as this was Dorsett's first major demonstration of the machine, the company had to either adapt other publishers' material or create teaching material in the course of the year. Thus, for Dorsett, the Texarkana project was an opportunity both to demonstrate the machine's capabilities and to develop instructional materials concurrent with instruction. (Mecklenburger, 1972, p. 12)

Second, the project emphasized individualized instruction and a clinical model of teaching. The learning system was based on efforts to "'diagnose' student learning needs, 'prescribe' what a student needed to learn and present him with a sequence of programmed instructional materials. The next year, several other educational technology companies used this same basic 'individualized instruction' concept" (Mecklenburger, 1972, p. 12). Third, these were pull-out programs—called Rapid Learning Centers in this case—where students worked for extended periods of time outside their regular classrooms, generally on basic skills instruction.

Fourth, the program emphasized the use of paraprofessional educators working with professional teachers. Fifth, the entire system was anchored on "motivational techniques borrowed from work of behavioral psychologists and referred to as 'contingency management'" (Mecklenburger, 1972, p. 12).

Tangible rewards were an especially important component of the program. Finally, there was the introduction of performance contracting, with a strong emphasis on accountability:

> Dorsett signed a contract with the school board stipulating that reimbursement should be directly related to students' achievement scores. If the students did not reach a certain level in a certain period of time, the company would not be reimbursed even for its costs. Because this arrangement rewarded the firm only for successful teaching, it came to be know as a performance contract. (Gramlich & Koshel, 1975, pp. 6–7)

> In order to performance contract on the basis of student "gain," a pretest was given each child when he entered the learning center. When it was judged he had achieved sufficiently, he was retested. If he had gained at least one year's growth, he returned to his regular classroom and another student entered. (Mecklenburger, 1972, p. 12)

> If a student reached this level in eighty instructional hours, Dorsett was to be paid approximately $80, roughly the cost of educating that student. If a student achieved this level sooner, Dorsett would be paid more and make a profit; if later, Dorsett would be paid less and lose; and if a student still had not graduated in 168 hours, Dorsett would get nothing at all. (Gramlich & Koshel, 1975, p. 7)

Early reports from the Texarkana project "indicated that educational achievement was increasing dramatically" (Lieberman, 1989, p. 87). Educators from every state in the nation visited the Texarkana experiment during the 1969-1970 school year. Although a scandal arose over student assessment in the program when charges were made that students had seen test items from the final examination in advance—allegations affirmed by two sets of auditors— more than 100 school districts adopted performance contracting for the 1970-1971 school year (Gramlich & Koshel, 1975). The most significant outcome, however, was a project initiated by the Office of Economic Opportunity (OEO)—"a national experiment to determine whether performance contracting as used in Texarkana would serve to fulfill Pres. Nixon's demand for 'accountability'" (Mecklenburger, 1972, p. 14).

The OEO Experiment

> This qualified interest in performance contracting, the President's pleas for accountability, and another theme in the same presidential message on education that the government should not adopt policies until there was assurance they would work finally led to the decision to conduct a social experiment in educational performance contracting. (Gramlich & Koshel, 1975, p. 9)

> The major experiment with performance contracting…began in April, 1970, when two Office of Economic Opportunity officials visited Texarkana to review first-hand

the project that had introduced a "shaft of light" into their analysis of compensatory projects. (Blaschke, 1972, p. 20)

The goals of the OEO project have been described by Blaschke (1972) as follows:

The major objective of the OEO experiment was to determine if any of the six different instructional systems used by performance contractors could produce significant results in math and reading for poor, underachieving students. A second goal was to determine the feasibility of performance contracting as a technique for conducting a large-scale field experiment. And, in light of the scanty information [available],…a third purpose was to establish some benchmarks and standards for school officials to judge firms' proposals in the future. (p. 21)

The OEO experiment incorporated important features of the Texarkana project. The focus was on compensatory education. Incentives for program participants and accountability for the contractor were emphasized. As in Texarkana, contractors were to be compensated based on student learning gains. Particular pedagogical and curricular innovations were highlighted, including individualized instruction and programmed materials (i.e., teaching machines), clinical teaching, and the use of paraprofessionals (Blaschke, 1972; Lieberman, 1989; Mecklenburger, 1972).

The general theme underlying the instructional programs of the six companies was to increase student motivation. All programs attempted to avoid the allegedly stifling traditional classroom atmosphere where the teacher worked with the entire group, students were at attention, and desks were neatly lined up in straight rows. The performance contracting programs instead featured individually prescribed lesson plans, students working on their own projects at their own pace, a much more casual classroom atmosphere, and also much noisier classrooms. Rather than having one fully licensed teacher in every classroom, many of the companies tried to replace and supplement these teachers as much as possible with aides, paraprofessionals, and a range of teaching machines, audiovisual tutors, and cassette recorders. The firms also insisted on refurbishing the classroom facilities with small tables and chairs or learning carrels, which could be grouped in many ways depending on the day's activities; sometimes there were carpets to cut down noise. (Gramlich & Koshel, 1975, pp. 23–24)

The initial trial consisted of six contractors operating in three districts each, for a total of 18 sites (see Table 2.2). In addition to the contracts with the six "educational technology companies" (Mecklenburger, 1972, p. 25), OEO also entered into agreements with three affiliates of the National Educational Association. At each of the original 18 sites, contractors taught 100 students in six grades—the first, second, and third and the seventh, eighth, and ninth—for a total of 600 youngsters. In each district, there was also a matched control group of 100 students in the same six grades. In total, then, over 21,000 students were involved in the experiment (Mecklenburger, 1972).

TABLE 2.2.
Contractors and Sites for the OEO Experiment

Alpha Learning Corp.	Quality Educational Development
Hartford, CT	Anchorage, AK
Grand Rapids, MI	Dallas, TX
Taft, TX	Rockland, ME
Learning Foundations	Singer/Graflex
Bronx, NY	McComb, MS
Duval County, FL	Portland, ME
Hammond, IN	Seattle, WA
Plan Education Centers	Westinghouse Learning Corp.
Athens, GA	Fresno, CA
Selmer, TN	Las Vegas, NV
Wichita, KS	Philadelphia, PA

The incentive contracts employed in the project provided payments to companies based upon student achievement gains during one academic year. As Gramlich and Koshel (1975) report, due largely to overconfidence on the part of the companies, the contracts themselves "were quite unfavorable to the firms...there was much for the contractors to lose and little for them to gain" (pp. 14, 16). The typical contract was crafted in such a manner that no payments were made for students who failed to gain one grade equivalent. An increase of 1.6 grade equivalents was needed for a contractor to break even, and "all students in the entire class would have to gain an average of 1.9 grade equivalent units for the firm to earn its maximum payment, which would exceed its total cost by only 15 percent" (p. 15). Given that, in the past, students in the experiment had gained approximately .64 grade equivalents per year, the requirements in the contracts were arduous, to say the least (Gramlich & Koshel, 1975).

Two hundred school districts that appeared to be interested in performance contracting were invited to apply. Seventy-seven of them requested to participate in the trial. This list, in turn, was winnowed down to 18 on the basis of five criteria:

1. At least 80 percent of the district population had poverty-level incomes, as defined by Title I of the Elementary and Secondary Education Act.
2. District students were below national norms in reading and mathematics.
3. The district enrolled the required numbers of students in the grades covered by the study.
4. The district had recent, valid, and reliable test achievement data so that it was feasible to assign students to experimental and control groups.
5. The absence of any problems that might interfere with the experiment. (Lieberman, 1989, pp. 87–88)

Individual schools within the districts were selected on the basis of the severity of academic deficiency: "The most academically deficient schools in a district were typically assigned by OEO to the experimental groups and the next most deficient to the control groups" (Gramlich & Koshel, 1975, p. 19). Individual students were selected using the same criterion: "Students judged to be most deficient academically were selected for the experiment" (p. 19).

The most important issue to be determined by the experiment was "whether or not private companies did in fact outperform the public schools in the control group" (Gramlich & Koshel, 1975, p. 32). Evaluations designed to answer this question found the effects of the experiment to be quite disappointing, especially in light of the extremely high expectations held by nearly everyone associated with the project. The report of Battelle Laboratories, the non-profit agency that conducted all the student testing for the trial, concluded:

> There is very little evidence that performance incentive contracting, as implemented by the technology companies at the 18 school districts in this study for a period of one year, had a beneficial effect on the reading and mathematics achievement of students participating in the experiment, as measured by a standardized achievement test. (cited in Lieberman, 1989, pp. 88–89)

The OEO report itself was equally disheartening:

> The single most important question for all concerned with the experiment is: Was performance contracting more successful than traditional classroom methods in improving the reading and math skills of poor children? The answer is: No.
>
> While we judge this experiment to be a success in terms of the information it can offer about the capabilities of performance contractors, it is clearly another failure in our search for means of helping poor and disadvantaged youngsters to develop the skills they need to lift themselves out of poverty. (cited in Mecklenburger, 1972, p. 23)

The specifics from which these conclusions were drawn have been summarized by Lieberman (1989) as follows:

> Using each grade at each site as a unit of comparison, the test results showed that the experimental groups scored better than the control groups in 28 cases, or 13 percent of the total number of comparisons. In 60 cases—28 percent of the total— the students in the control group scored higher than the experimental group. In 124 comparisons—59 percent of the total—there was no significant difference between the two groups. (p. 88)

Thus, under even the most optimistic review of the data, the "evidence indicates that performance contracting was not successful" (Gramlich & Koshel,

1975, p. 50) in the OEO project. Even when there were gains, they were marginal, and they "fell well short of what would be required to eliminate the achievement of differences of the students" (p. 41).

As is the case with any major policy initiative, the OEO project has been the subject of considerable ex post facto analysis. In particular, a good deal has been written about the fact that conditions operating at the time—lack of adequate time for preparation, confusion over project goals, testing problems, teacher resistance, poorly conceptualized contracts, and so forth—greatly hindered the viability of the experiment (see especially Lieberman, 1989, and Mecklenburger, 1972). In short, reasonable questions about the findings themselves and about the policy conclusions drawn from the trial have been raised over the years. For example, a 1973 General Accounting Office study of the OEO project concluded that "because of a number of shortcomings in both the design and implementation of the experiment, it is our opinion that the question as to the merits of performance contracting versus traditional educational methods remains unanswered" (cited in Lieberman, 1989, p. 98).

For our purposes here, three points can be made by way of a conclusion. First, "as a result of this negative evaluation, educational performance contracting virtually disappeared" (Lieberman, 1989, p. 89). On the demand side of the equation, "districts that had been contemplating similar projects dropped their plans to do so; districts that had contracts usually did not renew them" (p. 89). On the supply side, interest in contracting also plummeted:

> Whether rightly or not, the firms became very disillusioned with the whole idea of performance contracting and were not at all mollified by the rather generous final settlement of the contracts proposed by OEO. Of the six firms in the experiment, one went bankrupt, two more dropped direct classroom work, and all six stopped accepting incentive-based contracts. (Gramlich & Koshel, 1975, p. 54)

Second, "given the enormous difficulties in planning and implementation, it is still difficult to know how much credence to place in the results" (p. 31). Certainly, the claim that performance contracting as a policy intervention is incapable of enhancing student performance was drawn prematurely. Third, while there are many commonalities (Richards et al., 1996), there are also distinct differences between the contracting out via performance contracting of the OEO project and the contracting out via privatization initiatives that dot the policy landscape today (Lieberman, 1989; Richards et al., 1996).

The Banneker School Project

While a number of performance contracts were operational during the 1970-1971 academic year, the most noteworthy project other than the OEO trial was occurring at Banneker Elementary School in Gary, Indiana. This experiment is famous because it was the first and, until 1990, the only contract involving an entire school (Mecklenburger, 1972; Richards et al., 1996), thus making it "the most extensive illustration of performance contracting" (Gramlich & Koshel, 1975, p. 74) until the recent experiment in Baltimore. "The contract involved more money, more responsibility for the contractor, and a longer period of time than any other performance contract" (Mecklenburger, 1972, p. 28). Gramlich and Koshel (1975) provide the following overview of the project:

> Here a private teaching firm, Behavioral Research Laboratories (BRL), was given a performance contract to teach the entire elementary student body for three years. Parents in the neighborhood served by this school were free to send their children to other schools if they chose, and other parents in the district were free to enroll their children in Banneker. The firm was supposed to conduct all instruction in the school, though because of the difficulty in measuring gains in some subjects, the contracts stipulated that payment would be based only on achievement test scores in reading and mathematics. At the end of three years, the Gary contracts guaranteed the firm about $2,400 for every student attaining the national norms in standardized reading and mathematics tests, but—like the contracts in Texarkana and in the OEO experiment—it got nothing for the others. (p. 35)

Two strategies were central to the BRL program at Banneker. First, the professional workforce was restructured through differentiated staffing. Twenty-one full-time, paraprofessional aides (along with additional materials) were substituted for 13 certified teachers, leaving 21 licensed teachers, five of whom were "curriculum managers" responsible for a specific subject area and 16 of whom focused directly on classroom instruction. At the helm were two administrators, a center manager, and a learning director. Second, a "total systems approach" to learning was implemented. As with other performance contracting initiatives, BRL emphasized clinical instruction, individualized education, programmed instructional materials, the use of paraprofessionals, and learning centers. The program was ungraded, and "the day was organized on the basis of 20-minute modules of instruction" (Mecklenburger, 1972, p. 32).

Difficulties experienced at other contracting sites also visited the Banneker experiment. The teachers union (AFT) objected to a number of elements of the "total systems approach," especially changes associated with differentiated staffing. The State Board of Education challenged what it viewed as non-compliance with state regulations in the areas of staffing (pupil-teacher ratios) and curriculum (Mecklenburger, 1972). Results of the project in terms of student test scores have been summarized by Mecklenburger:

> During the first year at Banneker, 72.5%, or 396 of the 546 children in the program in grades 2-6, made average or better-than-average gains in reading, mathematics or both. Thirty-two percent, or 176 pupils, made 1.5 years' gain or more. In addition, 90%, or 72 of 80 kindergarten children in the program, scored at or

above national academic "readiness" norms, indicating the likelihood of their future success in school.

In the 1970–71 school year, student performance was measured in terms of gains between October 1 and June 1 administrations of the Metropolitan Achievement Tests. The 546 pupils measured in grades 2–6 in the Banneker program averaged 9.5 months growth in both reading and mathematics during the eight months between the two tests. (p. 31)

Overall, these results are much stronger than those recorded by most other performance contractors of this era. Although it must be noted that, since BRL was paid only for performance in mathematics and reading, instruction was heavily skewed in favor of those subjects (Gramlich & Koshel, 1975). Nonetheless, the project was terminated "in the fall of 1972, a year ahead of schedule because of the same contractual and educational problems encountered in the OEO experience" (p. 74).

CONTRACTING OUT EDUCATIONAL SERVICES: THE PRIVATIZATION ERA (1990→)

Then, what is the nature of the emerging privatization of public education in America? The privatization movement is one in which public schools are being asked to "contract out" for services beyond the traditional privatization of hard services, such as securing transportation, food services, paper and other similar items, and are now entering into agreements with private vendors for instructional services (human services). (Brown, 1995, p. 120)

Some see it as a means for improving student achievement and increasing the schools' abilities to fulfill their roles and responsibilities; others view it as a management-for-profit venture that is inappropriate in running the public schools. (NSBA, 1995, p. viii)

In the not so long run, public school management may come to view contracting out instruction as a necessity instead of as an option. (Lieberman, 1989, p. 115)

The Development of a Movement

We find that public schools have always contracted with the private sector for goods and services, but is just beginning to contract with private for-profit vendors for the purpose of providing students with regular instructional programs. (Brown & Hunter, 1995, pp. 112–113)

The next round of school outsourcing has begun: delivering instruction, in part or in toto. (Cooper & Doyle, 1996, p. 48)

A variety of indicators suggests that the markets are expanding. (Richards et al., 1996)

A New Focus

As we noted in the last section, the difficulties experienced with performance contracting in the early 1970s came close to destroying interest in contracting out educational services. For the remainder of the 1970s and throughout the 1980s, districts were very "reluctant to look for outside help in instructional services" (NSBA, 1995, p. 3): "The idea of private contractors remained dormant until the early 1990s" (Lamdin, 1996, p. 3). Particularly noteworthy, as both Whitty (1984) and Lieberman (1988; 1989) remind us, is the fact that the educational reform movements of the 1980s paid almost no attention to contracting out as a strategy for school improvement. As a consequence, districts continued to produce rather than purchase instructional services, looking to private contractors only when they had no recourse (e.g., in the case of certain special education students for whom districts were unable to provide services) (Lieberman, 1988). Indeed, moving into the mid-1990s, it was still the case that "instructional programming represent[ed] a very small part of the privatization market" (NSBA, 1995, pp. 2-3), with special education being "the only area of instructional programming to receive double digit percentages (14 percent)" (p. 3). Not unexpectedly, therefore, "contracting of public education only recently has attracted the attention of policy analysts. Neither demand side movement by districts, nor supply side activity by contractors was detectable until fairly recently. No local districts were engaged in this practice, so there was nothing to study empirically" (Lamdin, 1996, p. 3).

However, the confluence of the privatization forces described in Chapter 1 and a seemingly intractable set of problems in the educational industry is leading "a growing number of school districts...[to] look to the private sector for basic educational services" (Beales & O'Leary, 1993, p. 19): "Today...a growing number of school districts are expanding the concept [of contracting] to more fundamental educational services" (David, 1992, p. 2). As Lamdin (1996) characterizes the phenomenon, "seemingly spontaneous, and necessarily simultaneously, both contracting districts and operating contractors have emerged" (p. 3). What is new about this interest in contracting out "is the scope of the services and programs offered by business, up to and including the management of the district and its academic programs" (NSBA, 1995, p. iii), "the request to use private organizations to conduct and manage the regular program" (Brown & Hunter, 1995, p. 108).[4]

Contracting out initiatives that focus on the educational production function are generally of two types (Walsh, 1996b). The first, known as Educational Management Organizations (EMOs), are comprehensive in nature (Wenger, 1994) and include "companies that offer to manage entire school systems or entire schools" (NSBA, 1995, p. 1). Some of the best known of the EMOs, such as Educational Alternatives, Inc. (EAI) and the Edison Project, are profiled below. These "firms typically are given the same per-pupil funding as the public schools and assume full responsibility for all aspects of school operations, including administration, teacher training, and noninstructional functions such as building maintenance, food service, and clerical support" (Beales & O'Leary, 1993, p. 19). A second group of firms are known as Specialty Service Providers (SSPs). These businesses contract to fulfill specific educational functions (e.g., delivering professional development) or to provide selected educational services (e.g., foreign language instruction). SSPs include small "mom-and-pop" operations and individual entrepreneurs working out of their homes as well as larger firms such as the Sylvan Corporation, which has contracts with over a dozen school districts and works with over 3,000 remedial students. Before we turn to more detailed descriptions of EMOs and SSPs, we review briefly the developing infrastructure of the education contracting movement, describing the development of the American Association of Educators in Private Practice, the Education Industry Conference, and the *Education Industry Report*.

A Growth Industry

In 1990, when the American Association of Educators in Private Practice (AAEPP)[5] was formed, it had 16 members. By 1994, it had over 200 members (Yelich, 1994). A year later over 400 enterprises were in the fold, ranging from the larger and more well-known firms such as Berlitz and the Edison Project to small businesses and individual teachers. The AAEPP started a national newsletter, *Enterprising Educators*, in the fall of 1990, and in 1992 brought its annual conference, "Edventures," on line. The conference regularly draws educators, entrepreneurs, and investors from throughout the nation.

In February 1996, Lehman Brothers sponsored the First Annual Education Industry Conference "to introduce investment clients to promising companies that focus on education" (Walsh, 1996b, p. 1). In the brochure for the program, Mary C. Tanner, Managing Director, and Michael T. Moe, First Vice President—the firm's leading analysts on education-related companies—argued that "although the education sector is one of the last government-run monopolies in America, we at Lehman Brothers believe that private sector involvement is on the verge of significant expansion" (p. 2). They averred that the conference would "give investors some sense of a $600 billion industry and perhaps draw some parallels to the delivery of healthcare in this country only 20 years ago" (p. 2). The conference featured senior management from 40 corporations "in school management, software, child care, postsecondary education, and corporate training" (Walsh, 1996b, p. 1), including such well-known enterprises as Walt Disney Corporation, the Children's Television Network, and KinderCare Learning Centers, Inc. Over 350 persons attended the conference ("Education Industry Conference," 1996).

John McLaughlin[6] founded the *Education Industry Report* in 1993. Today the *Report*, which is designed to chronicle key issues in the area of private-public partnerships, reaches some 500 subscribers. It has become the leading source of investment information on the quickly developing contracting out movement.

Profiles of EMOs

Few issues in education today seem at once so appealing and so frightening as the notion of a local school district hiring a private company to come in and run its schools. ("Education, Inc.: Perspectives," 1994, p. 55)

Private management is the primary way that public schools can improve both educationally and financially and still remain public schools. (Golle, 1994, p. 60)

Edison Project

The Edison Project is the big and bold experiment we need. The size of it will really test our ideas. (Michael Kirst, cited in Walsh, 1992, p. 18)

If they are successful, they will have put the first nail in the coffin of public education as we know it. (Jonathan Kozol, cited in Walsh, 1992, p. 18)

Roots and evolution. In May 1991, Chris Whittle, the founder of Channel One, launched the Edison Project, an ambitious endeavor to create a blueprint for a new American school system (Walsh, 1992) and to incorporate that design into a system of for-profit schools (Brodinsky, 1993; see also "Edison Project's Core Team Named," 1992). The original plan was to start 200 schools by 1995 and to bring an additional 800 on line by 2010. Some $2.5 billion was to be invested in creating the "new educational infrastructure" (Brodinsky, 1993, p. 542), including the intellectual and physical capital. Schools were to be privately operated and funded—that is, tuition would be charged—at the equivalent of the cost of educating the average student in the United States. Campuses were to "be built in all types of communities, including the most desperate inner-city areas" (Whittle, cited in Brodinsky, 1993, p. 542). Twenty percent of the places in the schools were to be reserved for scholarship students and the student population at each site was to reflect the composition of the local community (Lyons, 1995). Educational innovations developed by the Edison Project were to be made readily available to public sector schools.

At the time of its launch, the Edison Project had $60 million (of the $2.5 billion needed) in seed capital from a variety of corporations, including Chris Whittle's parent corporation, Whittle Communications (Brodinsky, 1993; Walsh, 1992). The three-year task of creating the new model of schooling fell to a seven-member design team appointed in February 1992:

- Daniel Biederman, the president of the Grand Central and 34th Street Partnerships in New York City.
- Dominique Browning, an assistant managing editor of *Newsweek* magazine.
- John E. Chubb, senior fellow with the governmental studies program at the Brookings Institution.
- Lee Eisenberg, the former editor-in-chief of *Esquire* magazine.

- Chester E. Finn, Jr., professor of education and public policy at Vanderbilt University and former Assistant Secretary of Education, USDOE.
- Nancy Hechinger, the founder of an interactive multimedia production company and a former designer at the Apple Media Lab.
- Sylvia L. Peters, the principal of the Alexandre Dumas Elementary School in Chicago. (Walsh, 1992; "Edison Project's Core Team Named," 1992)

The initiative garnered considerable notoriety and prestige in June 1992 when it lured Benno C. Schmidt from the presidency of Yale University to take charge of the project (Walsh, 1992).

Plagued by difficulties in raising the required capital, Edison began to scale back on its original design to develop an independent system of for-profit schools (McCarthy, 1995). The major alteration came in the fall of 1993 when the Project put into abeyance its plan to enter into direct competition with public schools and instead "turned to competing with other private-sector educational contractors for contracts with public schools" (Farrell, Johnson, Jones, & Sapp, 1994, p. 74). The immediate goal became more circumscribed, to work with as many as 20 public schools by the fall of 1995 (Walsh, 1993b).

One year later, Edison's prospects looked dim indeed. Money to fuel the initiative continued to be in short supply. Progress in lining up and locking in public school partners was painfully slow. Whittle was experiencing considerable financial difficulties with his other companies, a condition that limited his own ability to contribute to the project as well as his appeal to the investment community. Rumors of differences between President Schmidt and Chairman Whittle began to surface in the press (Applebome, 1994a; Walsh, 1993b, 1994c). The original design looked totally unreachable, while even the scaled-back plan appeared to be floundering badly. Critics, in turn, were emboldened, averring that the entire adventure was "an oversold fantasy that would use America's school children as bait for investors" (Applebome, 1994a, p. 83). Applebome summed up the situation—for Edison:

> Three years after promising to combine entrepreneurial razzle-dazzle with cutting-edge education, it has come to this for the Edison Project of for-profit schools envisioned by the media entrepreneur Chris Whittle: Either the project raises $25 million to $50 million within the next two months or it dies a very noisy, public death. (p. 82)

and for the contracting out movement in general:

> Also at issue is the future of the budding, if hugely controversial, movement to bring corporate America into the nation's classrooms. (p. 83)

Through the efforts of its new vice president, Deborah McGriff, a former superintendent of the Detroit public schools who was hired in October 1993, the Project began to improve its efforts to line up potential partner schools (Walsh,

1993d). A year-and-a-half later, four schools—in Boston, Massachusetts; Wichita, Kansas; Mount Clement, Michigan; and Sherman, Texas—were on line to join the Edison Project in September 1995 (McGriff, 1995; Walsh, 1993d, 1994b, 1995c). Also, by March 1995, a much-needed infusion of funds, some $30 million, was secured (Walsh, 1995a). This additional capital permitted the Edison Project to bankroll its first year of operation in four elementary schools. In December of 1995, the company appointed John C. Reid, a senior executive with the Coca-Cola Company, as its chief operating officer ("Edison Project," 1996).

Program design

A significant research and development effort that unfolded over three years provides the foundation for Edison's version of "new ways to conduct education in the United States" (Schmidt, cited in Brodinsky, 1993, p. 543). The design itself has been described by Edison officials (B. C. Schmidt, 1994; McGriff, 1995) and a number of educational analysts (Bingham, 1996; Brodinsky, 1993; R. L. Bailey, 1995; Walsh, 1993a, 1994a, 1995c; Wichita State University, 1996). The three overviews offered below provide a fairly detailed snapshot of the essence of the Edison Project.

McGriff (1995) offers a particularly helpful synopsis of the design:

> The essentials of our school design build on the work of the most effective reform efforts in public and private schools around the globe. Our school organization will allow teams of diverse teachers to work with the same small group of students for several years. World-class curriculum standards, instructional methods that motivate, performance-based assessment, a longer school day (one or two hours longer), a longer school year (approximately a month more), and technology for an information age will create a new and exciting learning experience.
>
> Our technology curriculum requires a computer in the home of every Edison family, a laptop in the hands of every teacher, and technology at the fingertips of students and teachers any time of the day. Four computers will be installed in each regular classroom, and one computer will be available in each specialty classroom. The library/media center will have 10 permanent computers and possibly loaners.
>
> The Common, our online computer network, will link educators, students, parents, and communities, giving them access to a vast array of resources and learning tools. Parents and citizens will participate in the day-to-day operation and governance of partnership schools. A parent advisory council and a board of friends will meet regularly to discuss school issues and hear families' concerns and suggestions.
>
> Most importantly, Edison partnership schools will be accountable to their communities, which will be able to dismiss the Edison Project at any time if they are not satisfied with the performance of the corporation or the students. (pp. 75–76)

B. C. Schmidt (1994) has outlined 12 highlights of the Edison school design. From our perspective, the first four components and the last element might best be thought of as the foundation of the plan, while items 5 through 11 can be considered implementation components and strategies:

1. A basis in research
2. Clear and defining values (liberty, diversity, dignity, and character and virtue)
3. High standards for all children
4. A far larger role for school in the lives of children and parents
5. Curriculum in five domains (math and science, humanities and fine arts, health and physical fitness, morality and ethics, practical skills and arts)
6. Truly professional teachers
7. Proven—and individualized—instructional methods
8. Intelligent uses of powerful technology
9. Organized for success
10. True accountability
11. Parent and community participation
12. The benefits of system and scale. (pp. 61–63)

An especially user-friendly picture of the key ingredients of the Edison school design has been provided by Bingham (1996) in her review of Dodge Elementary School in Wichita:

1. A computer placed in the home of every student so children and parents can easily communicate with the school.
2. A longer school day and school year, providing more learning time for students.
3. Organization of the school into smaller units called houses, consisting of 110–120 students of mixed ages. A team of four teachers leads each house, staying with the same students for two or three years.
4. A reading program already shown by controlled studies to significantly raise reading levels. Ninety minutes of reading a day in groups of no more than 15, with extra tutoring for children who need it.
5. Lessons in character building.
6. Emphasis on ensuring that all students master the fundamentals of reading and math by second grade.
7. Instruction in Spanish for all students beginning in kindergarten.
8. Language arts, math, science, social studies, art, music, physical fitness and health.
9. Ninety minutes of planning and professional development time for teachers each day.
10. A laptop computer for every teacher, and 4 computers and one TV/VCR combination per classroom.
11. Quarterly learning contracts signed by teachers, students and families. (p. 89)

According to McGriff (1995), these essential elements and values compose about 70 percent of any individual school's design. The Project "then collaborates with parents and educators in each community to customize the remainder of the school design locally" (p. 75).

Evaluation

As Lamdin (1996) reminds us, the future of contracting out educational services "is difficult to assess. Thus far it has been implemented only on a limited experimental basis. Because experiments take years to implement and evaluate, and more such experiments are necessary to make confident general assessments, the success or failure of contracting will not be resolved any time soon" (p. 21). In short, the data on the impact of recent contracting out initiatives are quite thin (Richards et al., 1996).

Nonetheless, given the highly controversial nature of private management in public education, the school districts that have contracted with the Edison Project are under very close scrutiny. After one year of experimentation, preliminary reviews of the Edison Project on a quite limited number of indicators tend to be positive. Hard evidence on student achievement is not readily available (Wichita State University, 1996) and the company acknowledges that any "profit is likely years away" (Walsh, 1996d, p. 11). On measures of customer satisfaction, preliminary results are encouraging for the supporters of the Edison Project (Wichita State University, 1996). Waiting lists to enter the existing four sites are the norm. Each of the four initial sponsoring districts have agreed to expand into the middle grades for the 1996-1997 school year. In addition, four other communities have signed contracts with Edison, bringing the total number of schools to 12 for the 1996-1997 school year. Finally, on the labor front, while the two national teachers unions continue to follow these initiatives closely, "neither has declared war on the Edison Project" (Walsh, 1996d, p. 11) as they have on the EAI and Alternative Public Schools experiments.

Educational Alternatives, Inc.

Because of the scope of its work and its current experience managing public schools, EAI is widely seen as an important test case for private management in public education. (American Federation of Teachers [AFT], 1995, p. i)

What we're going to have left is nothing for the children. You treat them like so much livestock. This is an invitation to corruption. (Steven Fournier, a parent in Hartford, Connecticut, quoted in Innerst, 1994, p. 59)

But even if it survives only in a small way, Educational Alternatives could change the way in which the nation operates its public schools. (P. Schmidt, 1992b, p. 13)

In the mid-1980s, a Minnesota computer company, Control Data Corporation, spent more than two years and $1 million in development funds to create an approach to learning known as the Tesseract Way, which was to provide the foundation for a group of innovative new schools. After deciding to abandon that endeavor in favor of providing more attention to its core computer operations, Control Data sold its education business, USSA Private Schools, to John Golle. During its early years as an independent entity, the firm's goal was to build a chain of 20 private schools that would compete directly with public schools (Richards et al., 1996). The high costs of building and developing facilities, however, soon caused the company to shift "its strategic focus to providing school management, consulting services, and educational products" (P. Schmidt, 1992b, p. 13). In May 1991 and June 1992, EAI made its first common stock offerings—1,663,690 shares at $4 each in May and an additional 425,000 shares at $7 each in June. By the end of 1992, about 4 million shares were outstanding (P. Schmidt, 1992a, 1992b).

The basic strategy of EAI, as is the case with most EMOs, is to improve the quality of education while relying on the extant per-pupil cost structure, usually the average per-pupil cost in the district. In a company brochure, EAI describes the goal as follows: "Our mission is not to replace or compete with public schools but to be the public schools—and to fundamentally change the dynamics of the learning environment" (cited in P. Schmidt, 1992b, p. 13). When EAI enters into an agreement with a school or district, the "teachers, administrators, and other public school employees remain public but are subject to the private company's management" (Brodinsky, 1993, p. 547). In the framework presented earlier, the policy and service provision functions remain in the public sphere, while the administration function is privatized (Ismael, 1988).

The initial aim of EAI is to reduce costs about 25 percent, mostly by garnering available efficiencies in operational support areas (e.g., plant and maintenance, food services) and administration (e.g., secretarial services, school management) (Hunter, 1995a). To reach this goal, EAI works in tandem with three partners: Johnson Controls, which specializes in the maintenance dimensions of the school plant; KPMG Peat Marwick, which focuses on the school's financial and administrative systems; and Computer Curriculum Corporation, which provides instructional software. The company then invests 20 percent back into the school's educational program and keeps 5 percent as profit (General Accounting Office [GAO], 1996).

EAI's first foray into the public sphere—and "the deal that put EAI on the map" (Richards et al., 1996, p. 22)—came in 1990 when the firm was awarded a 5-year, $1.2 millon contract in *Dade County, Florida,* to manage the 800-pupil South Pointe Elementary School—"the first such business/public-school partnership in the country" (David, 1992, p. 7). As part of the contract, "EAI agreed to reduce student-teacher ratios, expand teacher training, increase the use of technology in the classroom, and implement its own innovative curriculum program, Tesseract" (Beales & O'Leary, 1993, p. 19).

Two years later, in June 1992, EAI inked a five-year, $140 million contract to operate eight elementary schools and one middle school for the *Baltimore*

Public School System—roughly 4,800 students at a per-pupil cost of approximately $5,500 (David, 1992; Williams & Leak, 1995). A caravan of problems soon visited "Baltimore's grand experiment" (N. J. Walsh, 1995, p. 195) in privatization, however. The teachers union, which "cooperated with EAI when it entered the schools" (AFT, 1994a, p. i; see also GAO, 1996), very quickly turned against the initiative. Indeed, it declared "an all-out war against the firm" (P. Schmidt, 1994c, p. 27). Union members boycotted EAI's training programs and engaged in protests against the firm (P. Schmidt, 1992a). At the heart of the conflict were widespread, teacher objections to EAI's "decisions to change school schedules, mainstream special education students, and replace veteran paraprofessionals with instructional interns" (P. Schmidt, 1992b, p. 13)—all actions that threatened the job security of teachers and teacher aides. The most serious source of friction was EAI's plan to replace 160 paraprofessionals with interns who would earn 40 percent less salary and receive no benefits (GAO, 1996; P. Schmidt, 1994c).

In December 1993, a year and a half into the agreement, the teachers union filed a lawsuit that challenged the legal status of the contract. It averred that the arrangement violated the city charter and prevented citizens from exercising their rights in determining how the nine schools should be operated (Richardson, 1993b). Later, the union sent letters to the U.S. Department of Education claiming that there were "improprieties in EAI's management of Chapter I and special-education programs" (P. Schmidt, 1994c, p. 28). Union opposition to EAI solidified into animosity, and by 1994, both the AFT and the NEA were fighting to prevent the firm from expanding its experiment in Baltimore or entering into new agreements elsewhere (P. Schmidt, 1994b; 1994c). Negative reports of EAI activities continued to be released by the AFT.

Baltimore superintendent Walter G. Amprey rushed to the defense of EAI. The district accused the AFT of inventing "groundless ploy(s) to throw cold water on the privatization efforts" (Amprey, quoted in Richardson, 1993b, p. 13) and "mounting a deliberate campaign of misinformation" (unnamed district source, quoted in P. Schmidt, 1994c, p. 28) to undermine the company.

By the end of the second year of the contract, the caldron of controversy had boiled over. In addition to the conflict within the district, the experiment had become a lightning rod for conservative and liberal factions in the larger society. In Baltimore, the school district is a department of city government, and Mayor Kurt L. Schmoke was an important player in the EAI experiment. Although, in the past, he had remained in the background, he was now pulled into the foreground of a roiling controversy. Claims of success and failure, some supported and others not, were bandied about freely (P. Schmidt, 1994b, 1994c; Walsh, 1994b; N. J. Walsh, 1995). Particularly damaging were: (1) a news release from EAI that exaggerated the academic progress of students in the EAI-managed schools; (2) claims of financial improprieties brought forth by the Baltimore comptroller's office; and (3) continued accusations of corporate guile, irresponsibility, and callousness leveled by the AFT (AFT, 1994a, 1994b, 1995, 1996).

In June of 1994, Superintendent Amprey announced that he was backing off his long-term plan of expanding the EAI presence in the district. In March 1995, Mayor Schmoke, citing the company's lack of progress in demonstrating substantial gains in student achievement, suggested that the contract be rewritten to include tough new performance standards. He also cautioned that the contract might be cancelled (AFT, 1995; P. Schmidt, 1995a). In November of that year, the axe fell. The three and-a-half year experiment in privatization via contracting out in Baltimore ended (Walsh, 1995e, 1995g).

During the time of the Baltimore experiment, EAI was also pursuing contracts to manage the operations of entire school districts. In October 1994, it found what it was seeking when the *Hartford, Connecticut,* school board voted 6 to 3 to contract with EAI "to manage every facet of the district's [32] schools" (P. Schmidt, 1994d, p. 1) and its $200 million annual budget—"the first city and the first school district to put the education of all its public school children in the hands of a private, for-profit management company" (Innerst, 1994, p. 58). Despite what some observers saw as a good venue for this comprehensive test of contracting out—a high per-pupil expenditure ($8,500), extremely low student achievement scores, a medium-sized city, and the political support of the mayor (P. Schmidt, 1994d)— the controversy that plagued EAI in Baltimore was quickly transported north. Both teachers unions were strident opponents of the agreement, with the AFT's Shanker denouncing it as "a scandal in the making" (cited in Innerst, 1994, p. 58). Critics condemned the board's action as a desperate measure (Evans & Carroll, 1995). The unneeded "corporate flubs" (Larrabee, 1994, p. A3) and "perceived missteps" (P. Schmidt, 1995b, p. 10) evident in Baltimore were soon visible in Hartford. Relations between the superintendent, Eddie L. Davis, and EAI officials frayed. School principals joined with teachers in expressing displeasure with EAI's long-term plans (P. Schmidt, 1995b). Not surprisingly, as the first year of the contract came to a close in June 1995, Hartford was in turmoil:

> Educational Alternatives Inc. has proposed laying off 300 school personnel. Crowds of angry parents and teachers have shut down public meetings by jeering city officials and company executives.
>
> EAI hasn't been paid a penny, the innovations it promised have been slow to materialize, and opponents of the company's five-year contract are getting more of a hearing. (Larrabee, 1995, p. A3)

Frustration on all sides was pervasive.

The debate over the EAI contract was brought to a head in the fall of 1995 with the approach of school board elections (P. Schmidt, 1995d). Entering those elections, the board was split seven to five in favor of the EAI contract, with the seats of five supporters up for grabs. Grueling non-partisan primary and general elections reduced the majority but still left a pro-privatization board (5 to 4) in place (P. Schmidt & Lindsay, 1995). No sooner had the election been decided than the spotlight of controversy was refocused on a set of issues that had been only slightly off center stage for much of the past year, namely, "an ongoing dispute between city and company officials over control of the school system's budget" (P. Schmidt, 1995d, p. 6) and payments to the firm (Walsh, 1995d). Because of the dispute, the company never realized control of the $200 million budget which was "the central part of the deal" (Sanchez, 1995, p. A15). In addition, questions about some of the EAI charges meant that, as of December 1995, the company had not received any payments for its services (Walsh, 1995d). Despite a reimbursement of $3 million to EAI in early 1996 (Gamble, 1996), the dispute festered, accommodation was impossible to secure, and "the nation's most extensive experiment in private management of public schools sputtered to an end" (Walsh, 1996a, p. 1).

The Baltimore and Hartford failures left EAI considerably weakened. Its stock, which had peaked at $48.75 in November 1993, closed at $4.25 on January 25, 1996, soon after the announcement of the cancellation of the Hartford contract. Its management team had been decimated by the loss of three top officials—David Bennett, President; William F. Goines, Chief Operating Officer; and Franklin L. Kuhar, Chief Financial Officer (Gamble, 1996; Walsh, 1995d). Worse still, EAI had no contracts to operate public schools (AFT, 1996; Walsh, 1996a), although, in February 1996, it did secure a contract to develop a budget for the Wappingers (New York) Central School District (Walsh, 1996c).

Program Design

The heart of the EAI educational program is an instructional system known as the Tesseract Way. According to EAI's former president, "The Tesseract program uses differentiated staffing to lower the adult-student ratio, and computer assisted learning to empower students to take responsibility for their own learning" (Bennett, 1994, p. 76). Technology, cooperative learning, continuous training for teachers, and active parental involvement are heavily emphasized. The focus is on student-centered learning and teaching (David, 1992; GAO, 1996; Molnar, 1994). The cornerstone of the Tesseract program is "individual attention with one teacher and one instructional intern working with each group of 30 students, and teachers developing a 'personal education plan' that sets educational goals for each child" (P. Schmidt, 1992b, p. 13). The program requires students "to derive much of their learning from computers, books, and real-life experiences" (p. 13).

EAI portrays the Tesseract Way as follows:

Every child has gifts and talents. We accept the challenge to find and nurture these qualities in each child.

1. Each student experiences success in school every day.
2. Parents are partners in their child's education.

3. A Personal Education Plan is developed for each student.
4. Real-life experience is the basis for learning.
5. Students take responsibility for their own learning by planning, accomplishing, and evaluating their own work, and making the best use of their time.
6. Technology helps students learn and teachers teach.
7. Hands-on projects provide experiences upon which students establish a solid foundation of understanding.
8. Cross-disciplinary and thematic units produce learning that is relevant and challenging.
9. All areas of curriculum are important.
10. Students learn productive and positive behaviors.
11. Creativity is fostered and celebrated.
12. Learning styles vary. Teachers design and present learning experiences in a variety of learning modalities.
13. Teachers use flexible grouping to meet the changing needs of individual students.
14. Students develop communications skills through a literature-based program that includes phonics, reading, writing, and spelling.
15. Receiving instruction in a world language enriches students' understanding of other cultures and extends their language skills.
16. Students develop a global perspective, learning to appreciate and accept all peoples of the world.
17. Homework is a natural extension of classroom activities.
18. Students, staff, parents, and the community work, learn, and share together. (in Williams & Leak, 1995, p. 82)

Evaluation. Of all of the EMOs, we understand the most about the workings and the impact of EAI, which we shall discuss in two ways. We begin by analyzing EAI's financial success. We then examine the impact of EAI on its nine contract schools in Baltimore.

As a for-profit firm, an important evaluation criterion is the company's financial health. After the first five years of operation (1986-1991), P. Schmidt (1992b) summed up the picture as follows:

> For its first five years, Education Alternatives failed to turn a profit, generate a positive cash flow, or succeed in its pursuit of a contract to manage an entire district. It has invested more than $8.5 million, but still has not demonstrated that it can profitably run public schools at their current funding levels. (p. 13)

The story for the last five years has been a bit brighter, although the company was hammered rather badly in 1995 and 1996. At the close of the 1996 fiscal year, EAI had 150 employees and 2,000 stockholders sharing some 7,352,352 shares of common stock. Revenues increased from $2.9 million in 1992, to $30.0 million in 1993, to $34.4 million in 1994, to $213.5 million in 1995. The value of EAI's stock, which is listed on the NASDAQ stock exchange (under EAIN), has been extremely volatile over the last five years, reaching a

TABLE 2.3.
EAI Earnings

	Net Income (Loss) (in millions)	Earnings (Loss) Per Share
1991	—	(1.06)
1992	(1.6)	(0.44)
1993	1.1	0.14
1994	2.5	0.08
1995	(7.4)	(1.01)
1996	(9.4)	(1.28)

Source: Valueline (June 21, 1996), S & P Marketscope (May 3, 1996), Piper Jaffray Research Department Quickview (May 6, 1996), Phone interview with EAI (September 12, 1996).

high of $48.75 a share in November 1993 and a low of $2.44 on July 15, 1996. At the time of this writing (September 13, 1996), the stock was selling for $3.75 per share. Earnings data are reported in Table 2.3. Considerable losses overshadow profits earned in 1993 and 1994. In addition, it appears certain that multi-million dollar losses will continue for EAI into the future. In sum, the conclusion: "There is no evidence yet that EAI can make a profit running schools" (Richards et al., 1996, p. 89).

The most thorough external reviews of EAI activities are the assessments conducted by Williams and Leak (1995) for The Center for Educational Research at the University of Maryland - Baltimore County; the General Accounting Office (1996); the American Federation of Teachers (1994a, 1994b, 1995, 1996); and Richards, Shore, & Sawicky, 1996. Williams and Leak and their team of investigators studied inputs, processes, and outcomes in the nine EAI schools and a matched group of seven comparison schools for the first three years of the privatization experiment, 1992-1993 through 1994-1995. The GAO (1996) investigators followed a similar strategy, focusing on seven of the nine EAI schools and a matched set of nonprivately managed public schools. They attended to three issues: (1) the requirements and expectations embedded in the contract, (2) activities in the district as the contract played out, and (3) the impact of private management on students. As with most comprehensive reviews of this magnitude, the reports contain language that will buoy the spirits of both opponents and advocates of contracting out. It is difficult to capture the complexity of the findings in a summative statement. Perhaps the closest one can come is to underscore the summary phrase "less-than-complete success" provided by Williams and Leak (1995, p. 116) as well as their concluding statement:

The accomplishments of Educational Alternatives, Inc. in the management of seven elementary schools in Baltimore City are considerable, particularly in the area of change in classroom instructional practices toward varied activities, flexible grouping and a focus on the individual student. The initial test score decline was substantial, with the lost ground recovered only by the end of the third year. (p. 113)

Thus, while the EAI experiment was not the complete failure many claimed it to be, neither was it the key to significantly improved education for Baltimore's urban school children. Even given enriched funding (Richards, Shore, & Sawicky, 1996), after three years, it had not led to "the expected level of transformation" (Williams & Leak, 1995, p. 114). Assessed against the comparison schools, EAI schools did some things better and some things worse. In the words of the General Accounting Office (1996), it "yielded mixed results" (p. 3). A thorough examination of the data shows that the EAI schools are largely undifferentiated from the comparison schools, that "Tesseract and comparison schools [are] more alike than different" (Williams & Leak, 1995, p. 113). The most important input and outcome findings are highlighted in Table 2.4.

In closing, it is worth noting that one important criterion that must be applied to the EAI experiment is the standard of expectations. When this measure is employed, the positive hues visible in the mosaic of findings presented by Williams and Leak appear much less pronounced. The expectation upon entering the Baltimore experiment was that there would be significant improvements. These expectations were never achieved. EAI was not able to maintain current levels of student performance and client satisfaction at significantly reduced costs to taxpayers. Neither was the company able to dramatically enhance valued outcomes even with enhanced levels of funding. As was the case with the performance contractors in the OEO experiment, "the sale of unrealistic hopes" (Judson, 1995, p. 12) has contributed to the perceived failure of EAI in Baltimore—and elsewhere.

Alternative Public Schools, Inc.

Forget Baltimore. Forget Hartford. If you want to follow the most crucial story in the newly emerging relationship between business and public schooling, look to Wilkinsburg, PA. One year into its Turner School Initiative, the tiny Wilkinsburg school district—in the greater Pittsburgh area—has done more to shape the future of the private sector in education reform than either of the two big cities most associated with the idea of privatizing management and curriculum. (McLaughlin, 1995, p. 1)

One of the most important education reform battles in the country is being waged in a town just outside of Pittsburgh, Pa. The final outcome will help determine if competition and choice will be allowed to play a role in reinvigorating the nation's failing public schools. Along the way it will also help determine who has the right to run the schools—school boards elected by parents and other members of the community or teachers unions dedicated to preserving the status quo. ("Showdown in Wilkinsburg," 1995, unnumbered)

TABLE 2.4.
Findings From the EAI Baltimore Experiment, 1992–1993 to 1994–1995

INPUTS

Funding
Education Alternatives Inc. was afforded a significant financial advantage in the management of its nine schools. EAI's allowance per pupil is 26 percent above the district cost for elementary school students and 36 percent above the district cost for middle school students (Richards, Shore, & Sawicky, 1996, pp. 108–109, 114).

Parent Involvement
Despite the introduction of four new parent involvement activities into Tesseract schools, there appears to be little difference between parent involvement in Tesseract and comparison schools.... Tesseract schools obtained an average rating of 2.54 on the 13 measured parent involvement activities, with a range of 1.92–3.17. This is slightly lower than the comparison schools, which obtained an average rating of 2.63, with a range of 1.23–3.38 (Williams & Leak, 1995, pp. 88–89).

OUTCOMES

Enrollment
Enrollment has been declining in Baltimore City schools. Enrollment in grades one through five in Baltimore City schools was 95 percent of the 1991–1992 level, the pre-implementation year of the Tesseract program, while the Tesseract school enrollment was 94 percent of the 1991-92 level and comparison school enrollment was 88 percent of the 1991–1992 level. Tesseract schools maintained school enrollment better than comparison schools, a measure of parent satisfaction with the program (Williams & Leak, 1995, p. 14).

Attendance
Overall, our analyses of student attendance data showed little difference between attendance patterns of students in privately managed schools and students in comparison schools. We found no difference in the number of days absent for nonmobile students (those remaining in the same school for the 3 years in the longitudinal analysis) and little difference when the entire student population was considered in the cross-sectional analysis (GAO, 1996, p. 48).

Achievement
The Maryland School Progress Index—In 1993–1994, at the end of the second year of the Tesseract program, the Maryland School Progress Index, 11/12 of which is composed of the percentage of students scoring satisfactory on the academic areas of the Maryland School Performance Assessment Program, showed Tesseract schools minimally higher than comparison schools (Williams & Leak, 1995, p. 21).
The Comprehensive Test of Basic Skills (CTBS)—In 1994–1995 total reading NCE scores on the CTBS decreased one point from the pre-implementation year (1991–1992) scores for Tesseract schools but were unchanged for the comparison schools. Total mathematics scores increased one point for Tesseract schools and comparison schools (Williams & Leak, 1995, p. 4).

Overall
Our test score analyses of Baltimore's schools indicated that, overall, test scores of students attending privately managed schools were similar to those students attending the matched district managed, comparison schools....Overall, we found little difference between test scores in privately managed and comparison schools (GAO, 1996, p. 43).

Sources: Williams and Leak (1995) and The General Accounting Office (1996).

Roots and Evolution. After a series of futile efforts to improve education in Tennessee through political and administrative channels, two local business-men, William DeLoache and John Eason, started a for-profit firm known as Alternative Public Schools, Inc. (APS) to test their hypothesis that competition and the power of the private market could succeed in improving America's schools (interview with William DeLoache, April 5, 1995). Incorporated in 1992 and bankrolled initially by its two founders, the company spent nearly two years forging its educational platform and searching for a community where it could test its educational and managerial philosophy. As with the Edison Project, this process was tortuous. In addition to the general concerns about contracting confronting all EMOs, APS' task was made more difficult by the fact that it would only work in districts where it was given full control over the hiring process, including the termination of existing professional staff (inter-view with John Eason, April 3, 1995).

The break that APS needed and the initiative that was to "catapult them into the national limelight" (Thomas, Moran, & Resnick, n.d., p. 1) came in September of 1994 when the Wilkinsburg (Pennsylvania) school board under-took a nationwide search for a contractor to manage one of the district's schools—the 375 low-income-student Turner Elementary School. After the board reviewed the five proposals submitted, APS "emerged the leader" (McLaughlin, 1995, p. 2). A lengthy negotiation process that dragged on for the better part of the 1994–1995 school year resulted in the board voting in March 1995 to contract with APS to operate Turner School (Lindsay, 1995d).

The decision immediately ignited already smoldering political fires through-out the district, the state, and the nation. On the day of the board vote, the then president of the National Educational Association, Keith Geiger, appeared in Wilkinsburg to denounce the decision at a rally attended by about 250 anti-pri-vatization citizens (Lindsay, 1995d). The union, as promised, also immediately sued to block the district from following through on its decision to sign a con-tract with APS. On March 30, "a county judge…ruled that the arrangement was not legal in Pennsylvania and issued a preliminary injunction barring the 1,900-student district from signing the agreement" (Bradley, 1995a, p. 6). Concomitantly, a group of local citizens opposed to the APS initiative—Wilkinsburg Residents Against Profiteering—formed and began actively lobby-ing against incumbent board members and the district's proposed arrangement with APS. On the other side of the debate, the governor of Pennsylvania came out firmly in support of Wilkinsburg school officials, going so far as to draft leg-islation that would specifically authorize districts to enter into agreements with EMOs (Bradley, 1995a; Lindsay, 1995d). McLaughlin (1995) summed up the central issue in the struggle as follows: "What has evolved in Wilkinsburg is a showdown with serious implications for Pennsylvania and the rest of the nation. At its core [is] the question, 'Who controls the school district?'" (p. 2). The out-come, according to the *Wall Street Journal* ("Showdown in Wilkinsburg," 1995), had the potential to "have momentous consequences for school districts all across the country" (unnumbered). The fight over bringing the Turner School initiative to life continued in political and legal arenas throughout the summer. The March injunction was stayed in May and then put back into effect in July ("Showdown in Wilkinsburg," 1995). The board appealed to the Pennsylvania Supreme Court, a move which provided an automatic stay of the injunction. The 1995-1996 school year began with APS running the Turner School but with the legality of the relationship still very much in question. It was not until October that the Pennsylvania Supreme Court voted to permit the agreement to stand (Ponessa, 1996).

Program Design

The Turner strategy and the larger APS educational agenda were crafted by a design team assembled by DeLoache and Eason. As noted earlier, at the heart of the design is control by APS over the hiring of all school employees. At Turner, for example, 24 of the 30 teachers on staff in the 1994-1995 school year were dismissed (Thomas, Moran, & Resnick, n.d.). While nine of those were reassigned within the district, 15 others were eventually laid off (Zlatos, 1995). The school opened for the 1995-1996 academic year with 20 teachers, six aides, a nurse, a guidance counselor and family support person, an office manager, and a principal (Haynes, 1995).

Other elements of the design include: (1) an extended school year of 212 (as opposed to the regular 180) days; (2) salary that is linked to performance, including the opportunity for staff to earn performance bonuses; (3) before- and after-school programs as part of an extended school day that stretches from 7:00 a.m. to 6:00 p.m.; (4) a family support center to better connect students and their families to social services; (5) multi-age classes; and (6) an integrated curriculum (Bradley, 1995a; Ponessa, 1996; "Showdown in Wilkinsburg," 1995; Zlatos, 1995).

As with most EMO contracts, it is too early to ascertain whether the Turner initiative is working[7] or whether the APS program is likely to be viable in the long run—whether it is, as a *Philadelphia Inquirer* ("A Flawed Experiment," 1995) editorial proclaimed, a "flawed experiment" (p. A10) or a powerful new way of educating America's children. What we do know is that as the 1996-1997 school year sets to open, APS is still in charge at Turner and is scheduled to take over the management of a second school, in Massachusetts.

Other Providers

While Edison, EAI, and APS are the best known and most controversial of the EMOs, a variety of other firms are in the business of providing comprehensive private management of publicly financed schools and school districts. One such entity is the *Walt Disney Company,* which recently entered into an agreement with the Osceola County (Florida) school district to construct and manage a school in a mixed-use, 3,500-acre development being created by the Disney

Corporation. The educational complex, known as the Celebration Learning Center, consists "of a pre-K through twelfth grade school for 1,400 students and a 'Teaching Academy' offering professional-development sessions for educators across Florida and the nation" (Walsh, 1994b, p. 9). Disney donated 26 acres for the Center and is paying roughly 30 percent of the construction costs.

Another for-profit group, the *Sabis Foundation,* under Massachusetts charter school legislation, assumed operational control of one school in Springfield, Massachusetts, during the 1995-1996 academic year. The Foundation, which is based in Liechtenstein, manages 12 schools throughout the world, and "Sabis schools stress a college-preparatory curriculum with emphasis on mathematics, science, and world languages" (Walsh, 1995b, p. 3). To help school officials identify and address gaps in students' knowledge, Sabis also employs a powerful computerized assessment system that is tightly linked to the curriculum.

In the fall of 1993, the Minneapolis school board voted to approve an arrangement with the *Public Strategies Group* (PSG) and, in 1994, it signed a contract to hire PSG to manage the 44,000-student district (Lyons, 1995; Richardson, 1993a, 1994). PSG was founded in 1990 by two former Minnesota state financial officials, Peter Hutchinson and Babak Armajani. Under the terms of the contract, PSG's Hutchinson serves as the district's superintendent, leading a team of PSG employees and district office staff in operating the district.

The arrangement between the district and PSG can best be characterized as a "pay-for-performance" contract, similar to those we reviewed earlier in the section on performance contracting. Except for a monthly fee of $5,000 that the company received for serving as the district superintendent, compensation depended on the firm's meeting specific goals, objectives, and tasks specified in the district's improvement plan. For each goal, in turn, the district established indicators that were designed to assist in determining whether the objective had been achieved. Goals were formulated in a variety of areas, including: student test scores, student attendance, instruction, curriculum, and community involvement in the schools (GAO, 1996).

Profiles of Specialty Service Providers

The debate over utilizing private sector services has expanded into the instructional area. Private education contractors claim that they can provide instructional services in special areas, such as science, foreign languages, and special education, more efficiently, at lower costs, and with better educational outcomes than the professional public education sector. (NSBA, 1995, p. 2)

Companies providing foreign-language instruction, science programs, and remedial education now work with public schools to broaden course offerings for students. (Beales & O'Leary, 1993, unnumbered)

The Growth of Specialty Firms

What do we know about the provision of specialty education services in America's school districts? First, there is a growing belief that a wide array of educational areas lend themselves to private provision, everything from services to at-risk children to hiring substitute teachers to programs in vocational education (Beales & O'Leary, 1993; Thomas, 1996). Second, we know that, as of today, "instructional programs represent [only] a small percentage of the privatization market" (NSBA, 1995, p. 11). Third, there is evidence that interest in private provision of specialty services is growing.

Privatization of special education services is not unusual in school districts. In 1993, for example, over 100,000 special education students were being publicly supported to attend private schools ("Serving Difficult-to-Educate Students," 1996). Historically, however, the rationale for private provision in special education has had more to do with the absence of alternatives than it did with efforts to reap the advantages of the marketplace. Indeed, for many special education students, privatization may be the only option.

Districts, however, have recently begun to think more proactively about the benefits of private contracts for specialized instructional services. Instructional support areas that appear particularly ripe for expansion include professional development, testing, and instructional technology (Beales & O'Leary, 1993; Hunter, 1995b; Whitty, 1984). Curricular areas that are receiving heightened attention include driver education, foreign language, and science (Yelich, 1994). In foreign language instruction, for example, both Dialogos International Corporation and Berlitz International, Inc., are active for-profit specialty providers:

> In Raleigh, North Carolina, one private firm, Dialogos International, most commonly taught corporate executives. Recently, however, Dialogos received a contract with the Wake County Public Schools to teach French, German, Spanish, Italian, Chinese, and Japanese in kindergarten through fifth grade. This was after the state passed a law in 1985 requiring all children in grades K-5 to study a foreign language by the 1994-95 school year. The school board estimates the annual cost of a contract with a Dialogos teacher, at about $19,000, is 30 to 50 percent less than the annual salary of a classroom teacher. In Upper Saddle River, New Jersey, the Robert D. Reynolds School contracts with Berlitz International Inc., to teach languages to first- and second-grade students. The school spends $19,600 annually on the instruction, less than the cost of a full-time teacher. Because the language classes are considered an "enrichment" program rather than regular curriculum, union teachers have not opposed the hiring of Berlitz to teach the classes. (David, 1992, pp. 14–15)

A number of firms have also shown interest in providing science instruction. In Maryland, Science Encounters has teamed up with two public school districts to offer after-school programs (Beales & O'Leary, 1993). In Milwaukee, school officials entered into a contract with MacDonald Research "to develop a pilot program for students in grades four to eight at eight elementary schools. The program includes a touring mobile science laboratory, a central equipment resource, a mentor program for teachers and students, and summer workshops designed to aid science teachers. The cost of the program is estimated at $6,250 per year, per school" (David, 1992, pp. 9–10).

No area in education is receiving more attention in the privatization literature these days than programs for youngsters at risk. Expansion is being powered here—as is the case in a number of program areas—both by start-up firms that have formed specifically to sell services to public schools and by existing companies that are shifting attention to the public domain. Ombudsman Educational Services in Libertyville, Illinois, is one of the best examples of a start-up business contracting to work with public school students at risk. Founded by Jim Boyle, Ombudsman serves students at both the middle and high school levels who are on the verge of dropping out of school. By the end of 1994, Ombudsman was helping 1,600 at-risk students in over 100 districts in seven states (Henderson, 1994; McLaughlin, 1995). Other for-profit firms in the business of serving at-risk public school students include Children's Comprehensive Services, Success Lab, Res-Care, and Youth International Services.

The largest private company that contracts with school districts to provide services for at-risk students is Sylvan Learning Systems. Sylvan is "in the business of diagnosing learning needs and offering instructional services to meet those needs. Essentially, the company provides supplementary educational services for children in school" (Whitty, 1984, p. 262). In the Sylvan program, students receive one-hour tutorials twice per week. The maximum student-teacher ratio is three to one. Students work with computers and other instructional materials and receive tangible reinforcements for completed work (Bowler, 1994; Hancock, 1995; Walsh, 1995f). Sylvan guarantees results in its performance contracts, "crediting the district with additional remedial instruction at the company's expense when students fail to meet goals specified in its contract" (Bowler, 1994, p. 56).

Originally chartered as a franchised learning system serving individual families concerned about the academic success of their children, Sylvan has made "quiet inroads into public schools" (Walsh, 1995f, p. 3) over the last few years. Expansion into the public sector began in 1993 when Sylvan signed a contract with the Baltimore public schools to provide remedial education to 660 students in five elementary schools. In 1994, Sylvan received authorization to begin working with students reading below the fourth-grade level in four Washington, D.C., high schools ("D.C. School System," 1994). Districts in Dorchester County, Maryland, and Pasadena, Texas, quickly followed the lead of Baltimore and Washington, D.C. By the end of 1994, Sylvan had contracts with public school districts in excess of $5 million and was serving over 2,900 public school students (Hancock, 1995). Contracts with public schools comprised 14 percent of the company's revenues (Magnum, 1996). During 1995, Sylvan entered into a $1.9 million contract to assist 11 schools in Chicago, began operations in Broward County, Florida, and St. Paul, Minnesota, and expanded services in Washington, D.C., and Baltimore (Walsh, 1995f). In early 1996, the company signed a three-year, $1.25 million contract with the Newark, New Jersey, public schools ("Newark Taps Sylvan," 1996).

Private-Practice Teachers

Independent teachers or teachers in private practice...remain a tiny fraction of the nation's teachers. But they are squarely on the fault line in education between those who want to open up multiple options for the way schools and teachers can operate and those who worry that the result will be less security for teachers and poorer education for children. (Applebome, 1995, p. 73)

One of the most interesting phenomena in the area of specialty service provision has been the growth of private-practice teachers. Beales (1994) defines private-practice teachers as "professional educators who provide their services to schools or other organizations on a contract basis" (p. 1). In reality, there is little difference between private-practice teachers and the specialty firms we described above. They both represent dimensions of specialty service provider contracting. We separate them here to highlight the growth of individual teacher entrepreneurs who are beginning to see themselves in a new light—not as employees of school systems or specialty firms but as individual contractors who sell their educational expertise as they see fit. The focus here is less on the development of alternative systems for delivering education and more on rethinking the connections between individual teachers and the organizations for which they work—a "look at private practice through the eyes of the teacher entrepreneur" (Yelich, 1994, p. 1). As thoughtful analysts of private-practice teaching remind us, while "teachers who 'hang out a shingle' remain a tiny fraction of the nation's teachers,...in seeking professional autonomy, they are pioneering new ways for teachers and schools to operate" (Yelich, n.d., p. 1). Indeed, as Beales (1994) observes, "Not only does private-practice teaching have the potential to transform the way education is delivered, it may also transform the careers of teachers" (p. 1).

David (1992) reveals that private-practice teaching can take a variety of forms. The most prevalent formats are by subject matter (e.g., music), unit of a course (e.g., the War Between the States), age group, targeted student groups (e.g., gifted student), learning approaches (e.g., phonics), or teaching methods (e.g., computer-assisted learning) ("A Lesson From Private Practitioners," 1991; Wenger, 1994; Yelich, 1994).

CONCLUSION

In this first of two chapters devoted to privatization via contracting, we provided descriptions of contracting out in action. We began by reviewing the development of private sector involvement in what are generally referred to as the support functions of schooling, for example, food services and pupil transportation. We then examined early initiatives in the contracting out of educational services. We analyzed in some detail the major experiments from the performance contracting era of education (1969-1972). We also portrayed the renewed interest in contracting for basic education services taking root today. Two lines of activity were profiled: the activities of Educational Management Organizations, such as the Edison Project, and the initiatives of Specialty Service Providers, such as Sylvan Learning Systems. In Chapter 3, we continue our discussion of privatization by examining the likely effects of these contracting activities.

3

Contracting Out:
What Can We Expect?

There is not enough information to predict with confidence that managing education under contract will or will not work. (Richards et al., 1996, p. 130)

I n this chapter, we extend the analysis of contracting out that began in
Chapter 2. There, the focus was primarily descriptive—developing a better
feel for the contracting landscape by reviewing historical and current contracting initiatives. Here, the focus is on two more speculative issues: the likely
effects of contracting and the conditions that make contracting most feasible.
Specifically, we answer the following two questions: First, if contracting out
works according to plan, what can we expect across an array of important outcome variables? Second, how good a candidate is the public education sector
for contracting initiatives, that is, does this sector adhere to important conditions necessary to ensure the likelihood of the success of market-based reform
initiatives such as contracting out?

CONTRACTING OUT: LIKELY EFFECTS

A decision to adopt a specific temporary privatization mode such as contracting out
should depend on expectations regarding the effects of privatization on efficiency,
quality of output and accountability for it, and distributional consequences.... The
basic consideration within this framework is whether privatization, as opposed to

government in-house production, will have either positive or negative effects on each of the factors. Summing over these factors will yield an estimate of the net benefit (or cost) of a particular temporary privatization mode. In the abstract, as long as the net benefit is expected to be positive, the government should adopt the corresponding temporary privatization mode and should contract out. Conversely, if contracting out is expected to yield a negative net benefit, the service should be produced in the public sector. (Hirsch, 1991, p. 124)

Supporters of performance contracting claim it encourages efficiency, serves as an incentive to good work and promotes rapid change. Others say it is wasteful of money and energy, promotes harmful competition and reinforces the most trivial education objectives. Some see the businesslike character of the contracts as a virtue; others find the business profit motive repugnant in education. (Mecklenburger, 1972, p. 3)

What are the likely effects of the most prevalent form of privatization—contracting out—on education? We preface our analysis with two comments. First, a number of theoretical and empirical building blocks suggest that contracting out the core business of education—the learning-teaching function—may not be the greatest idea in the search for school improvement, whether searching among the full array of school improvement possibilities or searching just among the array of privatization options. On this latter issue, it would appear: (1) that privatization advocates would do better to focus on areas like vouchers and deregulation to advance their agenda and (2) that opponents of privatization are right to be cautious about the ability of educators and other policymakers to keep contracting out linked tightly and continuously to school improvement. Here we put those discussions to the side, since the horse is already out of the barn. What concerns us here is the issue of what the horse is likely to do.

Second, our conclusions are drawn primarily from research on privatization of public functions other than education. It is important to acknowledge that this is only one of a number of useful frames for addressing the question at hand. For example, it would be helpful to supplement this analysis with reviews of studies of private schools (see Madsen, 1996), especially proprietary ones. When they become available, deeper analyses of the results of the contracting initiatives of the type we presented in Chapter 2 will also prove helpful.

Below, we examine likely effects of contracting out on the five most prevalent outcome variables in the privatization literature: costs, efficiency, quality, employees, and values.

Costs

In our view, cost benefit should be the basis of a school board's decision to enter into a public-private partnership. (Bennett, 1994, p. 77)

EAI is vulnerable to charges that it does not represent a cost efficient alternative to the Baltimore Public Schools. (Molnar, 1994, p. 68)

Without question, there is one "clear unifying thread" (R. W. Bailey, 1991, p. 236) in all the calls for privatization, especially contracting out: "maximization of efficiency" (p. 236). Or, as Hula (1990b) remarks, "The search for...market efficiency provides perhaps the most common justification for using markets in policy implementation" (p. 13). The basic logic here—"breakdowns rooted in the conflicting interests of principals and agents" (Donahue, 1989, p. 90)—was briefly overviewed in Chapter 1. In short, critics argue, because of the "weaknesses inherent in public sector organizations" (Pirie, 1988, p. 38)—especially monopolistic structures, political gamesmanship, and bureaucratic self-interest (B. W. Brown, 1992; Hemming & Mansoor, 1988)—"political control of a firm leads to gross economic inefficiency" (Ramsey, 1987, p. 98). "The above problems suggest that public enterprises will perform badly in terms of productive efficiency, because they are likely to have higher production costs at a given level of output than comparable enterprises in the private sector" (Hemming & Mansoor, 1988, p. 5). One reported result of this is that "potential efficiency gains [in the public sector] are allegedly substantial" (Pack, 1991, p. 286). Another is that increasing competition via contracting out strategies "can both directly improve efficiency and reduce the total costs of government service" (Hilke, 1992, p. 7), "while improving or at least maintaining the level and quality of public services" (Savas, 1987, p. 6).

What do we know about the viability of the cost savings argument that undergirds privatization? To begin with, while there is some skepticism on the issue (see Thayer, 1987), "the majority of experts would appear to agree that real financial savings are frequently possible, although they are neither automatic nor easily achieved" (Darr, 1991, p. 68). The collective data on cost containment and cost savings reinforce this expert judgment: "The privatization of individual public services frequently results in significantly lower costs" (Clarkson, 1989, p. 157). Indeed, "extensive research on privatization has revealed that private firms are almost always far more efficient than government enterprises in providing a wide array of services" (Bennett & DiLorenzo, 1987, p. 14). While it is difficult to aggregate studies across the various domains of contracting out, two summative conclusions can be drawn. First, because providing services by private firms in a competitive environment saves taxpayers between 15 and 40 percent over the cost of providing them publicly (Bennett & Johnson, 1980; Clarkson, 1989; Dudek & Company, 1989; S. Moore, 1987; Pirie, 1985), opportunities for cost savings in education from contracting loom large (Donahue, 1989; Clarkson, 1989; Hilke, 1992; President's Commission on Privatization, 1988). Second, contracting (and franchising) can help state and local educational agencies avoid or spread out large-scale capital expenditures (Roehm, Castellano, & Karns, 1991; Savas, 1987).

Thus on our first outcome—lowering costs—it appears that contracting out has considerable potential for education.

Efficiency

The difference between cost and efficiency merits treatment. Specifically, as a number of investigators remind us (De Hoog, 1984; Frug, 1991; Martin, 1993; Ross, 1988), cost savings are not synonymous with enhanced efficiency: "The debate over the cost advantages of privatization...often fails to distinguish between those savings that are net efficiency gains to society as a whole and those that represent transfers from one sector of society to another" (Gomez-Ibanez, Meyer, & Luberoff, 1990, p. 144); "They appear to equate cost reductions with efficiency increases. The two are not necessarily the same" (Hirsch, 1991, p. 124); "It is clearly inappropriate to identify efficiency as any reduction in cost" (Hula, 1990b, p. 14). Lower costs can result from either "greater efficiency or deteriorating quality" (Starr, 1987, p. 129)—from greater productivity or "from reducing the standard of service or by paying lower wages and imposing poorer work conditions on staff" (Bell & Cloke, 1990, p. 12). The goal "is not merely to cut costs but to do so without reducing benefits by a commensurate amount" (Gormley, 1991a, p. 7). "To the extent that cost reductions are achieved by reductions in level and quality of service, claims of increased efficiency are illusionary" (Hula, 1990b, p. 14). Thus "a finding that private firms have lower unit costs than their public counterparts does not necessarily imply that their contributions to social welfare are greater; questions relating to allocative efficiency and to the quality of goods or services provided also need to be taken into account" (Vickers & Yarrow, 1988, p. 40).

At the heart of the efficiency argument for privatization is the belief that because of three inherent sources of inefficiency in public ownership—"political interference and bureaucratic failure" (Hemming & Mansoor, 1988, p. 5) and "monopoly power" (B. W. Brown, 1992, p. 288)—"the public sector...is virtually by definition an inferior vehicle for pursuing economic activity" (Berry & Lowery, 1987, p. 5). The core tenet is that the private sector outperforms government by: (1) ensuring that the goods and services desired by consumers are the ones actually provided; and by (2) producing the same levels of outcome at lower costs (Bennett & Johnson, 1980; Hemming & Mansoor, 1988)—by "harness[ing] competitive efficiencies to the benefit of student welfare" (Beales & O'Leary, 1993, p. 28).

Efficiency is thus about two primary issues—how goods and services are allocated, or the mix of goods and services provided, and how goods and services are produced. The first point is concerned with "the price efficiency of optional resource allocation" (Hirsch, 1991, p. 76) and is known as allocative efficiency. The second issue focuses on "input-output production transformation" (p. 76) and is known as productive efficiency. Allocative inefficiency occurs when agencies "fail to allocate...assets to their best and highest uses" (Thompson, 1989, p. 205). The result is that agencies "produce the wrong mix of services, or even do not produce some valued programs at all" (B. W. Brown, 1992, p. 288)—"the quantity, quality, and other characteristics of goods and services are not those most valued by consumers" (Hemming & Mansoor, 1988, p. 5). Productive inefficiency, on the other hand, "occurs when more inputs (labor, raw materials, energy, etc.) are used than necessary" (Hilke, 1992, p. 139). "In the education context, a state of efficiency is one in which improved student achievement cannot be produced with a reallocation of the same resources (i.e., expenditure), or the same level of student achievement cannot be produced with fewer resources" (Lamdin, 1996, p. 6).

Efficiency benefits that are attributed to contracting out "do not rest in ownership or control of the vendor organization" (Richards et al., 1996, p. 181), nor are they dependent "on the suggestion that private operators are wiser, kinder, or harder working than people in government service" (Roth, 1987, p. 76). They are, however, based on two related propositions: (1) "that public education operates under a crushing burden of mandated inefficiency" (Lieberman, 1988, p. 7); and (2) "that scarce resources are more likely to be allocated to their most urgent uses if operated by profit-seeking owners than if administered 'in the public interest' by political bodies" (Roth, 1987, p. 76). Also, public agencies use more capital and labor than private-sector firms for a given level of output. The efficiency rationale rests upon five pillars: market incentives; structural productivity (especially issues of scale); labor productivity; management productivity; and capital productivity (see Lieberman, 1989; Murphy, 1996; Whitty, 1984).

While the chain of logic embedded in the efficiency argument is quite nicely developed, empirical results have lagged behind. What we can say at this point on our second outcome variable is that while the case remains open, there is reason to believe that the cost savings associated with contracting out are due, at least in part, to more efficient ways of doing business and, more forcefully, that "a substantial portion of total cost savings from privatization represents real resource savings" (Hilke, 1992, p. 133).

Quality

Although urban public school educators are not achieving the results their constituents would like, there currently is no evidence that for-profit educational companies will do any better or that they possess any special educational expertise in working with poor students of color. Private companies have no long-term track records of educational success. (Farrell, Johnson, Jones, & Sapp, 1994, p. 74)

The contracting system, in fact, ensures something that is not now possible in public school governance: unrelenting attention to the quality of instruction and learning in the lowest-performing schools. Contracting should, over time, substantially raise performance in the weakest schools and average performance levels of all district schools. (Hill, Pierce, & Guthrie, in press)

It does seem to have led to generally appropriate conclusions about performance contracting—that it is extremely difficult to implement such a system, and that the educational gains are not large and possibly not even positive. (Gramlich & Koshel, 1975, pp. 73–74)

The case is often made—and just as often challenged—that contracting will enhance the quality of the goods and services offered taxpayers. Before proceeding, we must underscore the importance of the quality dimension as it applies to privatization in education. While quality of service delivery usually places a distant second to efficiency as a principal rationale for privatization in general and contracting out in particular (Van Horn, 1991), as one moves into the social services—such as education—efforts to improve quality take on much greater significance (S. Brown, 1991; Gormley, 1991a; Lamdin, 1996). Thus, in some cases, "distributional and output quality concerns mute the importance of efficiency in production" (Pack, 1991, p. 296). In addition, the saliency of the quality dimension is heightened when attacks on the effectiveness of service delivery are paramount in the case used to support contracting initiatives (Butler, 1991). As we know, this is exactly the situation confronting education today. Concomitantly, because "quality in public service tends to be a complex matter" (Donahue, 1989, pp. 83–84), it is difficult to measure (Committee on the Judiciary, 1986) and difficult to monitor (Gormley, 1991b)—much more so than are costs. The issue of quality assessment in education under contracting is, therefore, laden with difficulties (Richards et al., 1996).

Advocates of a larger role for the private sector in providing public goods and services assert that contracting will "produce better quality services for the price paid" (De Hoog, 1984, pp. 6–7). They claim that, because of the dynamics of the marketplace and because "many of the forces which contribute to substandard performance by state enterprises will cease to operate after the transfer is made" (Pirie, 1988, p. 54), "privatization properly implemented offers tremendous opportunities for...providing better services" (Poole, 1985, p. 43). At the heart of the logic here is the proposition that "because of the sensitivity of the private sector to its customers, as opposed to the insensitivity of many publicly held operations to their customers, the private sector can assure more dependable services than can public ownership" (Butler, 1991, p. 19)—that privatization "ensures production of services that are demanded by consumers, not those chosen by government bureaucrats" (Smith, 1987, p. 183). Quality is thus supposedly enhanced by "more responsive service" (Savas, 1987, p. 98)— a responsiveness fostered through innovation, the development of an array of service options, and more direct attention to the needs of customers (Goldring & Sullivan, 1995; Kolderie & Hauer, 1991; Madsen, 1996). According to this line of argument, "contracting implies a commitment to diversity in educational offerings" [by ensuring that] "different tastes and preferences...find expression in different schools" (Hill, Pierce, & Guthrie, in press).

The quality of service provision is also expected to improve because of "the superior flexibility...of privatization" (F. L. Fixler & Poole, 1987, p. 177). Contracting would therefore heighten quality by taking advantage of the flexibility associated with markets. Particular aspects of such flexibility that are often cited include the ability to: off-load costly in-house functions (Butler, 1991)—"persons with specialized skills can be obtained as needed, and without the constraints imposed by salary limitations or civil service restrictions" (Peters, 1991, p. 58); "adjust the size of a program up or down in response to changing demand and changing availability of funds" (Savas, 1987, p. 109); "purchase new equipment more quickly" (S. Brown, 1991, p. 273); undertake new projects more easily (Peters, 1991); and "hire, promote, reward, and even out workload peaks" (S. Brown, 1991, p. 273).

Finally, proponents assert that contracting out will enhance quality by increasing accountability for the results of schooling. Indeed, as we noted earlier, it was the quest for heightened accountability in the early 1970s that made the initial contracting out experiments possible (Mecklenburger, 1972). According to Hill and his colleagues (in press), and other advocates of contracting, "A contract system creates pressure for performance in the same way it encourages initiative and responsibility among staffs—through competition....A system of contract schools *rearranges the incentives within the public education system to reward schools that improve student learning and penalize those that do not* [emphasis in the original]."

The belief that contracting and enhanced quality are tightly linked is not universally held, however. Indeed, "the contention that employing private contractors diminishes service quality" (S. Moore, 1987, p. 67) is frequently heard. While advocates of contracting acknowledge "the potential problem of reduced quality of service" (F. L. Fixler & Poole, 1987, p. 173), opponents talk in more strident terms, arguing that the "high financial stakes [of competition] bring with them a temptation to maximize profitability by skimping on quality" (S. Brown, 1991, p. 274) and that low cost also "buys lower quality and higher risks" (Thayer, 1987, p. 167)—that "the profit motive leads to cost-cutting practices that reduce the quality of the service" (Peters, 1991, p. 58). These critics rarely see contracting harnessed to "improve[d] public service quality" (Martin, 1993, p. 173). Where others perceive vistas of higher productivity and greater effectiveness, analysts in this camp are more likely to discern a much darker horizon—one colored by "the substitution of lower-quality resources and deliberate malfeasance" (Clarkson, 1989, p. 177).

Whether grounded in caution or anchored in critique, a number of specific arguments challenge the proposition that contracting will result in the production of higher quality goods and the delivery of higher quality services. Some analysts assert that, contrary to the claims of privatization advocates, "competitive environments...and competitive markets bring out the worst, not the best, in human behavior" (Thayer, 1987, p. 148). Economists have also been quick to point out that "the normal concept of a competitive setting mitigates against innovation...by dissuad[ing] firms from devoting resources to investments with delayed, uncertain payoffs" (Richards et al., 1996, p. 160). Other reviewers propose that contracting may lead to reduced services for certain types of consumers, especially poor ones (Hawley, 1995) and "clients who may be particularly difficult and expensive to help, such as disadvantaged clients" (Hatry, 1991, p. 265). Of particular concern to critics is the "fear that the rigors of the marketplace may result in unproductive cost cutting measures" (National School Boards Association, 1995, p. 11), that contractors' preoccupation with maintaining the necessary revenue streams...[will] take priority over their focus on the grave educational problems they are contracting to solve" (Farrell et al., 1994, p. 74). Thus critics argue that contracting firms may be more concerned with profits than with quality services (Lyons, 1995). A more refined worry is that contractors will engage in "practices that are educationally questionable" (Molnar, 1994, p. 69)—the homogenization of teaching, the pursuance of a very narrow educational focus (Gramlich & Koshel, 1975), and an emphasis on "rote-learning achievements without concern for [students'] overall development and psychological welfare" (Mecklenburger, 1972, p. 1). Of particular concern here is the worry that contracting out "threatens to interrupt and diminish the crucial bonds between teachers and students" (Richards et al., 1996, p. 78).

Still others base their apprehensions about lowered quality upon conditions associated with the process of contracting. They are quick to point out the "hidden public costs associated with monitoring delivery of services" (Clarkson, 1989, p. 179) and the deterioration of process safeguards, such as civil service regulations, associated with the production function in the government sector (President's Commission on Privatization, 1988). These reviewers also worry that privatization strategies such as contracting "may co-opt nonprofit social service agencies and cause them to downplay their role as a social conscience" (Peters, 1991, p. 59), again diminishing rather than enhancing service quality for customers.

Claims that contracting may lead to reduced, not enhanced, quality often highlight the issues of service vulnerability, risk, and accountability (Lyons, 1995; Richards et al., 1996). The vulnerability thesis posits that "contracting out renders public agencies vulnerable to undue pressure from contractors" (Lieberman, 1989, p. 112) and that these "contractors, grantees, and firms receiving franchises are more likely to curtail, interrupt, or cease operations due to such circumstances as financial problems, strikes, and rebidding of contracts" (S. Brown, 1991, p. 274). It is argued that these threats to reliability (Goldring & Sullivan, 1995; Gormley, 1991a) are likely to increase as financial constraints become more pronounced (Hatry, 1991; Peters, 1991).

Concerns about accountability are also interwoven throughout discussions of service quality in the literature on contracting out. While the critical reviews acknowledge the potential of greater accountability under contracting initiatives (F. L. Fixler & Poole, 1987) and while the more sophisticated analyses point out that both negative and positive effects in this area are possible (Hirsch, 1991), apprehension about diminished accountability remains a central strand of the contracting literature. For example, Richards, Shore, and Sawicky (1996) point out that accountability can be compromised because "private management is intrinsically more insulated from public view and control" (p. 169). They also argue that public policymakers can use contracting out as a vehicle to escape responsibility for unpopular decisions.

What can we say then about the likely impact of contracting out on the criterion of quality in schooling? First, the likely effect of contracting out on educational quality remains an open question. Neither side occupies the empirical highground, especially as one moves from support services to the core activities of learning and teaching. Second, the case that contracting out will lead to a reduction in quality in education is probably not very accurate. Given that the case for contracting is anchored primarily in efficiency and that the case for public provision is anchored primarily on the axis of quality and values, privatization via contracting out continues to look like an idea worth examining—it is likely to cost less, be somewhat more efficient, and, at least, neutral in quality.

Employees

Pension problems illustrate the point that the most difficult aspect of contracting out is its impact on public employees. (Lieberman, 1989, p. 104)

When these public enterprises privatize services, for-profit employers tend to reduce the number of public sector jobs. (Hunter, 1995b, p. 170)

On the other hand, it is undesirable to maintain an inefficient delivery system because some employees will be disadvantaged by change. (Lieberman, 1988, p. 22)

"Almost all of the literature identifies the employment issue as one of the most controversial aspects of contracting out services" (Dudek & Company, 1989, p. 15). In short, "the issue of jobs is a very sensitive one" (Pirie, 1988, p. 62) under contracting. It is also, as are many of the issues involved in privatization, long on opinion, short on analysis, and largely uninformed by reference to objective empirical data.

The subject of job displacement is "probably the most controversial issue associated with the policy of contracting out government services" (Dudek & Company, 1989, p. 47). The crux of the issue is: What becomes of public employees when their jobs are transferred to private contractors? Philosophically speaking, advocates of privatization, while acknowledging that contracting out is unlikely to slow the public expenditure express train significantly, believe that shifting work to the private sector will garner some cost savings and efficiencies. Opponents, on the other hand, assert that contracting out will lead to widespread unemployment and to an expanding emphasis on part-time work (Martin, 1993; Worsnop, 1992) as well as to fewer "protective workrules" (Gomez-Ibanez et al., 1990, p. 169) and to a reduction in the "plethora of job protection policies procedures, and practices [that] have become institutionalized" (Lyons, 1995, p. 158) in the public sector.

While drawing attention to variation among government agencies, Dudek and Company (1989) conclude that "private contractors generally pay lower wages than do the government agencies they replace" (p. 2). Reports tracking salaries in industries undergoing privatization via deregulation (e.g., the trucking and airline industries) uncover similar declines in wages (Thayer, 1987). Initial analyses of the effects of contracting on fringe benefits are even more pronounced: Because "the government usually provides much more generous fringe benefits than do contractors...the largest difference between the government and the contractor is in the level of the fringe benefits provided" (Dudek & Company, 1989, p. 3). In one of the most thoughtful discussions of this issue, Donahue (1989) demonstrates that, for most services, "lower labor costs—both wages and benefits—are a major part of the contractor cost edge" (p. 144; see also Molnar, 1994), especially for labor-intensive services such as education, where "total compensation for public school teachers averages 25 percent more than compensation for teachers in private schools (Lieberman, 1989, p. 55) and "districts with unionized teachers have higher costs by seven to 15 percent" (Lamdin, 1996, p. 12). Lamdin and Richards, Shore, and Sawicky lay out the most likely scenario for education:

> If a firm receives revenue equal to what the district would have spent at a given school, or set of schools, then cost savings are the only source of profits. Because personnel costs are by far the largest component of operating expenditure (both within schools, and as central administration), these must be reduced. It is unlikely that savings of a significant magnitude are available elsewhere. Some combination of reduced staff, reduced salaries and benefits, or a substitution of lower for higher paid staff must occur. (Lamdin, 1996, p. 12)

> Without controlling labor costs, they cannot hope to meet basic expenses, fulfill their sometimes extravagant promises to customers, and squeeze enough savings out of the system to turn a profit. (Richards et al., 1996, p. 40)

Because "governments tend to be more aggressive than private contractors about hiring and promoting minorities and women" (Martin, 1993, p. 179), some analysts are also concerned that "any negative effects of contracting out [will] fall with particular force on women and minorities who are employed in great numbers by public agencies and [who] often earn better pay than they could in the private sector" (Worsnop, 1992, p. 982)—"that privatization will cause proportionately more job losses and fewer opportunities for minority workers" (Savas, 1987, p. 102; see also Martin, 1993). Analysis on this point is limited, with some reviewers claiming that "the job opportunities for members of minorities appear to be pretty similar regardless of the arrangement" (Savas, 1987, p. 104) and other reviewers concluding that "contracting out might impede black professional employment opportunities" (Dudek & Company, 1989, p. 29). Indeed, Farrell and his colleagues (1994) argue that in districts with for-profit experiments, "people of color...appear to be bearing disproportunately the brunt of downward economic mobility that has accompanied privatization" (p. 75).

The issue of contracting's effects on professionalism in the workforce has not received much attention to date. Ismael (1988) maintains that "one impact of contracting out of public services to the private sector has been identified as the deprofessionalization of the public sector" (p. 7), and others raise this possibility as well (Committee on the Judiciary, 1986; Florestano, 1991). Yet, we have almost no data to test this hypothesis—a hypothesis with special significance for public sector fields like education that are more professional than bureaucratic.

What can we safely say then about the likely effects of contracting out on public employees? First, we do not know enough at this time to say anything with any degree of firmness on the issues of minority employment opportunities and the professionalism of the workforce. Second, much of the savings that result from privatization "comes at the expense of public employees. ... In short, a good deal of what taxpayers stand to gain from privatization comes at the expense of municipal employees" (Donahue, 1989, p. 145). The outcome in education is likely to be similar. Third, how one views the effects of contracting out on labor has a good deal to do with the mindset one brings to the problem. Those who see public employees as hard-working, dedicated civil servants tend to view privatization with considerable alarm. They believe that "commercialization has been employed mainly as a weapon against public sector workers" (Martin, 1993, p. 173). Likewise, those on the inside looking out (i.e., public employees) are extremely skeptical of privatization initiatives such as contracting out (Lieberman, 1995; Payne, 1995). They "fear losing control of their agency's performance, not to mention their own jobs" (Pack, 1991, p. 297). Players in both camps—defenders of public employees and those employees themselves—see privatization as "a modern and sophisticated version of what was once called 'scabbing' and associated with 'strike-breaking' and 'union-busting'" (Thayer, 1987, p. 168). Reviewers examining the information with different frames of reference arrive at quite different conclusions (Blaschke, 1972; Lieberman, 1988). Those who maintain that employees possess an unfair "advantage in the public sector in terms of job security, working conditions and fringe benefits" (Pirie, 1988, p. 59)—who believe that workers "are much better off in the public sector [and] know it" (Worsnop, 1992, p. 982)—discern gains from contracting out where defenders of the public sector see costs.

Values

> Thus, for society at large, the Chelsea struggle sheds light on the risks to the public "trust" that our gullible acceptance of privatization can bring. (Jacobs, 1993, p. 192)

> Defenders of the present system argue that market-oriented reforms, such as contract schools, would increase inequalities in public education. Nothing could be farther from the truth. (Hill, Pierce, & Guthrie, in press)

Sometimes lurking in the background and at other times at the forefront of the picture, questions of values are central to the debate on privatization, although they are more important with the more radical forms of privatization such as vouchers than they are with contracting out. While these value issues are often treated in a less sophisticated manner than are the other outcomes we have examined, such as efficiency and effects on employees, and are less informed by data from actual contracting initiatives, it would be inappropriate to complete our analysis without touching on the most central of these values: choice, equity, and community.

As Gormley (1991b) has observed, "choice is a popular value for both proponents and opponents of privatization" (p. 309). On the one side, advocates assert that "a large public sector...necessarily reduces the scope of total freedom by limiting economic freedom and by reducing the effectiveness of the countervailing force of the market on potentially tyrannical political power" (Berry & Lowery, 1987, p. 5). Such proponents believe "that privatization will enlarge the range of choice for individuals while serving the same essential functions as do traditional programs" (Starr, 1987, p. 131). By "maximiz[ing] individual preferences" (Hula, 1990b, p. 7), they assert, "choice offers the prospect of greater satisfaction with services freely chosen by those who will receive them" (Gormley, 1991a, p. 8). Even critics of privatization acknowledge the benefits of choice (Levin, 1987), recognizing that the severe restrictions imposed by uniform public programs—welfare loss due to collective consumption in economic terms—make choice "unquestionably the single strongest point in the case for privatization" (Starr, 1987, p. 131).

"The effects of the privatization decision on equity" (Hirsch, 1991, p. 69) are the subject of some debate and confusion—confusion increased by the fact that "equity can be interpreted and measured in many reasonable ways" (Ross, 1988, p. 15). Indeed, as Madsen (1996) reminds us, "Issues of equity in terms of school privatization have been debated in the literature for many years" (p. 14). The positive case for linkage between contracting and equity usually takes one of two forms. On the weaker end of the continuum, advocates simply argue that the current equity landscape remains largely unchanged when production is shifted from public agencies to private firms (Dudek & Company, 1989). More aggressively, they assert that because the rich currently enjoy privileges (such as better schools and better health care) not available to others, "greater freedom of choice will generally lead to a more just distribution of benefits" (Starr, 1987, p. 131).

Not surprisingly, critics of privatization strategies such as contracting out are less sanguine about the impact of privatization on the distribution of society's resources (Fine, 1993; Hawley, 1995; Jaeger, 1992). They feel that "when distributive justice is at issue, privatization signals a diminished commitment to include the poor in the national household" (Starr, 1987, p. 135). These analysts are concerned that rather than advancing the equity agenda, "a large-scale shift of public services to private providers would contribute to further isolating the least advantaged" (p. 134), leaving them with a poorer public sector providing services of a last resort (Fine, 1993; Starr, 1987, 1991). At the heart of this apprehension is the fear that "distributional social goals" (Pack, 1991, p. 304) that are a key aspect of many public services may be jettisoned when activities are contracted out (Ross, 1988; Pack, 1991). In particular, they worry that privatization arrangements like contracting out that include choice options "are likely to intensify a school's orientation to the private benefits of individuals over the public purposes of education" (Bauman, 1996, pp. 169-170).

While some analysts believe that "it is difficult to regard privatization as a threat to democratic government" (Gormley, 1991b, p. 317), "critics stress that contracting out to profit-making companies may have devastating effects, both direct and indirect, on the community" (Richards et al., 1996, pp. 71–72), arguing that "relying on the motives of private gain compromises democracy" (Jacobs, 1993, p. 178). They maintain that privatization will "further the fragmentation of America...according to religious beliefs, social class, race, ethnicity and political ideology" (Hawley, 1995, p. 741). Contracting proposals are "attacked as further eroding the sense of community in contemporary society and for intensifying the individualistic ethic of our time" (Kolderie, 1991, p. 257). Of particular concern is the fear that through "the removal of decisions from the public arena" (Starr, 1987, p. 132) and "by substituting private preferences for collective choices" (Gormley, 1991b, p. 317), contracting could "diminish the individual incentive for participation" (Starr, 1987, p. 132) and thus "drain much of the energy and life from local government" (President's Commission on Privatization, 1988, p. 22), "rob us of the advantages of public deliberation and discussion" (Gormley, 1991b, p. 317), and "weaken the foundations of local democracy" (Starr, 1987, p. 133; see also Jacobs, 1993). In particular, critics claim that "when communities contract out to private companies, they risk undermining community members' sense of personal, active responsibility for their public schools" (Richards et al., 1996, p. 77). According to R. W. Bailey (1987), the result will be that "a sense of public legitimacy will have been squandered for marginal productivity enhancement—a trade-off that not only is unquantifiable but is even more dangerous to effective governance" (p. 151).

What can we say about the effects of contracting out on these key values of choice, equity, and community? Most likely this: Because contracting out is a fairly mild form of privatization, neither the claimed benefits of the marketplace (e.g., choice) nor the putative deficiencies of privatization (e.g., fragmentation of society) are likely to be decisive factors in its success or failure.

In summary, it seems to us that on the basis of potential costs and benefits, the case against contracting out in education has not been made. On the other hand, contracting out, while not likely to be a grand solution, offers some promise of enhanced outcomes for schooling. The question to which we turn now is whether or not the educational industry provides a context conducive to contracting arrangements, i.e., a context in which possible benefits are likely to be realized.

CONTRACTING OUT: ITS FIT WITH THE EDUCATION ENTERPRISE

Each privatization arrangement requires certain conditions in order to be successful and fully effective. (Savas, 1987, p. 286)

Contracting is feasible and works well under the following set of conditions: (1) the work to be done is specified unambiguously; (2) several potential producers are available, and a competitive climate either exists or can be created and sustained; (3) the government is able to monitor the contractor's performance; and (4) appropriate terms are included in the contract document and enforced. (Savas, 1987, p. 109)

The more precisely a task can be *specified* in advance, and its performance *evaluated* after the fact, the more certainly contractors can be made to *compete;* the more readily disappointing contractors can be *replaced* (or otherwise penalized); and the more narrowly government cares about *ends* to the exclusion of *means,* the stronger the case for employing profit-seekers rather than civil servants. (Donahue, 1989, p. 97)

Privatization analysts have devoted considerable energy to uncovering conditions under which market-oriented approaches such as contracting out are likely to bear fruit (see especially Clarkson, 1989; Donahue, 1989; Gormley, 1991a; Hirsch, 1991). They have also described conditions that favor public delivery of goods and services. For purposes of discussion and analysis, we group these conditions into four clusters, those having to do with: (1) context; (2) task and outcome specification; (3) the nature of the service; and (4) the competitive environment.

Context

> Contracting can occur if four conditions are satisfied: (:) the government is under fiscal stress; (2) large cost savings are likely; (3) the act is politically feasible; and (4) a precipitating event upsets the status quo and requires change. (Savas, 1987, p. 272)

While extensive analyses of the internal dynamics appropriate for contracting out are available, discussions of the general context that facilitates contracting initiatives and that privileges this privatization tool over public delivery are less well developed. Nonetheless, a review of the literature in this area does reveal certain conditions that make contracting out in a particular sector of the economy a more appealing and potentially useful strategy than government delivery of publicly financed goods and services:

1. A crisis or major event challenges the status quo.
2. Customer satisfaction is low.
3. The government is experiencing fiscal stress—either decreasing revenues or increasing expenses, or both.
4. The service in question has a large budget.
5. Significant cost savings can be garnered.
6. Contracting out is legally permissible.
7. Contracting out is politically feasible.
8. There is strong political commitment from government.
9. Employees are not hostile to the idea.

Mapping these context variables onto the education industry reveals that the environment for contracting out is complex. The purported meltdown of public education reflected in the numerous commissioned reports of the 1980s and 1990s and the innumerable efforts to restructure, redesign, reculture, and reinvent schooling have created a crisis environment in which the seeds of privatization are taking root (Murphy, 1996). This seedbed of discontent has been enriched by regularly leveled claims—accurate or not—that customers are increasingly dissatisfied with the quality of public education.[8]

Turning to issues of funding, three points are clear. First, education does consume a very large share of the public budget. Second, although analysts ascribe quite different causes to the phenomenon—everything from insufficient public commitment to bureaucratic arteriosclerosis—many school districts find themselves in tight financial straights. Third, whether one agrees with the avenues likely to be followed in reaching the goal of enhanced efficiency, as noted earlier, real cost savings are possible under contracting out.

The political sector of the environment for contracting out in education is much less favorable than either the event or cost dimensions. To begin with, while contracting out is legally permissible, its use is heavily constrained. In particular, it is hemmed in by employee contracts and a plethora of government regulations that many analysts argue are unlikely to be jettisoned under contracting out arrangements (Pack, 1991; Richards et al., 1996). Also, when one steps back from the heat generated by the privatization debate, it is difficult to discern any large-scale political commitment from the relevant government actors to actively pursue contracting out initiatives. Or, stated alternatively, the demand side of the contracting out equation is not especially robust. Finally, the unions which represent educational employees are strongly opposed to privatization initiatives such as contracting out.

Task and Outcome Specifications

> Studies indicate that contracting out is utilized most efficiently when the service involved can be readily identified, measured, and evaluated. (Lieberman, 1989, p. 75)

> The choice between profit-seekers and civil servants to perform public duties hinges on two sets of concerns. The first is strictly task-specific. Is the product definable? Can performance be evaluated? (Donahue, 1989, p. 84)

As Ascher (1991) and other scholars in the area of privatization frequently remind us, "Due to the difficulties in specifying output and the importance of quality in determining customer satisfaction, not all services lend themselves to contractual arrangements" (p. 302). In general, the following conditions in the area of product specification and assessment favor contracting out. In their absence, the public sector offers a more viable alternative for providing services.

1. The service can be clearly defined.

To begin with, "contracting out is not feasible in the absence of consensus on the contractor's mission" (Lieberman, 1988, p. 16). In addition, contracting out is a more appropriate tool when the service being provided can be specified in advance and clearly defined (Hirsch, 1991): "When complexity and contingency are fundamental characteristics of the task, privatization's promise of simplicity will turn out to be illusionary" (Donahue, 1989, p. 129). In those cases where "duties can be less completely defined in advance, the more valuable is bureaucratic honor" (p. 89).

2. The outcomes can be specified.

Hirsch (1991) takes us to the heart of the outcome issue when he asserts that the "feasibility of temporarily privatizing a specific government service depends significantly on the difficulties incurred in measuring the characteristics that indicate its quality" (p. 99). When valued outcomes can be agreed upon and procedures for evaluating results clearly laid out, contracting out makes sense: "If a task allows for clear evaluation by results, then the bias should be toward turning the task over to profit-seekers instead of structuring elaborate performance incentives for civil servants" (Donahue, 1989, p. 83). On the other hand, "insofar as…'output' is hard to measure, the feasibility of contracting is diminished and the logic of public management strengthened" (Richards et al., 1996, p. 170).

3. Output characteristics are largely independent of the political process.

The more that output characteristics of a service or function are determined in the political arena, the less useful contracting out will be.

4. Output can be easily monitored.

The viability of contracting depends not only on the ease with which purchasers can specify outputs but also on their ability to readily monitor outcomes. As Hilke (1992) notes, "Services that are…easy to monitor for quality and price…make the best candidates for increased competition through outside contracting" (p. 135). "The easier it is to monitor output, the more likely it is that a service will be contracted out" (Hirsch, 1991, p. 96). Or, conversely, "as the costs of monitoring outputs rise still higher relative to the costs of monitoring inputs, there is an increased incentive to integrate activity within the government" (De Alessi, 1987, p. 30). According to privatization analysts, assessing outcomes is enhanced when there are: readily identifiable standards and criteria for evaluating success; tangible output characteristics; and objective, readily observable and quantifiable measures of performance (Hilke, 1992; Hirsch, 1991; Lieberman, 1989; Savas, 1987).

Given these four conditions about task and outcome specificity, it would appear that because "the educational 'product' is difficult to define" (Richards et al., 1996, p. 133) and because "service quality and effectiveness are not simply defined or measured" (De Hoog, 1984, p. 10), schooling is not an area where contracting out should flourish. To begin with, there is considerable lack of clarity about the appropriate mission and goals for schooling (Goodlad, 1984; Cohen, March, & Olsen, 1972). The criterion of goal consensus does not hold. Objectives abound. Weights for these desired states are rarely specified. Furthermore, it is difficult to describe the educational task in detail. As Richards and his colleagues (1996) observe, "The nature of the educational product is inherently complex and difficult to define" (p. 8).

At the same time, it is difficult to assess school performance, and definitions of performance that are used are highly dependent on the political process. This is the case because, in addition to problems with establishing

goals and describing tasks, it is often difficult to specify outcomes and to monitor results. Because education is a "post-experience" (Lamdin & Mintrom,
1996, p. 13) or a "trust good" (Hirsch, 1991, p. 94), "outputs are largely psychological and therefore not easily measurable" (Levin, 1987, p. 635).
Furthermore, with trust goods, the transaction costs of monitoring tend to be
high; that is, "the task of evaluating a contractor is complex and expensive"
(Richards et al., 1996, p. 148).

Nature of the Service

> The nature of the production itself is exceedingly important. (Hirsch, 1991, p. 126)

Certain characteristics of the service or function in question also shed light
on the appropriateness and usefulness of contracting out. The most important
of these elements are presented below in the format suggesting that public service delivery would be preferable to contracting out.

1. The process of production is as important as the product.

The central message here is provided by Donahue (1989). He argues that "the
less the government knows or cares about the means by which the public's business is accomplished, the looser the rein that can be granted to profit-seekers to
devise efficient and innovative ways of delivering specified results" (p. 80).
Conversely, "the rationale for bureaucracy is control over means, either when
means are more definable or observable than ends, or when means are important ends in themselves" (p. 83). The same bias in favor of public provision
holds, according to Pack (1991), when it is difficult "to separate the way in which
the social service is produced from the quality of what is produced" (p. 300).

2. The production function is characterized by uncertainty.

When the industry in question is characterized by "well understood technologies" (Hilke, 1992, p. 5), it is often a good candidate for privatization. On
the other hand, the absence of a well-established production function estab-
lishes "a limitation upon our use of contracting with the private sector" (Wilson,
1990, p. 67).

3. The function in question is more discretionary than ministerial.

According to Hirsch (1991), discretionary services are those in which the
actors enjoy a good deal of freedom in deciding how to complete a task.
Ministerial functions are those in which "workers basically follow standard regulations in performing tasks" (p. 19). Discretionary functions are less suitable for
contracting out than are ministerial ones.

4. The emphasis is on social services as opposed to physical services.

5. Credence services are involved.

Credence services are "soft" services in which quality is difficult to assess. As Hilke (1992) notes, "The production of credence services most closely corresponds to an inherently governmental service and is therefore the most likely candidate for in-house production by the government" (p. 9).

6. The service is a core function, is essential, and is central to the mission of governance.

Core services are those which are at the heart of a government program—as opposed to peripheral functions that build up around a core activity. The centrality criterion relates to the basic mission of government—as opposed to services that are not primarily public goods. Essentialness refers to the presence or absence of substitutes and to the costs of disrupted services. According to Hirsch (1991), where only limited substitutes are available and the potential of significant damage caused by interrupted supply is high, in-house production is politically preferable to contracting out.

7. Procedural fairness matters as much as efficiency.

8. The service has a significant regulatory dimension.

Functions with a strong regulatory component—such as the judicial system— underscore the state's moral authority. These services warrant greater emphasis on government provision.

9. Accountability is important yet difficult and costly to establish.

10. There is limited potential for the service to be improved significantly by innovation.

11. The service in question is not commonly produced by private firms.

As was the case in the areas of task definition and output specification, the conditions associated with the nature of the service suggest that contracting out may not be a good policy tool for education, that is, that public delivery may make more sense than privatization. While there are legitimate points of difference around the interpretation of these conditions, the bulk of the scholarship supports the position that the production function in education is unclear and that means in the educational enterprise matter as much as outcomes. Likewise, examining education through the lenses of conditions 3 through 7 above reveals that in-house delivery is preferable to contracting out. Both sophisticated empirical and theoretical analyses (Bradford, Malt, & Oates, 1969) and thoughtful historical reviews (Cuban, 1984) call into question the premise that education can be dramatically improved through innovative technologies (condition 10). The evidence on items 8 (regulatory aspects of a service) and 9 (importance and cost of accountability) is less clearcut. A reasonable case can be constructed on both sides of the issue. Finally, since there is a good deal of private provision of schooling in this country (although few proprietary institutions), condition 11 would suggest that contracting out may be a useful way to deliver educational services. In total, however, the set of conditions associated with the nature of the service favors public delivery over private contractors.

The Competitive Environment

> Perhaps the first question about privatizing some government function should be, "Is competition possible?" The second should be, "Will officials be willing and able to maintain competition over the long term?" (Donahue, 1989, p. 127)

> For contracting to provide the economic benefits commonly ascribed to it, governments must have a variety of choices and organize the contracting process to exploit competitive forces. (Richards et al., 1996, p. 2)

For contracting out to be effective in securing some of the benefits we described earlier, especially efficiencies, there must be "competition both in the environment and the procedures" (De Hoog, 1984, p. 32). Contracting works best when it is yoked to "service[s] which allow sustained competition, either because there are already multiple players or because a competitive market can be created" (Savas, cited in Richards et al., 1996, p. 145). Indeed, the great bulk of the privatization literature maintains that "the real issue is not so much public versus private; it is monopoly versus competition....It is the introduction of competition that makes the difference" (Savas, 1985, p. 23). Or, as Donahue (1989) puts it, "most of the kick in privatization comes from the greater scope for rivalry when functions are contracted out, not from private provision *per se*" (p. 218).

To further ascertain whether the benefits of privatization are likely to be realized in education, an analysis of the competitive conditions outlined below needs to be undertaken. We present each of the seven conditions in the format favoring contracting. To the extent that we discover that these conditions do not hold, in-house (government) delivery of education becomes a more appealing option.

1. There are a number of competing suppliers.

Contracting out is most effective when "many producers are already in existence or can readily be encouraged to enter the field" (Savas, 1987, p. 96).

Conversely, "competitive market pressures would certainly be minor when the number of potential providers is...limited" (De Hoog, 1984, p. 23). In particular, when there is a monopolist-monopsonist relationship (one characterized by a single buyer and a single seller), contracting out is not likely to be particularly helpful (R. W. Bailey, 1987). The underlying premise here is that "the fewer the viable alternatives available...the less the contractor must do to please the customer and earn a profit" (Richards et al., 1996, p. 158). Donahue (1989) sums up the situation as follows: "Those public services for which it is technically or politically impossible to keep contractors in a state of healthy insecurity offer, at best, limited potential for privatization" (p. 218).

2. There is limited existing competition with private providers.

As described above, it is the introduction of competition that advantages delivery by for-profit firms over provision by a bureaucracy. However, when the playing field between government and private providers is already characterized by considerable competition, additional gains from contracting out are likely to be limited (Hilke, 1992).

3. Competitive bidding arrangements are likely.

The benefits of contracting out arise not only from the availability of multiple suppliers but also from the presence of competitive bidding environments (Hirsch, 1991), contexts in which transparency can be introduced into the letting of contracts (De Hoog, 1984).

4. There are limited barriers to entry to service delivery.

The lower the costs of entering a market for contractors, the more likely sellers are to operate in a competitive environment.

5. There are few barriers against replacing contractors.

As B. W. Brown (1992) notes, "for markets...to work, clients should be able to switch contractors quickly and at low cost" (p. 294). Obversely, when considerable barriers confront buyers attempting to replace contractors, the advantages of contracting out are unlikely to be achieved.

6. The contractor does not invest heavily in the use of specialized assets.

Economists point out that competition is not likely to be viable under the condition of "asset specificity," that is, "when the seller invests in assets for highly specialized use such that the value of the assets in that use far exceeds that in alternative uses" (Hirsch, 1991, p. 59). Under such conditions, competition is weakened and opportunistic behavior on the part of both parties to the contract is possible. Specifically, both buyer and seller "develop an interest in continuing a relationship based on past accumulation of assets" (B. W. Brown, 1992, p. 294). Long-term contracts tend to get locked in. Competition is compromised.

7. There is minimal opportunity for a deterioration in the competitive environment over time.

As we have discussed in detail elsewhere (Murphy, 1996), there are inherent dynamics in contracting arrangements that undermine the resiliency of competitive environments. In fact, there may be an "evolution of the system from one explicitly designed to promote competition among private contractors to one that substantially inhibits competition" (Pack, 1991, p. 302). For example, "contractors often build up inside information or develop local knowledge that gives them a competitive advantage and reduces parity among bidders at times of contract renegotiation" (Starr, 1987, p. 129). A culture of accommodation may develop and "the relationship between specific providers and their clients [may] ossify over time" (Richards et al., 1996, p. 153). Indeed, "the fates of political leaders and specific vendors [can] become linked" (p. 155). Governments can become "captives of the private contractors providing services to their communities" (Van Horn, 1991, p. 273).

Competitive environments are also likely to degrade because "competition is costly" (Donahue, 1989, p. 165) and the energy needed to maintain it through contracting and monitoring often tends to diminish. In addition, corruption, cooptive politics, and the socialization of private delivery can all contribute to undermining the spirit of competition fueling effective contracting relationships (De Hoog, 1984; Gormley, 1991a; Van Horn, 1991).

Reviewers who evaluate the robustness of the competitive environment of contracting out educational services based on the seven conditions outlined above often reach quite different conclusions. While analysts such as Doyle (1994a, 1994b) discern a contracting landscape with significant competitive influences, others such as Richards and his colleagues (1996) are much less sanguine about the possibilities of developing and maintaining the competitive culture central to the health of contracting initiatives. Indeed, Richards and associates (1996) go so far as to assert that "the market for educational management bears little resemblance to real-world competitive markets, let alone ideal models of efficient markets" (p. 156).

Our own examination of the educational playing field leads us to conclude that there is a good deal of potential for creating competition in contracting arrangements. Given the low costs of entry, the potential supply of contractors appears to be quite large. We would also argue that few of the benefits of competition between the private and public sector have been realized. Because educational management is a non-durable good, the costs of replacing contractors are not onerous, nor is the possibility of a deteriorating competitive environment excessively high. In short, the conditions in this fourth area of analysis—the competitive environment—suggest that the benefits associated with privatization may be garnered through contracting out educational services.

CONCLUSION

In this chapter, we completed two assignments. First, based on what we have learned about contracting out as a privatization strategy, we constructed a framework for examining the potential costs and benefits of this policy tool. We then used that framework to discern where the advantages of contracting out in education were likely to occur. Second, we laid out 32 conditions on which the question of the viability of contracting out may best be determined. We then analyzed the extent to which these conditions favor either contracting out or government provision of educational services.

The story that emerged from our work is complex. We reported that contracting out offers the promise of real gains, especially in the areas of costs and efficiencies. At the same time, we found that those benefits will not come easily and that they are likely to be accompanied by real costs—unacceptable costs according to many critics of privatization. When we turned to the question of whether these benefits uncovered in other areas of government-financed services are likely to be found in the educational sector, we discovered a mixed picture. General context and competitive environment conditions generally support the assertion that contracting out may be a good policy tool for strengthening education. Conversely, analysis of the conditions associated with the educational task and with the nature of the production function in schooling led us to conclude that in-house production may enjoy many advantages over contracting with private providers.

So where does this leave us? First, for us, it suggests that those who have staked out strong positions on either side of the contracting out debate may be in trouble. The entire area is a good deal more complex and contested than many advocates on both sides of the issue would have us believe. Second, it suggests that contracting out may work well in some places and in some areas of schooling and poorly in others. Contracting out is neither a magic wand nor an inherently flawed policy mechanism. It is a tool that if used thoughtfully and with an understanding of its strengths and weaknesses, may be a useful addition to our school reform tool kit. The goal should be neither to demonize nor deify contracting out but rather to analyze where and how it advantages or disadvantages schools and the youngsters who attend them.

4
Educational Vouchers

E ducational vouchers, having first been proposed "more than 200 years" ago (Kirkpatrick, 1990, p. 163), are not the newest idea for school improvement. But as Ernest Boyer (1992) points out, "In the current school reform debate, choice has moved to the top of the national agenda" (p. xv). Levin (1990) identifies two systems of "choice": market choice and public choice. Market choice is associated with the use of a "voucher financing mechanism" (p. 247), generally to purchase private schooling, though Chubb and Moe (1990) see a voucher-financed school system comprising both private and public schools. Public choice is associated with a range of schooling options within and among public schools. In this chapter, we use interchangeably the terms "choice" and "school choice" to encompass both market choice (vouchers) and public choice, although our focus is on markets.

If there is any doubt that choice has moved to center stage of the school reform debate, one need only consider the following:

- Two state legislatures have passed voucher legislation that provides government vouchers to be used in parochial schools (Heritage, 1997, online).
- Thirteen state legislatures, by 1992, had adopted statewide school choice (Carnegie, 1992, p. 2).
- Twenty-eight states introduced and four enacted school choice legislation in 1995 (Heritage, 1997, p. 1).
- Thirty-five governors have supported some form of school choice (Heritage, 1997, p. 1).

Why has parent and student choice become such a hot topic? Lamdin and Mintrom (1996) see "calls for school reform, such as school choice plans,...[as being] most likely to occur in an environment of dissatisfaction with performance" (p. 10). "There are few areas of public activity," according to Coons and Sugarman (1978), "in which user vexation is more common than public education" (p. 15). "User vexation" with public education in the United States has been well documented—not to mention stimulated—over the last dozen years in a variety of commissioned reports. Consistent with the central tenet of this volume, Lamdin and Mintrom (1996) see "school choice policy as being swept along by the *Zeitgeist* surrounding privatization and deregulation in other sectors of the economy" (p. 10). Forceful moves to privatize education have raised strong opposition from many sectors of the education community. Boyer (1992) claims that the choice debate has taken on an "ideological...zealousness...that smothers thoughtful discourse" (p. xv).

In this chapter, we first present a brief history of educational vouchers. Next, we present the variety of forms of "choice," followed by an examination of positions on either side of the "choice" debate. Then we assess various implementations of "choice" programs. We conclude with some lessons that emerged from our analysis. As previously mentioned, we use the terms "choice" and "school choice" to refer to both private-school vouchers and public-school choice.

HISTORY

The view that the state should merely befriend and expedite education rather than determine and impose its forms is scarcely new. (Coons & Sugarman, 1978, p. 18)

In our limited exploration into the history of educational vouchers, we found antecedents to all the major rationales for vouchers that have emerged in the recent waves of educational reform: efficacy, equity, efficiency, and control of education. We uncovered historical debates regarding the purpose of government support of education, appropriateness of public funding of religious schools, and issues of personal liberty versus the common good. We also discovered that waves of interest in vouchers have risen in the last half of each of the last three centuries.

Early Conceptions

The history of educational vouchers is at least as old as the United States. In 1776, in England, Adam Smith proposed in his *Wealth of Nations* that selection of a school by parents would release a subsidy from the government to the school (Coons & Sugarman, 1978). Smith saw competition among schools for students as a remedy to the effects of school endowments that "not only corrupted the diligence of public teachers, but have rendered it almost impossible to have any good private ones" (Adam Smith, 1776/1996, p. 780). Similarly, Smith reasoned that unless part of a teacher's salary was paid directly by parents, the teacher "would soon learn to neglect his business" (p. 785). He saw a "voucher" plan as an efficient as well as effective way to improve education (Johanek, 1992).

Thomas Paine "brought Smith's ideas to America in the late eighteenth century, but added his own twist: that the poor should be given special aid and that parents should be required to purchase education for their children" (Lindelow, 1980, pp. 6-7). Paine carried the message of democracy to England, where his *The Rights of Man* was published in 1791, and to France, where it was published in 1792 (Foner, 1945). Thomas Paine championed "what today might be called a negative income tax scaled progressively in favor of the poor" (Coons & Sugarman, 1978, p. 19) that would enable lower class families to send their children to school. Under his plan, "every family would receive a specified amount for each child up to the age of fourteen" (Levin, 1990, p. 255). Adam Smith, like Paine, advocated for state-supported education for the lower classes and argued that an educated public was in the government's best interest (Smith, 1776/1996). However, unlike Paine, Smith lived under the rule of George III of England and thus distanced himself from "'Paine's yellow fever' or egalitarian 'democratical' philosophy" (Johanek, 1992, p. 149).

Thomas Paine's influence as one of the framers of the French constitution (Foner, 1945) may have planted the seeds for an 1870s voucher proposal in France. Alex Molnar (1996) relates that:

> [France suffered a] crushing defeat in the Franco-Prussian War.... [In] the social turmoil that followed many French citizens angrily attacked the public school system as the source of their woes and embraced the simplistic political declaration that it was 'the Prussian teacher [who] has won the war.'...In 1872 a French parliamentary commission recommended a religious school voucher plan remarkably similar to the ones currently championed in the United States. However, in 19th century France hostility to the idea of providing public money to support church schools was so widespread that the plan was never taken up by the French Assembly. (p. 1)

In Smith's and Paine's early calls for government subsidized choice, we see antecedents to the primary contemporary rationale for school vouchers: (a) school improvement or efficacy and (b) educational equity for the poor. We also see distrust for full support of education by the government and disagreement regarding the purpose of government subsidies. Two additional dynamics of the voucher debate were played out in France: (a) blaming education for the country's perceived lack of competitiveness and (b) hostility toward using public money to support religious schools.

In 1859, John Stuart Mill, in *On Liberty,* took up Thomas Paine's call for a minimum education (Mill, 1935). If parents could not provide adequately for their child's education, then Mill thought the state should pay the difference. Where Paine gave emphasis to the rights of parents, Mill focussed on the rights of the child. Coons and Sugarman (1978) would take up Mill's concern for the child a century later in *Education by Choice: The Case for Family Control.*

Consistent with his commitment to individualism, Mill thought that parents should be able to purchase their education wherever they chose and saw public education as just "one among many competing experiments carried on for the purpose of example and stimulus" (cited in Lindelow, 1980, p. 7). Mill "stressed personal liberty in arguing against the state actually providing the education. 'A general State education is a mere contrivance for molding people to be exactly like one another'" (Johanek [citing Mill], 1992, p. 149). Again, we see antecedents to contemporary privatization issues: (a) the argument that government need not be both the provider of finance and the provider of education and (b) a call for public schools to compete with private schools in order to stimulate change.

Emergence of Public Education

In the United States, "the somewhat contrasting emphases of Paine on the parental right and Mill on the child's right were both swallowed up after 1875 in the enthusiasm for compulsory public education" (Coons & Sugarman, 1978, p. 19). Lindelow (1980) writes that "the growing influx of immigrants, coupled with a strong American nativism, made the public schools essential to the goal of creating a unified American culture" (p. 7). At that time, "the task of the state (as some educators saw it then) was to break the power of the family over its children; to liberate the children from the narrow horizons, the dogmas, the language, the narrow subcultures, the self-serving power of their parents" (Coleman, 1990, p. xiv). Coleman concludes, "One might say, in 1990, that the state has succeeded all too well" (p. xiv).

In the late eighteenth and early nineteenth centuries, "schools were denominational in character and public support of religious education was common....But as education became more available, infighting developed among sects, and particularly between Protestants and Catholics" (Lindelow, 1980, p. 8). "Local control of schools within state systems provided a solution to the tensions between private and public goals by permitting substantial and systematic diversity within an overall system of common schools" (Levin, 1983, p. 23). "Private differences were permitted in an overall system of local common schools established within a broad institutional structure of formal educational standards and compulsory attendance requirements adopted by each state" (Levin, 1990, p. 253). At the same time, consolidation of rural schools and centralization of urban school districts was transferring control of schools from parents to elites and professional school managers (Weise & Murphy, 1995), thus preparing the ground for future tensions that would mobilize fringe and special-interest groups and organized religions.

Court Cases

In the early 1920s several states moved "to require *all* children to attend public school, even the children of the rich who could afford private education" (Lindelow, 1980, p. 7). In Oregon, a "referendum against private schools had been instigated by members of the Ku Klux Klan who had infiltrated the Scottish Rite Masons and were capitalizing on a wave of nativist and anti-Catholic sentiment in the years following World War I" (James, 1983, p. 65). James points out that "behind these extremists, however, was the fact that the use of public authority for expanded programs to assimilate and control masses of people had become the lingua franca of a dominant culture that had been trying to organize itself and its newcomers for a century" (p. 65).

In 1925, the U.S. Supreme Court ended legislative threats against private education with its decision in *Pierce v. Society of Sisters*. In this case, "the Court held that the Due Process clause of the Fourteenth Amendment protected private education and added that it gave the family a right to choose such education where it met reasonable state standards for quality" (Coons & Sugarman, 1978, p. 19). Since the 1925 *Pierce v. Society of Sisters* decision, "parental choice of private schools has enjoyed federal protection, and private school interests have lobbied for tax money to support the exercise of this right. *Pierce* has become the political symbol of the authority of parents over their children's education" (p. 22). However, the court's decision reinforced another right. Tyack (1990) points out that in "preserving the right of parents to send their children to private schools [the court] asserted the public interest in the civic education of all children" (p. 89).

Though Pierce protected the rights of parents to send their children to private school, throughout the first half of the twentieth century, control of the schools continued to become increasingly centralized and removed from the influence of parents (Weise & Murphy, 1995). During these years, the hope for a substantial role for the family in formal education "was kept alive first by church-related interest groups and later by Southern segregationists" (Coons & Sugarman, 1978, p. 19–20). In the era of desegregation following the Supreme Court's 1954 decision in *Brown v. Board of Education,* "Southern parents who wanted the right to send their children to racially segregated schools were among the strongest backers of school choice" (Smith & Meier, 1995, p. 315).

After the Supreme Court's ruling in *Brown,* many Southern school districts took extraordinary measures to avoid desegregation rulings, including ending public education altogether. A more common strategy was to institute "freedom of choice" plans "for all pupils who desired to attend an integrated school" (Peterson, Rossmiller, & Volz, 1978, p. 310). These plans, which initially were supported by the Department of Health, Education, and Welfare (HEW), purported to promote integration by allowing both black and white students to attend their school of choice. However, by 1968, HEW came to see "freedom of choice" plans as delaying tactics and called for their elimination. In 1968, the Supreme Court, in *Green et al. v. County School Board,* ruled "that 'freedom of choice' desegregation plans are inadequate when school districts are not desegregated as rapidly as by other available methods" (p. 310).

In its 1971 ruling on *Lemon v. Kurtzman,* the U.S. Supreme Court "erected a difficult hurtle for advocates of tax dollars going to religious schools" (Molnar, 1996, p. 2). The Court identified "three evils against which the establishment clause of the First Amendment was intended to afford protection—sponsorship, financial support, and active involvement of the sovereign in religious activity" (Peterson et al., 1978, p. 149). To be constitutional, the court held that any plan for state financing to "directly or indirectly aid sectarian educational institutions" (p. 149) had to "meet three standards: its purpose is not secular; its main effect is to neither advance nor inhibit religion; and it does not excessively entangle the state with religion" (Molnar, 1996, p. 2).

We see here how vouchers came to be identified with conservative groups seeking to preserve educational inequities, a legacy that impacts the current choice debate. In the 1960s, vouchers began to shed their racist trappings as leftist academics, community activists, and government officials came to see vouchers as a policy strategy for creating educational equity (Coons & Sugarman, 1978). This position has been adopted at the highest levels of the United States government.

Presidential Advocacy

Since the mid-1960s, voucher advocates have generally found support for their cause in the United States presidency. Molnar (1996) points to the administration of President Lyndon Johnson as the beginning of contemporary presidential advocacy for vouchers. The Johnson administration found a "vocal constituency not just from the right wing groups or segments of the business community, but also among...the left" (pp. 1–2, see also Coons & Sugarman, 1978), who found appealing "the chance to craft so-called 'regulated' voucher plans—ensuring that the poorest recipients got the largest vouchers" (pp. 1–2). President Johnson's Office of Economic Opportunity (OEO) developed a voucher proposal that did not get implemented during Johnson's tenure due to the "lack of grass roots enthusiasm for the idea" (p. 2) among the professional education community.

President Richard Nixon was a strong education-voucher advocate (Menge, 1994). His administration aggressively moved the Johnson administration's OEO plan forward, implementing a public-choice program in Alum Rock, California; planning "a New Hampshire free market education voucher test project" (p. 171); and openly promoting a plan, called "Parochiaid" (Molnar, 1996, p. 2) to publicly fund religious schools.

President Ronald Reagan also "actively supported" (Moe, 1995, p. 3) choice in various forms. The Reagan administration "tried unsuccessfully to move some form of voucher legislation through Congress" (Molnar, 1996, p. 2) in 1983, 1985, and 1986.

President George Bush advocated "sweeping away the old institutions and replacing them with new ones—break-the-mold schools" (Carnegie, 1992, p. 7). He claimed that "for too long we've shielded schools from competition and allowed our schools a damaging monopoly of power" (cited in Carnegie, 1992, p. 3). In June 1992, President Bush announced "a proposal to provide $1,000 tuition scholarships for low- and middle-income families in public or private schools. The Bush measure, termed the 'GI bill for children,' was later rejected by Congress" (Martinez, Godwin, & Kemerer, 1995, p. 75).

President Bill Clinton "has supported school choice within the public system" (Pitsch, 1996, p. 19) but "has generally been a foe of vouchers for private schools. He opposed the 1993 voucher initiative in California and…a proposal to give federally funded vouchers to students in the District of Columbia" (Editorial Projects in Education, 1996, online). Following his election to a second term, President Clinton appeared to have modified this position: "If you're going to have a private voucher plan, that ought to be determined by states and localities where they're raising and spending most of the money….If a local school district in Cleveland, or anyplace else, wants to have a private school choice plan, like Milwaukee did, let them have at it" (cited in Pitsch, 1996, p. 19). However, in his State of the Union Address on February 4, 1997, President Clinton advocated choice but made no mention of vouchers in his 10-point education plan. In his plan, he specifies that "one size does not fit all in American education. All students and their families need to be able to choose a public school that meets their needs, and schools must be given more flexibility in return for greater accountability to parents and the public for high standards" (U. S. Department of Education, 1997, online).

FORMS

Choice was also argued as a way to restore a more appropriate balance of power between families and schools. (Raywid, 1992, p. 12)

The terminology of "choice" debate is a labyrinth of overlapping meanings. Chubb and Moe (1990) point out that even among its supporters, "choice means many different things" (pp. 207–208). Smith and Meier (1995) "found a lot of people who favored school choice, but few who seemed to be talking about the same thing" (p. 313). Lack of clarity in terminology regarding choice has led to imprecision in assessing the extent to which choice has been implemented. As Lamdin and Mintrom (1996) observe, "one can define school choice in such a way that it is pervasive" (p. 1). While the focus in this volume is on privatization strategies in education, because the extant cases of educational choice that link public financing with private provision are limited in both number and scope (Smith & Meier, 1995), we shall examine both public and private financing and provision. To accomplish that, we employ the categories set forth in Chapter 1 and presented graphically in Figure 1.1. Specifically, we focus on quadrants 1, 3, and 4 of Figure 1.1—public finance and provision, public finance and private provision, and private finance and provision.

Public Finance and Provision: Public Choice

As with the general term "choice," the terms "public-school choice" and "public choice" (we use these interchangeably) have been "stretched to include almost any innovation in which categories of students, particularly those with special needs, can enroll in nontraditional programs" (Carnegie, 1992, p. 3). Public-choice strategies include "a wide range of alternative programs for gifted students, dropouts, and those who aren't making it in traditional classrooms" (pp. 2-3). The myriad of public-choice strategies may be subsumed under the six following categories: (a) alternative and magnet schools that provide a specialized educational program; (b) intradistrict choice plans that enable parents to select any school within the district; (c) "second chance" options for dropouts and at-risk students; (d) postsecondary options that allow high school students to take college courses; (e) interdistrict choice plans that allow students to attend any public school in the state (Young & Clinchy, 1992), and (f) charter schools that "grant teachers and others the opportunity to create their own schools" (p. 51).

In this chapter, we highlight four of the six public-choice categories identified by Hakim, Seidenstat, and Bowman (1994): alternative and magnet schools, intradistrict plans, interdistrict plans, and charter schools. We drop their "second chance" and "postsecondary options" categories in order to focus on "those pre-collegiate choice programs designed to serve all students within a state or district...[and] in which parents are free to select the schools their children attend" (Carnegie, 1992, p. 3).

Alternative and Magnet Schools

"Alternative" and "magnet" schools were the first choice options (Young & Clinchy, 1992), and many contemporary choice plans are built around the magnet school concept (Chubb & Moe, 1990). Alternative schools were introduced as a public-choice option in the 1960s by "individuals dissatisfied with the conventional education offered in public schools" (Young & Clinchy, 1992, p. 4) and as a response to the private but leftist "free school" movement[9] of that period. Alternative schools, typically less academically structured than traditional schools, had no neighborhood attendance boundaries and enrolled students districtwide. In the 1970s, school district officials came to see these schools as important strategies to avoid court-ordered desegregation plans. "Magnet" schools, alternative schools that offered specialized programs not available in traditional schools, were placed in inner-city neighborhoods. School district officials hoped to "entice white families to enroll their children voluntarily in schools with high minority populations" (Henig, 1994, p. 101). In 1978, Coons and Sugarman, examining Minneapolis's alternative schools plan, reported "So far,...minorities are well distributed among the schools in that part of the district" (p. 118). However, 14 years later, Young and Clinchy (1992) analyzed more than a dozen studies of alternative and magnet schools and found that, in general, because of the limited numbers of schools involved and inadequate information distribution, magnet schools had "limited success in promoting desegregation" (p. 24). If magnet schools were an ineffective desegregation strategy, they proved to be a more effective strategy for educational improvement.

While these public-choice options began primarily as integration strategies, they "emerged," says Henig (1994), "through a gradual and pragmatic process of administrative adjustment and the growing recognition of choice as a politically useful tool for achieving other goals of educational reform" (p. 101). In their meta-analysis, Young and Clinchy (1992) found the following effects: improved attendance; social, security, and self-actualization needs met; fewer student behavior problems; higher teacher satisfaction; high quality education; improved student achievement; lowered dropout rates; greater on-task behavior; and more positive attitudes.

Intradistrict plans

The "intradistrict" or "districtwide" model of choice "permits parents and students to select a public school within their home district" (Carnegie, 1992, pp. 1-2). Young and Clinchy (1992) note that "the oldest and most frequently found intradistrict model is that of open enrollment....[Under this strategy,] all students are assigned initially to neighborhood schools, after which they may enroll in other district schools on a space-available basis" (p. 6). They identify "a newer and increasingly popular intradistrict model" (p. 6) called "controlled choice":

> In this model there are no neighborhood schools. Most or all schools become alternative or magnet schools. Attendance boundaries for individual schools are replaced by several attendance zones that contain a number of schools, or by one zone that contains all of a district's schools. Students and their parents may apply to any school within their attendance zone or districtwide depending upon the configuration. (pp. 6–7)

In some districts (e.g., Cambridge, Massachusetts), each school must maintain the racial distribution of the district as a whole (Young & Clinchy, 1992). Chubb and Moe (1990) describe a less restrictive intradistrict choice plan. Under this "simple" model, "there are no neighborhood schools or attendance areas. Parents and students are free to choose any schools in the district" (pp. 210-211).

Interdistrict Plans

Interdistrict or "statewide" choice plans "allow families to choose schools outside the district in which they live. Tuition costs for the transferring student are paid to the district of choice by the resident district, the state, or the student. While students have the right to transfer, districts that are at maximum enrollment cannot be forced to take additional students. If districts have openings, however, they must accept all students" (Young & Clinchy, 1992, p. 7). In addition to available-space restrictions, selections may be restricted by "desegregation requirements, and by the students' ability to travel to preferred schools" (Carnegie, 1992, p. 2). Districts that lose students generally lose state funding as well. In the Implementation section (below), we see how not providing travel can limit participation for some populations.

Charter schools

Chubb and Moe (1990) describe the following as characteristics of charter schools:

- Teachers may put forward "proposals, and, with the district's involvement and consent, form their own schools" (p. 212).
- Schools may no longer be associated with buildings, a building may house a number of different schools.
- Schools may control their admissions, setting their own criteria and making their own decisions about whom to accept and reject.
- "Formal rules imposed through collective bargaining and democratic control have [often] either been waived or ignored" (p. 213).

Districts usually charter schools on the condition that they meet certain performance criteria and attendance projections. If the schools fail to meet their objectives, the district "puts them out of business" (Chubb & Moe, 1990, p. 213). In some advocates' plans, the charter school model provides the means by which private schools might receive public funding (see Public Financing and Private Provision below). "In 1991, the Minnesota legislature inaugurated the nation's first 'charter' schools program, which grant[ed] teachers and others the opportunity to create their own schools. These charter schools [would] be state funded but largely free of government control. They [had] three years to live up to achievement goals or risk losing their charters" (Carnegie, 1992, p. 51). Since that time, the number of charter schools has grown to nearly 500, and the movement has expanded to include a variety of authorizing mechanisms and private provision in the form of contracting.

Public Finance and Private Provision: Government Vouchers

Government vouchers are the "most hotly disputed form" (Carnegie, 1992, p. 2) of school choice, and we find little agreement, even among voucher advocates. The range of proposals, for example, is very broad—from Coons and Sugarman's (1978) highly regulated voucher model, designed to ensure equity for the child, to Chubb and Moe's (1990) voucher plan that rejects the notion of democratic regulation and control of schools in favor of allowing schools to be shaped by the economic forces of the market place. Although some choice factions find merit in public choice, they have little common ground concerning vouchers. As Chubb and Moe point out, "any choice plan that upsets the traditional structure of public education generates intense opposition from established groups" (pp. 207–208). In a later section, we describe more fully the broad range of positions of voucher advocates and opponents.

In its most simple incarnation, private-school choice, "often called a voucher plan, permits parents to send their children to private schools, using public funds" (Carnegie, 1992, p. 2). Voucher programs, as most often proposed, are characterized by melding government funding with both public and private *provision*, competition for students, and deregulation of public schools, with only minimal regulation of private ones. Although theoretical voucher models proliferate and legislative voucher proposals seem to increase exponentially, to date, only Wisconsin and Ohio have passed voucher legislation. The Milwaukee program, which began operation in the fall of 1990, was the first voucher program in the United States to provide substantial subsidies to private schools (Witte, Sterr, & Thorn, 1995), but these subsidies were provided only for nonsectarian schools (see Implementation below).

In 1995, both Wisconsin and Ohio passed legislation that would allow vouchers to be used in parochial schools. In Wisconsin, implementation in Milwaukee was blocked by a district court judge following a three-to-three tie of the justices on the Wisconsin Supreme Court. The Ohio program also was challenged in court by a "coalition that has traditionally opposed vouchers, including the major teachers' unions and groups advocating strict separation of church and state" (Walsh, 1996e, p. 20). To date, the Ohio legislation has been upheld by a county court, and an appeals court judge has refused to issue an injunction pending a ruling by the state appeals court. Thus, the program began in the fall of 1996. Over 1,900 low-income families received vouchers, out of more than 6,200 applicants. The vouchers, valued at up to $2,500, could be used to pay for up to 90 percent of tuition in private schools or public schools in adjoining districts; however, no suburban districts chose to participate. In the first year, the program was open only to children in grades K through three (Walsh, 1996f). The Ohio program "marks the first time that government tuition vouchers are going to religious schools in any significant number" (p. 18).

In our discussion of public financing and private provision, we use the following issues to focus our discussion of this "choice" model: (a) state allocations and "add-ons," (b) admissions and tuitions, (c) governance and regulation of school operations, and (d) regulations restricting entrance by providers and limiting the supply of schools.

State Allocations and "Add-ons"

In most voucher proposals—as opposed to implementations—the state would provide families with a voucher that they could use to purchase education at the school of their choice: public or private, secular or parochial. The size of the state's allocation for each voucher might be the same for all students or weighted to favor a particular population (e.g., low-income families). For example, the Milwaukee Parental Choice Program was designed "to provide an opportunity only for relatively poor families to attend private schools" (Witte, Sterr, & Thorn, 1995, p. 4). Witte, Sterr, and Thorn report that "a payment from public funds equivalent to the [Milwaukee Public Schools] per member state aid...is paid to the private schools in lieu of tuition and fees for the student" (p. 1).

The value of a voucher is determined by the per-student base amount allocated by the state and by the availability of "add-ons." "Add-ons" are additional funds that school districts or families may add on to the voucher to increase its value. The state can determine the availability of add-ons and can set limits. We see four means for determining the vouchers final value: (a) vouchers are not weighted in favor of low-income families; (b) vouchers are weighted in favor of low-income families; (c) "add-on" amounts are available—determined by individual districts or families and within limits set by the state; or (d) no add-ons are available. In the matrix below (see Table 4.1), we present the four possible combinations of these elements for determining voucher size and the possible effects that different combinations have on different classes of families. One effect in particular stands out: There is only one combination—no weighting, no add-ons— that does not penalize middle-income families. Two combinations each favor low-income families and families living in upper-income school districts.

TABLE 4.1.
Impact of Voucher Weighting Systems and Add-Ons

	Vouchers Not Weighted	Vouchers Weighted in Favor of Low-Income Families
No Add-Ons	Equal vouchers for all families	Larger vouchers for low-income families
Add-On Amount Determined by Individual Districts	Larger vouchers for families in upper-income districts	Larger vouchers for low-income families and for families in upper-income districts

Chubb and Moe (1990) advocate allowing individual districts to add on to the size of vouchers that are awarded by the state. However, like most voucher advocates, they "think it is unwise to allow [families] to supplement their scholarship amounts with personal funds. Such 'add-ons,' threaten to produce too many disparities and inequalities within the public system, and many citizens would regard them as unfair and burdensome" (p. 220).

We note that Chubb and Moe (1990), who oppose democratic control of education, maintain the historic geographical structures of school districts in their radical plan to restructure education. Another possibility would be to eliminate school districts and have vouchers awarded only by the state. In this case, we would see a shift in the distribution of public-education funds away from families in upper-income school districts and toward middle- and low-income families. (We assume that any legislated voucher plan would not explicitly be weighted to favor middle- and upper-income families.) Any statewide voucher plan that would both retain school districts and allow add-ons would, by and large, maintain the existing distribution of educational funding that results from individual school districts' determining the allocation of resources for education.

Admissions and Tuitions

The capacity of schools to set tuitions and "make their own admissions decisions, subject only to nondiscrimination requirements...[is an] absolutely critical" (Chubb & Moe, 1990, p. 221) part of most voucher proposals. Additionally, advocates generally support schools' being able to "expel students or deny them readmission" (p. 222) and to "put a ceiling on the size of its student body" (Coons & Sugarman, 1978, p. 135). However, all recognize that "the state will have to assure each child access to a place in a public or private school" (p. 135).

Governance and the Regulation of Operations

Reducing or eliminating government regulation of school operation is at the heart of the governance-driven case for vouchers, and Chubb and Moe have brought high visibility to this perspective (Raywid, 1992). They argue that "each school must be granted sole authority to determine its own governing structure" (Chubb & Moe, 1990, p. 223), that only minimal certification requirements— "corresponding to those that, in many states, have historically been applied to private schools" (p. 224)—be imposed on teachers, and that schools be held accountable for student performance "from below, by parents and students who directly experience their services and are free to choose" (p. 225).

Regulations restricting entrance by providers and limiting the supply of schools

Most voucher proponents agree that criteria for entry "should be quite minimal" (Chubb & Moe, 1990, p. 219). In regard to school accreditation to participate in a voucher program, Chubb and Moe prescribe regulations "roughly corresponding to the criteria many states now employ in accrediting private schools—graduation requirements, health and safety requirements, and teacher certification requirements" (p. 219). The degree and form of regulation of schools by the state would, in part, determine the supply of private schools in any voucher plan.

Many voucher proponents see a thousand flowers blooming with the lifting of supply-side restrictions on schools (for example, see Hakim et al., 1994). This expansion of providers is not nearly so clear to opponents who point out that current private-school enrollment accounts for only 11 percent of children enrolled in schools. Cookson (1992) foresees that not only is the supply of private schools limited, but the number of empty seats in existing institutions makes it unlikely for voucher programs to have a significant effect on the public-school student population, at least without a major expansion of new schools. Such an expansion would be contingent on "the availability of entrepreneurs to supply private education[, which] is a relevant factor that affects the prevalence of private provision" (Lamdin & Mintrom, 1996, p. 3). Hakim, Seidenstat, and Bowman (1994) project that "if the voucher system is put in place, then many new schools will be established" (p. 3). Witte, Thorn, and Pritchard (1995) concur but caution: "It is unclear how many new schools would spring up, where they would be located, and what type of clients they would seek" (online)—or in what time frame they would appear.

Private Finance and Provision: Private Vouchers

Private Schools

Privately financed and provided education is the oldest form of education and comprises both sectarian and nonsectarian schools. Hakim and colleagues (1994) provide perspective on the scope of private education in the United States. They identify five types of private schools: parochial schools, prep schools, home schooling, Afrocentric schools, and "for-profit/not-for-profit schools" (p. 6). "Approximately half the private schools in the United States" (Witte, Thorn, & Pritchard, 1995, on-line) are Catholic parochial schools, forming "the largest non-public education system in the nation" (Hakim et al., 1994, p. 6). However, the number of students in the Catholic system decreased by 56 percent between 1964 and 1991—from 5.7 million to 2.5 million. According to Hakim and associates, prep schools are characterized by "rigorous academic standards, and...usually emphasize liberal arts courses" (p. 6). There are 1,500 nonreligious prep schools educating 400,000 students. Home schooling "is usually practiced by conservative Christians who stress the Bible and believe in the integration of family life and education" (p. 6). As noted in Chapter 6, it is estimated that over one million students are home schooled in the United States. Afrocentric schools "stress African and African-American culture" (p. 6). 50,000 students attend 300 such academies nationwide. By "for-profit/not-for-profit schools," Hakim, Seidenstat, and Bowman refer to entrepreneurial educational corporations, such as the Edison Project discussed in detail in Chapter 3.

Private vouchers

A new variation of private finance and provision arose in the 1990s. Beginning in 1991, coalitions of individuals, businesses, and religious organizations in several cities established educational foundations to test the viability of awarding vouchers to low-income families and allowing them to select the private school of their choice. While scholarships to private schools for low-income children is not new, these foundations are attempting to provide demonstrations that will propel government funding of vouchers (Moe, 1995).

In his book *Private Vouchers*, Moe (1995) identifies a private-voucher movement in the United States that is "in important respects a political as well as a philanthropic movement" (p. 8). He acknowledges J. Patrick Rooney, chief executive officer of the Golden Rule Insurance Company in Indianapolis, as its "founder and guiding spirit" (p. 9). Rooney, in August 1991, announced the creation of the Educational Choice Charitable Trust, the first private voucher program in the country. Its purpose is both "to provide financial assistance—private vouchers—to low-income children within the Indianapolis public school system" (p. 9) and to launch a "consciously orchestrated outreach effort" (p. 11). Since its formation, it has become a model for private voucher programs across the country. The voucher programs in Milwaukee and San Antonio, which began operation the following year, "were explicitly designed in accordance with the Golden Rule model" (p. 12). Partners Advancing Values in Education (PAVE) in Milwaukee is the largest private voucher program in the country. The Children's Educational Opportunity (CEO) Foundation in San Antonio was established by the Texas Public Policy Foundation, "a conservative policy organization" (p. 12). Moe points out that "the leading figures of the private voucher movement ... share a common vision ... of the political picture" (p. 8). CEO America, the political arm of CEO, has become "a centralizing entity ... to provide institutional leadership for the movement ... and challenge grants (on a matching basis) of up to $50,000 to initiate programs in new cities" (p. 16).

Moe (1995) reports that, as of 1995, there were 6,500 children receiving private vouchers, 5,400 of which were in four cities—Indianapolis, San Antonio, Milwaukee, and Los Angeles. He identifies 17 cities with private-voucher programs and reports that programs are "on the drawing boards in some thirty other cities" (p. 14).

POSITIONS

The "correct" answer on choice all too often depends on the ideological prism through which it is viewed. (Smith & Meier, 1995, p. 313)

> A paucity of relevant data limits the public debate surrounding the educational voucher issue. (Heise, Colburn, & Lamberti, 1995, p. 103)

The merits—or lack thereof—of choice programs have come wrapped in the political wrangling that has surrounded privatization issues in other arenas. Because "choice is one of the major tenets of both a market economy and democratic society" (Levin, 1990, p. 248), it is a closely held value of both proponents and opponents of school choice. While there has been a general acceptance of public-choice programs (Carnegie, 1992), the same cannot be said for voucher programs (Moe, 1995). School choice based on a market system of educational vouchers brings into juxtaposition the individual right of choice versus broad social rights: the right of parents to shape "the social, moral, and intellectual development of their children" (Coleman, 1990, p. x) versus "the right of a democratic society to use the educational system as a means to reproduce its most essential political, economic, and social institutions through a common schooling experience" (Levin, 1990, p. 252).

The virtues of choice have been extolled by proponents. Some foresee the emergence of "attractive and interesting schools [that] are everything that you and your friends can imagine, plus much more that may not even occur to you" (Nelson, Palonsky, & Carlson, 1990, p. 42). In 1986, the National Governors' Association enthusiastically endorsed public-school choice in its report, *Time for Results*, declaring that:

> There is nothing more basic to education and its ability to bring our children into the 21st century than choice. Given a choice in public education, we believe parents will play a stronger role in our schools. Innovative programs will spring to life. Parents and the whole community will become deeply involved in helping all children learn. Teachers will be more challenged than ever. And, most importantly, our students will see immediate results. (National Governors' Association, cited in Young & Clinchy, 1992, p. 2)

With such momentum behind them, it is little wonder that four years later, Chubb and Moe (1990) were able to write that "choice *is* a panacea" (p. 217) for problems of education.

Opponents of educational choice argue that a voucher system would not produce the conditions necessary for sustaining democracy, that it would increase current social inequities, and that it would not result in the efficiencies projected by choice proponents. Choice critics see a voucher system as weakening the educational scaffolds of consensus, detracting "from the creation of cultural unity among Americans" (Mereman, 1990, p. 84). Opponents foresee market systems of choice fraught with a variety of threats to integration. Witte (1990b), for example, warns that "free-wheeling schools could either blatantly or subtly discriminate" (p. 42). They charge that a market-based choice system goes against traditional educational values (Tyack, 1990). It has "adverse distributional consequences" (Elmore, 1990, p. 285) because it increases segregation (Lindelow, 1980), handicaps economically and educationally disadvantaged parents (Levin, 1990), stratifies by merit (Coleman, 1992) and promotes elitism (Cobb, 1992). The merits on which choice has most often been debated follow the framework described in Chapter 3—including the relative efficacy, equity, and efficiency of public schools versus market-driven schools, and the purpose and control of education—including the educational requirements necessary to promote democracy, cultural unity, and consensus. In this section, we briefly examine the merits of the positions through the lenses of the proponents and opponents of choice.

Efficacy

As with almost every issue surrounding choice, there is little agreement as to whether or not there is a problem with the schools, and if there is, what it is, and what should be done about it. "Virtually all choice advocates agree that public schools are failing and that the institutional structure of public education is a root cause of this problem" (Smith & Meier, 1995, p. 314). Chubb and Moe (1990), for example, decry the declining quality of the public education system and identify "the single most important symbol of the underlying problem...to be the monotonic decline, from the mid-1960s through 1980, in the scores of high school students on the national Scholastic Aptitude Test, or SAT" (p. 8).[10] However, voucher opponents counter that "the major reason that SAT I scores have fallen over the decades is the changing demographic makeup of the test-takers. Beginning in the late 1960s, those who took the SAT I became less white, less well off, and less likely to have graduated in the top 20% of their high school classes" (Smith & Meier, 1995, p. 314).

Chubb and Moe (1990) see the organization of schools as having "a significant impact all its own" (p. 186) on student performance. They state that "ineffective performance is really a deep-seated institutional problem that arises from the most fundamental properties of democratic control" (p. 191). "We believe existing institutions cannot solve the problem, because they *are* the problem—and that the key to better schools is institutional reform" (p. 3). Voucher proponents argue that "transforming parents into education consumers will force the school[s] to shape up or lose customers" (Heritage Foundation, cited in Carnegie, 1992, p. 3). It encourages professional educators "to improve instruction and toughen standards" (p. 3).

Voucher opponents find little evidence to support proponent's claims. The Carnegie Foundation (1992) in its study of school choice concluded that "the educational impact of school choice is ambiguous at best" (p. 20) and that "evidence about the effectiveness of private-school choice, limited as it is, suggests that such a policy does not improve student achievement or stimulate school renewal" (p. 16). Other researchers take a more cautious approach. Henig (1994) finds that "the evidence regarding the consequences of school choice is mixed and uncertain" (p. 145), and Murnane (1990) sees a "paucity of solid evidence concerning the effects of particular choice plans" (p. 332). Even voucher advocates admit that "there is little hard evidence to document whether children are actually better off as a result of vouchers" (Moe, 1995, p. 33). Witte, Sterr, and Thorn (1995) suggest that a different "way to think about [efficacy] is whether the majority of the students and families involved are better off because of this program. The answer of the parents involved, at least those who respond to our surveys, was clearly yes. This is despite the fact that achievement [of Milwaukee Parental Choice Program students], as measured by standardized tests, was no different than the achievement of [Milwaukee Public School] students" (p. 14).

Equity

Witte (1990b) states proponents' core argument for the equity benefits of choice: "The current situation is the epitome of inequality because it provides choice primarily to the middle- and upper-income families who can afford a home in the suburbs or the price of private schools for their children[, and] because choice already exists for many, government choice plans...must be instituted to further equity" (p. 42). Carnegie (1992) dismisses the equity benefits argument: "The choice process tends to work much better for those who are most advantaged economically and educationally" (p. 14). In examining the effects of statewide public-choice programs on school districts, Carnegie concludes that they "tend to widen the gap between rich and poor districts" (p. 25). Bennett (1990) points out a design conundrum: "Not everyone holds the same definition of equity, so manipulation of the plan to solve one definition may do injury to another" (p. 145; see also Coons & Sugarman, 1978). In the Implementation section (below), we show how program design influences equity for various populations.

Efficiency

Many proponents believe that school choice will improve the efficiency of the education system because schools "that falter will find it more difficult to attract support and they will tend to be weeded out in favor of schools that are better organized" (Chubb & Moe, 1990, p. 190). They also see choice eliminating costly regulation and administration. However, in analyzing the efficiency of a market-choice approach, Levin (1990) hypothesizes that "the overall costs for sustaining the information, regulation, and other parts of the market system while providing, at least, minimum social protections look high to prohibitive relative to a public-choice approach" (p. 247; see also Murphy, forthcoming). Three important factors identified by both sides of the debate that lead to new and/or higher costs are transporting children to their new schools of choice, providing useful information to parents in a form that will enable them to make sound decisions about schools, and establishing controls to prevent selection inequities (Moe, 1995).

Control of Education

According to Coons and Sugarman (1978), "the question for the state is whom it shall empower to decide what is best" (p. 45). They argue eloquently for the "family as being in the best position to observe the outcome of an educational decision, to learn by the experience, and to experiment with a new solution" (p. 60). Chubb and Moe (1990) take an extreme position on public control of schools: "Democracy is essentially coercive. The winners get to use public authority to impose their policies on the losers" (p. 28). They propose "a new system of public education, one that is built on school autonomy and parent-student choice rather than direct democratic control and bureaucracy" (p. 186).

Opponents of market choice argue that a voucher system would lead to increased fragmentation of society (Kozol, 1992). Witte (1990a) sees market incentives as leading directly to either blatant or subtle race and class discrimination by schools and families. Indeed, findings of inequities in existing private voucher programs even may be turning staunch advocates for free markets in favor of increased control. Moe (1995), for example, avers that "the absence of controls threatens to produce certain problems: internal skimming, the possible exclusion of especially needy children, the possible inclusion of bad or mediocre schools, and so on" (pp. 33–34).

IMPLEMENTATION

When choice-based reforms actually get adopted, they tend to be...political concoctions, built up through a patchwork of compromises. (Moe, 1995, p. 7)

If school choice is viewed as a minimally regulated, market-based system of education, then no such entity currently exists. (Smith & Meier, 1995, p. 313)

In this section, we examine the limited research that has been conducted on various implementations of public choice, government vouchers, and private vouchers.

Public Finance and Provision: Public Choice

Public-choice programs have been in existence two decades longer than either government or private voucher programs. There are many sites, and several have been studied extensively. We selected one implementation each of intradistrict and interdistrict choice plans that serve as exemplars of this form of financing and provision.

Intradistrict

The "controlled-choice" plan of Cambridge, Massachusetts, has received accolades from across the choice political spectrum: "one of the most exciting developments in American public education" (Chubb & Moe, 1990, pp. 211-212); "minority students are outperforming white students" (C. H. Russell & R. C. Clark, cited in Henig, 1994, p. 123); and one of "the nation's 'stars of choice'" (Carnegie, 1992, p. 29). In 1981, Cambridge implemented its 'controlled' choice plan as part of a then recent desegregation effort (Young & Clinchy, 1992). "The concept is simple. There are no neighborhood schools or attendance areas. Parents and students are free to choose any schools in the district. To assist them in gaining information and making wise decisions, the district provides a Parent Information Center " (Chubb & Moe, 1990, pp. 210-211). Schools may not have admission requirements; they are "selected on the basis of parent and student interest" (Young & Clinchy, 1992, p. 30). However, criteria for student assignment by the district exist, including racial balance, proximity of home to school, and school assignment of siblings (Young & Clinchy, 1992). Generally, 90 percent of all families receive their first choice. This occurs "in part because students often prefer schools that are close to their homes, but also because the Cambridge schools offer distinctive programs that have differential appeal" (Chubb & Moe, 1990, p. 211). The fact that "families must provide their own transportation" (Young & Clinchy, 1992, p. 30) is also a factor, which raises the question of controlled choice's impact on desegregation.

A review of desegregation evidence in Cambridge "suggests that the voluntary system has led to better racial balance than before, that no school has drifted toward resegregation, and that the proportion of school-age students attending public over private schools has increased" (Henig, 1994, p. 123). Young and Clinchy (1992) report that "all 13 of the district's schools are within 10 percentage points plus or minus of the districtwide averages for race and ethnicity" (p. 31). However, Henig (1994) cautions that choice studies often make claims that are too strong and that "it may be that a more modest conclusion—that controlled choice can allow for *sustaining* desegregation progress begun using more authoritative governmental means—is more appropriate" (p. 140).

Claims of improved academic performance for Cambridge have been impressive. Young and Clinchy (1992) find that "improved student performance is associated with Cambridge's intradistrict 'controlled' choice plan based on results of the 1984–1985 and 1987–1988 California Test of Basic Skills in math, reading, and writing" (p. 31). "By eighth grade," say Alves and Willie, "minority students are outperforming white students in math and reading citywide in 60% of the public schools, and similar academic gains have been reported for low income students in 50% of the schools" (cited in Henig, 1994, p. 123). The "percentage of students passing the district's basic-skills test increased from 72.8 to 87 over the first four years of the controlled-choice program,...[and] scores continued to increase through 1988" (p. 123). Young and Clinchy (1992) speculate that "the district's ability to attract students from private schools has probably helped to increase districtwide test scores" (p. 31).

Young and Clinchy (1992) conclude that Cambridge's "'controlled' choice model appears to hold the most promise for promoting accountability, equity, and diversity" (p. 31) and that "the only additional improvement Cambridge might make to enhance equity further would be to provide free transportation to all of its schools" (p. 31). Cambridge has "proven that choice in a single district can stimulate creative planning and promote widespread satisfaction" (Carnegie, 1992, p. 46).

Interdistrict

Interdistrict choice enables parents to select schools outside of their district. In "statewide" choice, they may choose any public school in the state. In 1987, with its Open Enrollment plan, Minnesota became the first state to implement a statewide choice model (Carnegie, 1992). Both "elementary and secondary students are allowed to attend schools outside their own districts, with state and local money—up to a minimum or 'foundation' set by the state—following them, as long as the receiving district has room and racial balance is not adversely affected" (Chubb & Moe, 1990, p. 210). In addition, "except for the three cities with desegregation court orders (Minneapolis, St. Paul, and Duluth), districts could not bar any students from leaving their district to attend school in another district" (Rubenstein & Adelman, 1994, p. 217). While such broad choice may have benefitted many families, it created liabilities for some districts.

Student shifts led to dire consequences for some school districts. The town of Motley, for example, "lost half of its five hundred students to the larger nearby town of Staples" (Henig, 1994, p. 133). Superintendents cited that the biggest change brought about by Open Enrollment "was an increase in average class size, either because new students were entering a district or because student departures from a district forced program or teacher cuts" (Carnegie, 1992, p. 52).

The Carnegie study reveals that "the reason for the shifts were usually not for academic reasons" (Carnegie, 1992, p. 58). Hakim, Seidenstat, and Bowman (1994) concur: "Most parents in Minnesota...chose schools by proximity to home or work" (p. 11). These findings differ from those of Rubenstein and Adelman (1994), who found in their study of Open Enrollment that "parents select non-resident schools primarily because of their strong academic reputations" (p. 223). However, they acknowledge that parents "also give serious consideration to a schools proximity to the family's home" (p. 223), which is "a factor of some significance in a rural state like Minnesota, where a farm may be twenty miles from the resident school, but only two miles from a school in an adjoining district" (p. 223). "Roughly the same pattern holds true for minority families" (p. 223).

"In Greater Minnesota, minority and low-income families were proportionately represented among Open Enrollment participants" (Rubenstein & Adelman, 1994, p. 220). This has not been the case in the cities. For example, in the Twin Cities, "minority family participation was limited by a variety of factors, including the existence of intradistrict choice and limited access to transportation and information" (p. 220), and "minority families may have been uncomfortable sending their children to suburban schools where they might be the only minority student in their class, if not the school" (pp. 221-222). Additionally, to maintain racial balance, "Minneapolis has had to deny transfers to 88 percent of white students seeking to leave" (Henig, 1994, p. 123).

Another reason that probably contributed to the low level of minority participation in the cities was the "lack of congruence between most districts' strategies for disseminating information to parents, and minority parents' most common sources of information on schools" (Rubenstein & Adelman, 1994, p. 223). Though the "original Open Enrollment statute stated that school districts 'are responsible for informing students' about options programs…the state did not monitor compliance with this requirement, so districts responded in many forms, some far less effective than others" (p. 222). Reports of inadequate information dissemination are repeated in most of the studies we examined.

Rubenstein and Adelman (1994) found in their surveys that parents and secondary students generally were pleased with their selections and that:

> At least 50 percent [of the parents] said that their child had shown improvement in the following areas: academic performance, motivation, self-confidence, and sense of responsibility. Parents also said that they were more directly involved in their children's education but were less involved in the PTA and other school or district organizations. (p. 223)

The Carnegie Foundation (1992) reports that "in Minnesota, some thirteen thousand students attended public schools outside their district in 1991–92 under open enrollment—about 1.8 percent of the student body" (p. 49). However, in its study of school choice nationally, it found no correlation between statewide choice programs and improvement of students' academic performance. In assessing the Minnesota reform, Chubb and Moe (1990) lauded the effort, but they felt that it did "not go nearly far enough, failing to free up the supply of schools, continuing to control them from above, and leaving all the traditional institutions in place" (p. 210).

Public Finance and Private Provision: Government Vouchers

As noted previously, only two states, Wisconsin and Ohio, have voucher legislation that enables public school students to attend private schools at government expense. The Milwaukee Parental Choice Program (MPCP), begun in 1990, was the first choice program in the country to fund private-nonsectarian schools. Like the private voucher programs, it is limited to low-income families. In 1995, the enabling legislation was amended "(1) to allow religious schools to enter the program; (2) to allow students in grades kindergarten through three who were already attending private schools to be eligible for the program; (3) to eliminate all funding for data collection and evaluations" (Witte, Sterr, & Thorn, 1995, p. 2). The amending law was blocked by a lawsuit brought by the American Civil Liberties Union and the Wisconsin affiliate of the National Education Association.

The MPCP is a highly regulated government voucher program that has survived court challenges. Witte (1993) cautions that because the MPCP is "a targeted program that represents a compromise in design between the extreme of an open-ended, unregulated market system of education and a system in which the public role is limited solely to conventional public school governance,…[it] should not be used as evidence, either pro or con, for evaluating more inclusive choice programs" (p. 103).

Key characteristics of the MPCP program are as follows: (a) only nonsectarian schools that will accept the voucher as full payment ($3,209 in 1994–1995) may participate; (b) schools may not select students on the basis of gender, religion, or academic performance (Beales & Wahl, 1995); (c) private schools "initially had to limit choice students to 49% of their total enrollment" (Witte, Sterr, & Thorn, 1995, p. 1), but this was increased to 65 percent for 1994–1995; (d) "new choice students must not have been in private schools in the prior year" (p. 1); and (e) although initially no more than 1.0 percent (approximately 1,000) of Milwaukee Public School (MPS) students could enroll in MPCP, this limit was increased to 1.5 percent (approximately 1,500) for 1994-1995 and to a maximum of 15,000 students in the 1995 legislation that was ruled to be unconstitutional.

One result of the limitations on the supply of schools is that the maximum voucher allotment of 1,000 had not been achieved by the 1994–1995 school year, although there was a waiting list of eligible students (Witte, Sterr, & Thorn, 1995). September enrollments grew from 341 to 830 from 1990–1991 to 1994–1995. The number of schools participating grew from seven to 12 for the same period. These numbers contrast sharply with those of PAVE, Milwaukee's private voucher program, which enrolls many more students and has many more participating schools.

John Witte of the University of Wisconsin was in charge of annual data collection and evaluation from 1990 to 1995. We have drawn heavily from his reports on MPCP. Witte, Sterr, and Thorn (1995) report that "the program has had the greatest impact on African-American students, who comprised 74% of those applying to choice schools and 72% of those enrolled in the first five years of the program,…[and that] Hispanics accounted for 19% of the choice applicants and 21% of those enrolled" (p. 4). Regarding marital status, "choice families were much more likely to be headed by a non-married parent (75%) than the average MPS family (49%) and somewhat more likely than the low-income MPS parent (65%)" (p. 4).

The average MPCP family income for the first five years was $11,630; however, in 1994, it increased to $14,210 (Witte, Sterr, & Thorn, 1995). "A unique characteristic of choice parents was that despite their economic status, they reported higher education levels than either low-income or average MPS parents....Over half of the choice mothers reported some college education (56%), compared with 40 percent for the entire MPS sample and 30 percent of the low-income MPS respondents" (p. 4). Not surprisingly, parents' educational expectations for their children were also somewhat higher for choice parents than MPS and low-income MPS. Witte, Sterr, and Thorn's findings are consistent with those of Schneider, Schiller, and Coleman (1996). Using the National Education Longitudinal Study of 1988, Schneider and colleagues find that "students whose parents had low levels of education were least likely to consider choosing a public or private school other than the one to which their child would be assigned on the basis of residence" (p. 19).

Witte, Sterr, and Thorn (1995) found that choice parents expressed much higher levels of dissatisfaction with their prior schools than MPS parents. However, their "frustration with prior public schools, although not unimportant, was not as important a reason for applying to the Choice Program as the attributes of the private schools" (p. 4). Indeed, survey results reveal that the primary reasons for participating in MPCP were the perceived educational quality and teaching approach of the private schools, followed by the school's disciplinary environment and general atmosphere. Parental involvement, "which was more frequent than for the average MPS parent in prior schools, was even greater for most activities in the choice schools" (p. 12). Beales and Wahl (1995) suggest "that there is something about either the school chosen or the act of choice itself that is a motivator in its own right" (p. 59).

Witte, Sterr, and Thorn (1995) find little to differentiate MPCP student performance from that of nonvoucher students, other than that they "had lower prior achievement test results than the average MPS student" (p. 5). Key findings for the fifth year of the program (the most recent available) show that outcomes "remain mixed...achievement-change scores varied considerably in the first five years" (p. 12). In addition; "regression results...generally indicated that choice and public school students were not much different" (p. 12); attrition was comparable to that found in Milwaukee Public Schools. Witte and colleagues conclude: "Obviously the attrition rate and the factors affecting attrition indicate that not all students will succeed in these schools, but the majority remain and applaud the program" (p. 14).

Two recent studies of the MPCP program presented different conclusions than did Witte's. Paul E. Peterson and Jay P. Green found that students who remained in the program at least three years scored three to five percentage points higher in reading and five to 12 percentage points higher in math than did students who applied to the program but remained in the public schools (cited in Olson, 1996). In a subsequent study of MPCP, Cecilia E. Rouse reached the more modest conclusion that "math scores of students in the private schools likely increased by 1.5 to two percentage points each year over what they would have been had those students remained in public schools" (cited in Olson, 1997, p. 5), but "the results for reading were mixed and not statistically significant" (p. 5). Both studies compared applicants selected for MPCP with those who where not selected and remained in public schools. A key difference in the two studies is that Peterson and Green "did not include students who were selected for the program but never enrolled or who subsequently left the private schools and returned to the public schools" (p. 5). Some critics, including Witte, say that those omissions biased the Peterson and Green study, "since students who were not being well-served by the private schools were more likely to leave" (p. 5). Rouse's study is seen by some as being "definitely a corrective on the grand claims that Paul Peterson and Jay Green were making" (Bruce Fuller, cited in Olson, 1997, p. 5).

In a recent study comparing MPCP students with randomly rejected applicants, Witte (1997) reached a similar *initial* conclusion as did Rouse: no significant difference for reading scores but a significant difference, favoring the MPCP students, in mathematics scores. However, Witte then examined the characteristics of his sample and found that one part of the sample, the randomly selected rejects of the applicants to MPCP, were an anomaly. The rejects were outscored not only by the MPCP recipients who attended private school but also, and to an even greater extent, by the eligible low-income students who never applied to MPCP and remained in the public schools. Examining the students over a four-year period, Witte reports that the MPCP students and the eligible but nonchoosing MPS students were similar across the four years studied, while the MPCP rejects began much lower and continued to decline over time. Witte (1997) asks, "To whom would we generalize these results even if they were valid? Certainly not to the MPS low-income students....That group far outperformed the [MPCP] *Rejects*" (online).

Private Finance and Provision: Private Vouchers

In this section, we examine findings from studies of three of the largest private-voucher programs. We draw heavily from the research of Heise, Colburn, and Lamberti (1995), Beales and Wahl (1995), and Martinez, Godwin, and Kemerer (1995) for our reports on private-voucher programs in Indianapolis, Milwaukee, and San Antonio, respectively, and from Moe (1995), the editor of the *Private Vouchers* volume in which these studies are found.

Both the Milwaukee and San Antonio plans incorporate the basic tenets of the Indianapolis model (see below). In addition to these basic tenets, we found that all three of the private-voucher programs had a number of additional characteristics in common. Despite a lack of data about the performance of students in voucher programs, the programs are very popular with both parents and students, as indicated in part by the long waiting list for each program. The lack of data concerning student performance contrasts with the rather extensive data researchers collected on participant characteristics and preferences and operational issues. Parents of voucher recipients are less poor and have higher educational levels and higher educational expectations for their children than nonchoosing low-income parents. Educational quality is the primary reason parents participate in voucher programs, and they perceive private school quality to be higher than that of public schools. Fifty percent of voucher recipients attended private school the year prior to receiving a voucher. Since the voucher programs examined pursue no information distribution strategy, churches and private schools became significant information sources.

For each of the three voucher programs we provide the following information, if available: participant statistics, observations on methodology, demographic characteristics, and additional conclusions. Demographic characteristics include: race, marital status, religious education availability and preference, educational attainment of parent, how families learned about the program, parental attitudes, parental satisfaction, and academic performance. Because of our reliance on single studies for these implementations, we present more detailed information about research methodology in this section than we have previously.

Indianapolis

J. Patrick Rooney built his Educational Choice Charitable Trust, or "Golden Rule" program, around several basic tenets. The vouchers pay up to half the cost of tuition with a cap on the maximum and "with parents responsible for paying or raising the remainder" (Moe, 1995, p. 9). Vouchers are awarded only to low-income families to send their children to private sectarian or nonsectarian schools. Children may be already attending a private school. Students apply for admission directly to their school of choice, and schools decide whom to enroll. There are "no requirements, academic or otherwise, aside from the admissions standards of the specific schools they choose to attend" (p. 10). Students are awarded vouchers on a first come, first served basis. We shall see that the first and last tenets are potential sources for inequity in the distribution of vouchers.

Observations on methodology. Heise, Colburn, and Lamberti (1995) identify partial funding for their research as coming from a grant from the Lilly Foundation, a contributor to Educational Choice Charitable Trust. They do not identify to whom the Lilly grant was made (e.g., the trust or university) or other sources of support. They say that they based their research on surveys that are conducted annually; however, they do not identify the source of the surveys. Demographic comparisons were made between low-income participants and the whole population of public-school families—rather than comparable low-income public-school families. We have not reported these comparisons. Heise and his colleagues caution that their evaluation "has not yet reached midpoint" (p. 105), that their data are "preliminary, the analyses descriptive" (p. 105), and that "little can be reasonably concluded from these preliminary data" (p. 117).

Participation statistics. From the beginning, the trust had a long waiting list of students who had applied for a voucher. Within three days of Rooney's initial announcement, more than 600 families had applied, followed soon after by an additional nine hundred (Moe, 1995). The original plan to award 500 vouchers the first year was expanded to 744. In the second year of the program (1992–93), vouchers were awarded to 874 students to enroll in 60 private schools. Of these, half previously attended private school. Vouchers were capped at $800 the second year.

Religious education availability or preference. "Catholic schools account for just under half the total number of schools selected by voucher parents," report Heise and associates (1995, p. 116); however, Catholic schools enroll two-thirds of the trust students. No data were provided on the other participating schools. Part of the reason for high enrollment in Catholic schools was related to how parents found out about the program.

How families learned about the program. The researchers identify a problem with the trust's information distribution: "Information reached different people at different times. Because…grants are allocated to eligible families on a first-come, first-served basis, those families that learned about the availability of grants early gained an important advantage" (Heise et al., 1995, p. 117). As was true with the MPCP initiative, the Indianapolis "program did not pursue a formal outreach or dissemination strategy. As a result, the importance of alternative information dissemination mechanisms increased" (p. 112). The primary sources of information in their order of frequency were friends and relatives, private schools, newspaper, churches, and TV and radio. "The reliance on news coverage along with an informal dissemination effort by the Catholic schools' leadership played an important role in determining who heard about the trust program and when" (p. 102). The Catholic church's "incentive—to increase Catholic school enrollment—is clear. The number of trust recipients attending Catholic schools reflects the diocesan's efforts" (p. 114).

Educational attainment of parents. Trust-program parents are more highly educated than nonparticipating, low-income parents. Heise and colleagues (1995) conclude that "as a result, the trust program might not be reaching the least advantaged among the eligible low-income families" (p. 118). Researchers of other programs have not reported a correlation between parent income and education; however, they have found that participant parents tend to be more highly educated.

Parental attitudes and behaviors. Ninety percent of parents identified educational quality as a "very important" reason for participating (Heise et al., 1995). Additionally, 70 percent of parents described as being "very important" reasons:

"financial considerations, school safety, general atmosphere and religious values of the selected school, and discipline" (p. 115).

Parental satisfaction. Researchers found a "general absence of significant frustration with Indianapolis public schools voiced by those parents whose children left public schools" (Heise et al., 1995, p. 115). This stands in sharp contrast to the research findings for the San Antonio voucher program, which showed high levels of parental dissatisfaction with the public schools (Martinez et al., 1995).

Academic performance. Heise and associates (1995) acknowledge the "paucity of relevant data...surrounding the educational voucher issue " (p. 103). Although they identify vouchers "effect on student academic achievement" (p. 118) as being the "perhaps most important" (p. 118) unanswered question, they provide no findings on student performance. This lack of information on student outcomes is puzzling considering the extensive data collected on participant characteristics and operational issues. The absence of data on such an important issue begs the questions: Was performance data collected? If not, why not? Heise and his colleagues (1995) note, "Important questions about the efficacy of educational vouchers remain" (p. 118).

Milwaukee

In 1992, business and religious organizations united to establish Partners Advancing Values in Education (PAVE). PAVE was "not built from scratch;...rather, the Milwaukee program arose from an institutional base, the Milwaukee Archdiocesan Education Foundation, that had been set up earlier to provide aid to children and Catholic schools in the inner city" (Moe, 1995, p. 12). The Foundation "formed a more broadly based coalition—representing the full range of private schools in the city, religious and nonreligious, Catholic and non-Catholic—for the purpose of raising funds to support private education and low-income students in Milwaukee" (p. 13). The Foundation contributed its $800,000 trust toward the establishment of PAVE. Other foundations and businesses also made major contributions. PAVE began operations in the 1992–1993 school year and functions in the same city as the nation's first public voucher system. However, PAVE "is not encumbered by the debilitating design restrictions that distort the operation of vouchers in the public program" (pp. 13–14).

Observations on methodology. Information about the PAVE program came from surveys of parents whose children received scholarships. The surveys were commissioned by the Lynde and Harry Bradley Foundation, were conducted by Family Service America, "a national nonprofit corporation providing services, education, and advocacy for families in need through its 290 member agencies" (Beales & Wahl, 1995, p. 47); and were based on John Witte's survey for the Milwaukee Parental Choice Program (MPCP). The Bradley Foundation has been a major contributor to PAVE. Note that this study does not focus on a particular school year or set of school years. Sometimes, Beales and Wahl identify the *First Year Report of the PAVE Scholarship Program* as the source of their data and at other times, the second year report, without explaining why particular years were selected for certain analyses. Beales and Wahl compare their data on PAVE with that collected by Witte on MPCP, and we report those findings.

Participation statistics. During PAVE's first year of operation, 1992–1993, it funded 2,089 children (Moe, 1995). In 1993–1994, PAVE selected 2,370 recipients (83% elementary) from 4,000 applicants. Awards totaled $1,645,000. Participating in the program were 110 schools (90 religious). PAVE capped individual vouchers at $1,000 for elementary school and $1,500 for high school (Moe, 1995). Consistent with other programs, about half the PAVE scholarships were given to low-income students who were enrolled in private schools before the advent of PAVE (Beales & Wahl, 1995). Beales and Wahl report that PAVE's overhead was 7 percent.

Race. In 1992–1993, PAVE awarded vouchers to a higher percentage of white children (46 percent) and a lower percentage of African-American children (37 percent) than represented among the low-income population of the Milwaukee Public Schools—29 percent and 55 percent, respectively. The percentage of Hispanic recipients (13 percent) was slightly higher than represented in the population of low-income MPS students (10 percent). Beales and Wahl (1995) note that although 42 percent of low-income children in Milwaukee are white, only 29 percent of low-income students in the public schools are white, and thus it can be seen that many low-income white families have already fled the public schools.

Marital status. Forty-two percent of PAVE parents are married, a larger percentage than for other low-income parents in Milwaukee public schools (Beales & Wahl, 1995).

Religious education availability and preference. Beales and Wahl (1995) report that almost 95 percent of PAVE students attend religiously affiliated schools, with 60 percent enrolled in the 50 Catholic parochial schools participating in the voucher program. They also report that PAVE is having a greater financial impact on other denominations. In participating schools, the percentage of the total student body that was funded by vouchers was as follows: Catholic—12.5 percent; non-Catholic Christian—25 percent; Jewish—25 percent; and Muslim—almost 50 percent (Beales & Wahl, 1995). The economic impact on participating religious schools of even this relatively small voucher program—compared to the total number of students in public schools—cannot be overlooked.

Educational attainment of parent. The parents that participate in PAVE are better educated than are other low-income parents in the public schools. They are half as likely to have dropped out of high school and are almost twice as likely to have attended college. Beales and Wahl (1995) suggest "that educated parents are more likely to seek educational opportunities for their children and that school choice is perceived as such an opportunity" (p. 53).

How families learned about the program. Beales and Wahl (1995) found that "the most common source of information about the PAVE program was the private schools themselves" (p. 54). Sixty-five percent of PAVE families learned about the program from private schools or churches; whereas, 68 percent of MPCP families learned about the MPCP program from friends or relatives and newspapers. The role of the church in information distribution is apparent. The top three sources of information about PAVE were private schools (54 percent), friends or relatives (14 percent), and churches (11 percent). The top MPCP sources were friends or relatives (44 percent), newspapers (24 percent), and private schools (22 percent).

Parental attitudes and behaviors. PAVE parents have higher educational expectations for their children than do other low-income parents in Milwaukee public schools, which may in part explain their higher level of participation in the schools' activities. Beales and Wahl (1995) found that "96 percent of PAVE parents and 97 percent of MPCP parents reported attending parent-teacher conferences compared with 84 percent of Milwaukee public school parents" (p. 59). It appears to Beales and Wahl that "participation in choice, be it the MPCP or PAVE, is a better predictor of parental involvement than whether the parent must pay for that choice" (p. 59).

Parental satisfaction. Educational quality was foremost among the reasons that parents gave for participating in PAVE. Sixty-five percent of PAVE parents "indicated that 'frustration with the public schools' was a very important reason for their choice" (Beales & Wahl, 1995, p. 56). Parents were highly satisfied with their new schools with 90 percent rating with an A or B the schools they had selected.

Academic performance. Examining data collected by Family Service America, Beales and Wahl (1995) report that "twice as many PAVE [seventh-grade] students, in percentage terms, score at or above the 50th percentile on the Iowa Tests of Basic Skills (Iowa Basics) than do low-income Milwaukee public school students" (p. 60). Additionally, they report that 52 PAVE students who attended public schools in the previous year "consistently [scored] lower in math, reading, and on the composite score" than did 47 PAVE students who had always attended private schools. They caution that their data were limited, that they were "not able to control statistically for factors such as income levels or parental education" (p. 60), that bias may have been introduced in the selection process and in survey and test evaluation processes, and that "additional variables (such as spirituality and socioeconomic status within the low-income parents)...may alter these conclusions" (p. 63). However, they suggest that "private schools have a positive impact on the academic performance of low income students" (p. 63).

Beales and Wahl findings for seventh-grade students who attended elementary school in predominantly Catholic schools contrast with earlier findings reported by Marie Rohde, religion reporter for the *Milwaukee Journal,* who wrote on August 1, 1991:

> Minority students enrolled in Milwaukee's Catholic elementary schools suffer the same lag in achievement test [Iowa Test of Basic Skills] scores as their counterparts in the public schools, according to test results made public for the first time....[The scores] run counter to longstanding claims by most Catholic educators that they are doing a superior job of teaching disadvantaged children. (Rohde, cited in Shanker & Rosenberg, 1992, p. 139)

San Antonio

Children's Educational Opportunity (CEO) Foundation was founded in 1992 by James R. Leininger, a physician, chief executive officer of Kinetic Optics, and head of the Texas Public Policy Foundation (Martinez et al., 1995). CEO America, an offshoot of CEO, has spearheaded the drive to develop voucher programs in cities across the country (Moe, 1995).

Observations on methodology. Martinez, Godwin, and Kemerer, faculty members of the University of North Texas, initiated a comprehensive external evaluation comparing CEO participants with two other populations: low-income nonchoosers in the public schools and choosers of a public-choice, multilingual program[11] that had an academic-performance criterion but no restriction on the income of participant families. They gathered data with English and Spanish versions of a mail questionnaire and interviewed a stratified random sample of nonchoosing families by phone. Martinez and her colleagues (1995) caution that "because the low-income population of San Antonio is heavily Latino, we are constrained in generalizing to other low-income racial and ethnic groups" (p. 80).

Participation. In its first year, 1992–1993, CEO awarded vouchers to 936 recipients from more than 2,200 applicants. The vouchers were valued at up to $750 to pay for up to half the cost of tuition. As with the other two programs, 50 percent of the recipients had attended private schools the previous year. At 99 percent sectarian, CEO had the highest enrollment in parochial schools of the three most prominent voucher programs.

Race. Martinez and associates (1995) found that "a demographic factor that is related to the probability of being a private school chooser is ethnicity. Twelve percent of private school choosers are Anglo compared with only four percent attendance-zone families [nonchoosers] and six percent of multilingual school families [public-choice choosers]" (p. 84).

Marital status. The Martinez research team (1995) discovered "no significant difference in marital status of San Antonio choosers and nonchoosers" (p. 84). However, they find that chooser families—both voucher recipients and public-choice families—were both smaller in size and had relatively higher incomes. They anticipate that if a publicly funded voucher program "does not pay the full cost of a child's tuition and no adjustment is made for family size, then the program will discriminate against large families" (p. 84).

Religious education availability and preference. Private schools in the low-income areas of San Antonio are predominantly parochial and Catholic. Participant schools were 60 percent Catholic, 30 percent Baptist and other Protestant, nine percent other denominational, and one percent nonsectarian. Martinez and associates (1995) conclude that "more-religious parents want to place their child in a school that teaches the values that are important to the parents, which leads them to look for alternatives to public schools" (p. 94). They also argue that "when comparing the importance of education with the importance of maintaining religious practices and ethnic traditions, private-school families are more likely to stress goals other than education" (p. 88).

Educational attainment of parent. Martinez and her colleagues (1995) found that "regardless of race, income, program design, and recruitment strategies, educated mothers are more likely to search out alternatives to attendance-zone [public] schools" (p. 92). The data indicate that, compared with nonchoosing parents, voucher parents are nearly three times as likely to have completed some college and public-choice parents are nearly twice as likely. The researchers conclude that choice programs "empower parents whose education leads them to want alternatives to their current public school but whose income does not allow either private schools or residence in wealthy neighborhoods and school districts" (p. 92).

How families learned about the program. One equity problem reported by the researchers was that "the program was advertised only in English-language newspapers, probably reducing participation by families in which English is not the primary language" (Martinez et al., 1995, p. 80). "Churches provided the other most important source of information about the program, perhaps biasing participation in favor of more-religious families" (p. 80). We find in all of these implementations of voucher programs that when information dissemination is not planned, informal information networks fill the void, favoring particular populations and, therefore, limiting information dissemination to—and thus the participation of—other populations.

Parental attitudes and behaviors. The educational aspirations and expectations of parents who exercised a choice option "far exceeded the expectations of parents who [did] not" (Martinez et al., 1995, p. 85). Indeed, "more than half of choosing parents expect their children to attain graduate and professional degrees, compared with 17 percent of the [nonchoosing] respondents" (p. 85). Parents responded that the leading reason for their choice "was educational quality" (p. 89). Tying for the second most important reason in the selection process of private-choice parents were "discipline, the general atmosphere of the chosen school, and religious training" (p. 89).

Parental satisfaction. In contrast to Indianapolis but consistent with Milwaukee, "more than half of CEO parents gave their child's previous public school a grade of C or lower" (Martinez et al., 1995, p. 87). By comparison, "less than one-fifth of nonchoosers gave their child's school a grade of C or lower" (p. 87). Choice parents' "key areas of dissatisfaction with public schools were the amount their children learned and school discipline" (p. 88). Only 13 percent of these parents gave the new schools a grade of C or lower.

Academic performance. Surprisingly, Martinez and colleagues (1995) provide only a short paragraph discussing one of "the biggest difference[s] between choosing and nonchoosing families" (p. 85): student scores on standardized tests. Examining average normal curve equivalent (NCE) scores, they found that public-choice student scores in math and reading were significantly higher than voucher student scores, and both were much higher than the scores of students from nonchoosing families. They point out that the higher public-choice scores are "not unexpected given the academic performance criterion of the public program" (p. 86).

Income of participating families. Martinez and associates (1995) show that income as well as family size can be a barrier to participation. They report that the "CEO respondents are slightly better off than [nonchoosing] families" (p. 83): "More than twice as many nonchoosing families receive public assistance (35 percent) as do either public- or private-choosing families (15 percent)" (p. 84). According to the investigators, "The San Antonio data demonstrate that a public-choice program that recruits on the basis of academic achievement and does not intensively recruit low-income students will take the higher-income children" (p. 83). A voucher program "which covers only a portion of school costs will not attract the lowest end of the low-income population" (p. 83). To increase participation by the lowest-income groups, Martinez, Godwin, and Kemerer argue that "a private school scholarship or voucher program must cover a larger portion of the costs and make adjustments to scholarships that account for both income and the number of children in a family" (p. 94).

LESSONS LEARNED

Lack of consensus has not halted the progress of educational choice in the United States. Across the nation, public-choice programs have been implemented and voucher programs initiated. Proponents make strong claims for the increased efficacy, equity, and efficiency of choice, while opponents counter that data does not support efficacy claims, that choice increases, not decreases, inequity, and that any efficiency gains are offset by new expenses incurred in the interest of equity. Proponents claim that families should have the right to decide which values their children will learn. Opponents counter that the democratic need for a common education supersedes the interests of individual family values. An ever-present wedge between choice proponents and opponents is the historical support of vouchers by advocates for segregation of education by race or religion. Entrenchment on both sides of the choice debate provides little opportunity for considered discourse. Only in the domain of public-school choice have combatants found any measure of common ground.

Efficacy, equity, and efficiency are the frames through which we examined voucher positions and through which we now consider the empirical lessons learned to date. In general, we found that little data exists regarding test results to support claims of improved student performance; however, parent and student satisfaction with choice schools appears uniformly high across all forms of choice programs, whether public choice, government voucher, or private voucher. All the choice programs we examined, with one exception, appear to create inequities for part of the target population. The exception appears to be the "controlled-choice" plan in Cambridge, Massachusetts, which demonstrates that careful design of choice programs can produce, or at least maintain, some level of equity. However, equity comes at a price, and claims that choice programs increase efficiency disappear once the costs of equity measures are included in the equation. Equity-producing/cost-increasing measures include adequate information systems, free transportation to school, and regulations to maintain the district's racial and socio-economic balance at each site. Such measures appear to reduce the "skimming" that generally takes place within choice programs.

Efficacy

Given the primacy of the efficacy issue, we are struck both by the lack of breadth and depth in the evaluation of student performance in choice programs and by the echoing call by researchers for more studies on student performance. However, Henig (1994) decries not the limited volume of research on voucher programs but the limited quality, and he calls for more rigorous studies.

One reason for the lack of research is the fact that Milwaukee, until recently, was the only government voucher program in the country available to study. The only ongoing research examining effects of vouchers on student performance was conducted by John Witte who tracked MPCP from 1990 to 1995. Although Witte found no difference in student performance between students in MPCP and low-income children in the public schools, recent research by Rouse indicates small gains by MPCP students. However, Witte also found high levels of parent and student satisfaction with their new schools of choice, which he does not discount as one measure of the efficacy of voucher programs. Similar levels of parent and student satisfaction have been reported by researchers looking at private-voucher and public-choice programs. Surprisingly, parent satisfaction with choice schools appears to occur irrespective of any initial dissatisfaction with the local public schools.

Witte concurs with voucher advocates that the highly regulated MPCP program should not be considered a fair test of the efficacy of government vouchers. Proponents of vouchers have long called for a substantial voucher trial to adequately demonstrate benefits and liabilities. There are, however, problems in doing so, one of which is the supply of private schools. Even if religious schools were allowed to participate, the available seats would fill up very quickly. Proponents point to the necessity of opening up the supply side for a fair trial. However, whether a voucher trial of limited duration could be structured in such a way that educational entrepreneurs would make the necessary investment is open to speculation.

All researchers agree that more and better research still needs to be done. However, legislatures are not waiting for the results. As Boyer pointed out in 1992, many of the "claims for school choice have been based more on speculation than experience" (p. xv). That appears to be even more true five years later.

Equity

Researchers are unanimous in reporting inequities in the choice programs that they examined. Despite the fact that all existing public and private voucher programs target low-income populations, researchers report that the parents of voucher students are more highly educated, have higher educational expectations for their children, and are less poor than nonchoosing, low-income parents. Additionally, within the unregulated private-voucher programs, children tended to be more white than the low-income population of nonchoosing students in the public schools. Several reasons account for choice favoring certain populations.

Each of the public and private voucher programs we examined as well as the statewide choice program in Minnesota were notable for their lack of a formal information distribution strategy. For each of these programs, researchers reported inequities in the awarding of vouchers and attributed these inequities, in part, to a lack of information in forms meaningful to each segment of the target population. As a result, more educated parents with higher educational expectations for their children tended to get information and act on it more quickly than less educated parents. The private-voucher programs' policy of first come/first served contributed to the advantage of better educated parents.

In the private voucher programs, churches and parochial schools filled the information void by providing information to parishioners and by actively recruiting students. As a result, sectarian schools, in general, and Catholic schools, in particular, received the highest proportion of enrollments. It should be pointed out that the dominance of Catholic schools in attracting voucher students is attributable, in part, to their being the most numerous private schools, in general, and the most representative of private schools in low-income neighborhoods.

Because private schools unilaterally set admissions requirements, racial balance was generally not maintained in the private-voucher programs. However, this need not be the case, as demonstrated both within the highly regulated public-voucher program in Milwaukee, where African-American children were found in significantly greater proportion than in the low-income public-school population, and within the "controlled-choice" Cambridge program, where each school reflected the demographic makeup of the district. Researchers report that lack of free transportation limited the choice of schools for some participating families—even in the highly acclaimed Cambridge program.

All these data suggest that voucher program design has the potential to either reinforce or alleviate the "skimming" that already takes place among private schools, including Catholic schools, which routinely "screen admissions in a manner that would tend to filter out probable poor performers" (Henig, 1994, p. 144). Additionally, when information distribution is left to chance, those institutions with the most to gain will maximize the opportunity to their own benefit but not necessarily to the benefit of the entire target audience of the choice program.

Efficiency

Private-voucher programs demonstrated that efficiency and equity may be mutually exclusive goals. With the intent to be models for how government vouchers should work, these programs imposed minimal restrictions on student applicants and participant schools—the primary limitation being restricting applicants to children from low-income families. To keep overhead expenses low, these programs ignored information dissemination and discrepancies of income, education, and family size within the low-income population. Additionally, neither the voucher nor the public-choice program subsidized transportation. We see that, in so doing, these programs awarded vouchers inequitably within the low-income target population. Any equitable voucher plan would have to incur expenses related to information distribution and to transportation. As Murnane (1990) has pointed out, "there are difficult tradeoffs in the design of a family choice plan" (p. 332). Equity and efficiency goals may represent one such tradeoff.

Can efficacy, equity, and efficiency be achieved through careful program design? It appears that we have, at least, one demonstration where equity was maintained through program design. Efficiency, however, appears to be connected to equity in such a way that gains in one arena result in losses in the other. And efficacy? The research has yet to appear that would answer that question.

In this chapter, we began by reviewing the history of proposals and found antecedents to virtually all contemporary rationale for and against choice. We then identified and presented characteristics of three forms of choice: public finance and provision, public finance and private provision, and private finance and provision. Next, we assessed the various positions of proponents and opponents of choice relative to the issues of efficacy, equity, efficiency, and who should control education. We followed this by examining studies done on specific implementations of public choice, government vouchers, and private vouchers. Finally, we shared lessons that we learned about choice over the course of our research relative to the frames of efficacy, equity, and efficiency.

5

School Deregulation

Imagine having a chance to restructure your schools—to alter or abandon restrictive regulations and local bureaucracy and shape the school program as you see fit. (Jenkins & Houlihan, 1990, p. 18)

The same people who loosened the government rules that regulated airlines, trucking and savings and loans now would like to rewrite the rules concerning teaching and schools. (Clabaugh, 1992, p. 53)

I n the move towards privatization of education, one means is deregulation. Following two centuries of growth in educational rules and regulations, many states are now exploring deregulation as a strategy for school improvement. In this chapter, we examine the growth of regulation and the forces that spurred it before turning to the arguments that are now propelling deregulation to the forefront of educational policy. We describe the various types of deregulation programs. After examining the effects of deregulation on schools, we present the ways deregulated schools have utilized their new freedom. Finally, we discuss barriers to the implementation and effective use of deregulation.

HISTORICAL CONTEXT

Though history does not repeat itself exactly, there is much to be learned about the viability of current reform proposals...by looking at how school systems have evolved historically. (Rogers, 1973, p. xiii)

When the U.S. Constitution was adopted, education was a matter reserved to the states; and when the state constitutions were adopted, *formal* responsibility over schools was vested in the state. (Wise, 1979, p. 51)

The Growth of Regulation in Education

The development of schools in the American colonies was strictly local in control. After the formation of the United States and the adoption of the U.S. Constitution, education was a right reserved to the states, although local control was maintained (Kaestle, 1983; Wise, 1979). There was a strong distrust of government and a fear that schools would be used by the politicians in power to indoctrinate students into their ideological beliefs (Spring, 1982). Nevertheless, over the last two centuries there has been steady growth in the regulation, bureaucratization, and centralization of the educational enterprise. In this section, we present a brief history of the growth of regulation in education and the forces that fueled it.

The Common Schools

The schools that were created, the so called common schools, had many characteristics of a tribal center designed to induct the young into the tradition of the tribe. (Schlechty, 1990, p. 17)

Generally considered to be the beginning of modern public school systems, the common school movement gained force in the 1820s (Kaestle, 1983; Spring, 1982; Tyack, 1974). During this period, "the idea of tax-supported, tuition-free schools, accessible to all, was entered into policies, laws, and state constitutions" (Warren, 1990, p. 64). Nevertheless, "the values of decentralized local government and participation by the common man were exemplified in the establishment of small school districts" (Cronin, 1973, p. 78). Edson (1982) notes that "in the nineteenth century, the chief goals of public education were to develop good moral character and teach the basics (p. 152). The three R's—reading, writing, and arithmetic—were the essence of the common school experience.

Historical analysts have shown that "the general trend...was towards a greater role for schooling in children's lives and toward ever more similar school experiences, in context and amount, for different children" (Kaestle & Vinovskis, 1980, p. 234). States attempted to expand their access to rural areas in order to standardize "curricula, teacher preparation, and the length of school terms" (Warren, 1990, p. 64) through regulations. Although most states slowly developed state education agencies, these bodies did not have any authority over the schools; their primary functions were to collect data on the schools, prepare reports and speeches, and distribute state funds (Tyack, James, & Benavot, 1987). Nevertheless, the goal of "less dissimilarity and more commonality among the schools" emerged as schools began uniform "oral and written examinations of teachers, school architecture and furniture design, curriculum, pedagogy, teacher training, and measures of student achievement" (Warren, 1990, p. 65).

Although the spread of common schools was largely decentralized and local, the common school era paved the way for the growth and expansion of state regulation. Indeed, by the time of the Civil War, the northern states had "something akin to state systems of public elementary schools" (Warren, 1990, p. 67). Since authority for local schools rested in "lay school boards" consisting of community leaders (Schlechty, 1990, p. 20), people forgot their fears that schools would be used for political purposes (Spring, 1982).

Reconstruction

> In this case, as in the past, schools gained attention obliquely via concern over particular social issues, in this case those related to rebuilding the union. (Warren, 1990, p. 60)

School reformers from the North blamed Southern secession on a "dearth of basic schooling in the states that had formed the Confederacy. If the people had been educated, the argument went, Southerners would have resisted their leaders' call to break the Union apart" (Warren, 1990, p. 69). Therefore, under Reconstruction, states created state educational agencies, and schools expanded into the rural South (Tyack et al., 1987; Warren, 1990).

Despite a general distrust of government after the Civil War, public education enjoyed a period of expansion and increased state financial support relative to other programs (Tyack, 1974). Federal land grants and state school funds were used "to stimulate local communities to build schools and as levers to secure compliance with state regulations. Although the first steps toward state control were halting, meager, and contested, they helped to persuade Americans to accept education as a proper function of the state" (Tyack et al., 1987, p. 54). As the century progressed, states created the beginnings of state school authorities—including state superintendents, state school boards, school funds, teacher certification, local taxes, and compulsory education laws. Some degree of standardization of systems emerged as states copied ideas from other states. However, states still had little power to enforce regulations (Kaestle, 1983; Tyack et al., 1987).

Large school systems underwent extensive centralization to become "large, coordinated, bureaucratic urban" organizations (Wise, 1979, p. 50). An increase in regulations accompanied the creation of hierarchal structures and an increase in centralization. However, new state "constitutions often contained elaborate blueprints of their own versions of the one best system, creating bureaucracies even while there were sometimes only a few thousand school children" (Tyack et al., 1987, p. 57). The "constitutional provisions and statutes governing education became more similar, complex and prescriptive by the latter half of the 19th century" (p. 61).

The Progressive Era

> Regulating a new society—using government and law to control the behavior of institutions, individuals, and groups—was a conspicuous feature of that outburst of state activism that we call the Progressive movement. (Keller, 1994, p. 1)

By the turn of the century, the "accumulation of industrial wealth and power within an elite group sharpened social class distinctions" (Warren, 1990, p. 71). "The influx of non-English-speaking and non-Protestant people, urbanization, and industrialization all had major impacts" (Schlechty, 1990, p. 21), which led John Dewey to advocate recognizing the new "complexity and diversity of the American people" (Keller, 1994, p. 46). Industry turned to a new means of organization in which "the production process shifted from the hands of the workers to the hands of the employers" (Edson, 1982, p. 146). Schools sought to meet industrial demands for employees with technical skills, "appropriate work behaviors," and "proper attitudes toward work" (Edson, 1982, p. 155). "The density and scale of urban population allowed, even demanded, new ways of organizing common schooling" (Kaestle, 1983, pp. 70–71).

One of the most significant results of the Progressive era for education was an increase in states' control over schools: "The state government became a fulcrum whereby reformers levered major institutional change. More than ever before, the state became an arena for designing broad social policies and centralized authority in changing social institutions" (Tyack et al., 1987, p. 125). Along with increased regulation of financial services, transportation, welfare, and criminal justice, "the expanded activity of various states in encouraging and organizing education was not an isolated governmental initiative" (Kaestle, 1983, p. 73).

A major change in school management took place during the Progressive era as the schools were modeled after corporations, with the superintendents acting as chief executives and the school board as the stockholders. Traditional responsibilities of the school board—such as textbook selection, curriculum, teacher employment, and annual student testing—were transferred to the administrative staff. By increasing their regulation of curriculum and by licensing teachers, the states centralized authority (Cronin, 1973; Tyack, 1974). Hierarchies arose, with each person assigned specific duties (Warren, 1990).

"The first generation of professional leaders educated in the new schools of education" (Tyack & Cuban, 1995, p. 17) believed "that administrative control was preferable to democratic control" (Spring, 1982, p. 92). As industrialists and professionals gained control of the schools, schools were viewed as factories, with students "as products to be molded, tested against common standards, and inspected carefully before being passed on to the next workbench for further processing" (Schlechty, 1990, p. 22). Responding to Frederick W. Taylor's "scientific management," the rhetoric of business efficiency was used as justification for the expansion of administrative powers (Beck & Murphy, 1993; Callahan, 1962; Murphy, 1992b) in the "popularization of measurement and organizational innovation" (Cronin, 1973, p. 90). Standards were set for all schools. Public high schools were created with tracks including vocational programs (Tyack, 1974).

During the Progressive movement, "regulations ballooned" (Tyack & Cuban, 1995, p. 19) and state educational agencies grew in order to carry out their new responsibilities. States used the incentive of state funds to provoke local districts into meeting minimum regulations, which "included the quality and safety of buildings, the qualifications of teachers, the length of the school term, congruence with the state course of study, and even the size of flags and pictures on the walls" (p. 20). There were reorganizations and centralizations of schools, the development of comprehensive secondary schools, and the addition of compulsory school laws (Keller, 1994; Tyack, 1974).

World War I offered the Progressives a chance for social reform, but new obstacles of "xenophobia, illiberalism, (and) pressure for conformity" (Keller, 1994, p. 51) emerged. Although the Progressive movement continued during the 1920s and 1930s, it diminished in velocity. There was a notable decrease in immigrants to the country and a decline in native birthrates—two factors that had helped spark the Progressive movement (Cronin, 1973; Keller, 1994).

The Civil Rights Movement

We conclude that in the field of public education the doctrine of "separate but equal" has no place. Separate educational facilities are inherently unequal. (*Brown v. Board of Education of Topeka*, 1954)

Coinciding with the technological challenge of Sputnik, "the emergence of a massive Civil Rights Movement between 1954 and 1968 was the major domestic event in American politics" (Berube, 1994, p. 47). Departing from a tradition of state and local control, the federal government became increasingly involved in public education in the interest of national security and equal opportunity (Clowse, 1958; Kaestle & Smith, 1982). The U.S. Supreme Court's rulings regarding segregation and Bibles in the schools brought education to the forefront of the American scene (Ravitch, 1983; Rippa, 1992): "It energized a cadre of mostly white education reformers who offered a wide range of solutions to American education. The key was poverty and the need for social mobility through the schools" (Berube, 1994, p. 62).

Led by the U.S. Supreme Court, a new era of equal rights and equal opportunities was ushered into education: "Dispossessed groups have *challenged* through legislation and the courts what they perceived as an unequal and unjust system of public schools" (Tyack, 1986, p. 213). "Moreover, civil rights leaders perceived the U.S. public school system as one that could more easily be influenced by legislation, court decisions, or street protests" (Berube, 1994, p. 48) than by administrative actions. From litigation and new federal equal opportunity laws, regulations were enacted regarding all aspects of schools: "The federal courts became aggressive in telling school boards what to do to remedy their constitutional violations" (Ravitch, 1985). Laws regarding integration, busing, and the education of handicapped persons emerged. The courts also opened up reforms of educational finance (Rippa, 1992).

The Reform Movement of the 1980s

> The nation's public schools are in trouble. By almost every measure—the commitment and competency of teachers, student test scores, truancy and dropout rates, crimes of violence—the performance of our schools falls far short of expectations. (Twentieth Century Fund, 1983, p. 3)

A state of crisis erupted in the late 1970s and 1980s with the publication of a number of reports critical of education. Most notable of these was *A Nation at Risk: The Imperative for Educational Reform* (National Commission on Excellence in Education, 1983), which triggered a "level of state policy activity...unprecedented in the history of American education" (Timar & Kirp, 1988). Reacting to the belief that the United States was falling behind in technology, productivity, and quality, the authors of the reports found schools to be inadequate and unsatisfactory (Murphy, 1990, 1991).

Because of the reports, states were spurred to enact massive, omnibus education reform acts (Murphy, 1990; Murphy & Beck, 1995). As noted by Swanson (1989), "higher standards for teachers, students, and the curriculum characterized these reforms. They further relied heavily on state-level legislation, regulation, and bureaucratic control in a top-down approach" (p. 268). Regulation was increasingly prescriptive (Murphy, 1990, 1991).

The Case for Regulation

Having briefly chronicled the rise of educational regulation, we now turn to an examination of the pressures behind the increase in rules and regulations.

Nation-building

> The educated character and tamed will of the individual was the foundation of civic virtue, a small *imperium* in the larger *imperio* of the state, a better guarantee of lawful behavior than regiments or constables. (Tyack et al., 1987, p. 45)

Democracy. In the earliest days of the republic, the common school was seen "as (an) efficient means to promote morality, loyalty, and economic sufficiency among the people" (Warren, 1990, p. 66). Based upon republican theory, schools "focused on the individual as the key to political stability and schooling as the means of shaping the citizen" (Tyack et al., 1987, p. 45). During the 1800s, "the chief goals of public education were to develop good moral character and teach the basics" (Edson, 1982, p. 152). Schools were the transmitters of "the white, Anglo-Saxon, Protestant republic" (Schlechty, 1990, p. 18) as espoused in books such as *McGuffey's Reader.*

In order to build the intellectual capital required by the new nation, "some of America's most eloquent political leaders looked to education—not just through the informal colonial modes of instruction but through schools organized and financed by the states" (Kaestle, 1983, p. 5). Noah Webster and Benjamin Rush saw schools as instrumental in developing nationalism and sustaining the republic (Cronin, 1973). With widespread concern about "regional loyalties," the nation's schools were seen as "devices that might be employed to weld its sections into a union" (Warren, 1990, p. 66). As states gradually created school funds to finance new schools, they sought to provide early regulation in the form of rules covering student classification and instruction (Kaestle, 1983; Tyack, 1974).

Assimilation. By the late nineteenth century, the primary concern of the nation was the assimilation of immigrants into the American culture for "social cohesion" (Keller, 1994, p. 66). A chief result of the Progressive movement was the fact "that corporations and the middle class sought to impose greater social controls on an urban-immigrant industrial working class thought to be dangerously susceptible to radicalism and/or social disorder" (p. 1). Schools were seen as a means of assimilating children that might otherwise "be unassimilable" into the nation (Tyack et al., 1987, p. 112). Since "education had to take on the daunting task of 'Americanizing' new immigrants and their children" (Keller, 1994, p. 44), "an expanded educational role for the state seemed justified and urgently needed, simply to accomplish traditional goals of morality and literacy" (Kaestle, 1983, p. 96). The result was increasing state regulations designed to make education more systematic and uniform (Tyack, 1974; Kaestle, 1983).

Creating Opportunity

Instruments of social reform. "Advocates of spending for public schooling portrayed the common school as the great preemptive social service, the public good that made other forms of social spending less necessary if not superfluous" (Tyack et al., 1987, p. 53). Schools "were to remediate social ills" (Schlechty, 1990, p. 18). In this view, the "purpose of schools was to serve as an engine of social reform—a means by which the injustices inherent in an urban industrial society might be addressed" (p. 18). Meeting the needs of minorities and the impoverished "for social mobility" (Berube, 1994, p. 62) became part of the school focus beginning in the 1950s. To address these issues, states made school attendance compulsory, centralized control of education in the hands of professionals, increased regulation so as to provide a systematic standardized education, regulated a differentiated curriculum, and implemented vocational education programs (Tyack, 1974; Kaestle, 1983).

Equity and access. From the era of the common schools on, there was expansion of a free, standardized education for all children (Warren, 1990). Initially limited to the North, public schools were established in the South during the Reconstruction. Horace Mann saw schools as the great equalizer of class society (Cronin, 1973). During the nineteenth century, the working class movement "wanted the schools to provide them with the intellectual tools to gain power" (p. 85). By the turn of the century, the administrative Progressives aimed to promote equity by "increased access to schooling for young people for ever longer periods of time" (Tyack & Cuban, 1995, p. 21). In the 1950s and 1960s, the focus of regulation turned to providing equality of educational opportunity for minorities. The issue of access to schooling remained key. The 1970s and 1980s saw enhanced efforts to equalize educational funding. Throughout the late 1980s and 1990s, access to learning opportunity became a key plank in the educational equity agenda (Murphy & Hallinger, 1989). Throughout each era, state regulation was seen as necessary for children to be afforded their "educational rights" (Tyack et al., 1987, p. 79).

Increased Complexity

Urbanization. With rapid population growth, urbanization, and industrialization in the late 1800s and throughout the twentieth century, schools have increased in their size and complexity (Kaestle & Vinovskis, 1980; Tyack, 1974). To manage these urban schools, better coordination was required and regulations proliferated to create the "one best system of education" (Tyack, 1974, p. 28). Adding better-trained teachers, extending school years, and developing more differentiated curricula, urban schools sought standardization and created bureaucracy to manage it (Kaestle, 1983). Analysts have shown that these "urban school districts typically were far in advance of state law in systemizing schooling; the campaign to use state law to standardize public education was aimed largely at one-room schools and often was spearheaded by school leaders from urban districts" (Tyack et al., 1987, p. 61). Tyack (1974) notes:

> They sought to replace confused and erratic means of control with careful allocation of powers and functions within hierarchal organizations; to establish networks of communication that would convey information and directives and would provide data for planning for the future; to substitute impersonal rules for informal, individual adjudication of disputes; to regularize procedures so that they

would apply uniformly to all in certain categories; and to set objective standards for admission to and performance in each role, whether superintendent or third-grader. (p. 28)

Changing funding patterns. Initial state support for public education came in the form of *"enticement,* as a way to persuade their fellow citizens through moral appeals so as to attract them through state subsidies to establish state schools and to send their children to them" (Tyack, 1986, p. 213). The administrative Progressives thought inadequate schools to be a result of "meager state and local taxation" (Tyack et al., 1987, p. 109); thus they advocated increased state financing of public education. Slowly, the financing of schools changed from private and charity funding to increasingly state-supported public schools (Kaestle, 1983). In the 1920s and 1930s, there was a major shift in school funding from the local to the state level, with state school budgets often doubling (Keller, 1994). With the increased litigation over education beginning in the 1960s, the courts have played a key role in the implementation of new regulations governing the distribution and utilization of school funds (Ravitch, 1985; Rippa, 1992). To increase equity and to provide additional funding, the percentage of school funding from state sources increased dramatically again in the 1970s (Doyle & Hartle, 1985). "Not surprisingly, as their share of the financial obligation for schooling increased, state interest in education increased" (Murphy, 1990, p. 20), and regulations followed that increased accountability while reducing the "flexibility and autonomy of local school districts" (Doyle & Hartle, 1985, p. 21).

Efficiency. As early as the common school movement, reformers viewed schools as a means to help children reach their full potential "as citizens and producers of wealth" (Tyack et al., 1987, p. 79). Reacting to a lack of supervision, inadequate teacher exams and poor performance (Cronin, 1973), "the administrative Progressives believed that school governance would be more efficient and expert if it were more buffered from lay control" (Tyack & Cuban, 1995, p. 18). Warren (1990) says the reformers wanted "to organize and manage schools according to sound business principles—efficiently, scientifically, professionally" (p. 72). They disregarded "the old idea that a common school grounding in the three R's would suffice for any career" (Tyack, 1974, p. 188). Adapting the methods of industrial production developed by Frederick W. Taylor, schools developed educational evaluations and achievement tests (Callahan, 1962). New state regulation required testing programs, extensive record keeping, increased supervision, programs for special populations, and vocational education (Cronin, 1973; Tyack, 1974).

Reaction to political corruption. During the rise of the Progressive movement, educational professionals accused school board members "of being corrupt or ignorant meddlers" (Tyack & Cuban, 1995, p. 18) in the selection of textbooks, the hiring of teachers, and the allocation of construction projects

(Cronin, 1973). Complaints of political favoritism in the hiring of teachers and administrators led critics to claim "that the schools were being victimized by political machines" (Spring, 1982, p. 89). As a reaction to "the assumptions that ignorance, waste, and corruption were fostered by localized political domination of schools" (Keller, 1994, p. 44), school boards became smaller, with members often elected citywide. Reform brought about new state regulations to consolidate rural schools, to move power from lay control to professionals, and to the creation of "new bureaucratic patterns of educational organization" (Tyack, 1974, p. 25).

Professionalization. Consistent with the economic theory of regulation in which certain occupations or industries attempt to improve their economic status by asking for increased regulation (Becker, 1983; Stigler, 1971), the administrative Progressives sought regulation to affirm their positions: "While they sought and won power for the professional, they believed that educators were not just another interest group but experts who understood and served the public good" (Tyack, 1986, p. 225). Entered into regulation, this belief led to the creation of organizational structures, established specifications for administrators, promoted the development of educational specialists, and set teacher qualifications based upon the level of training and function (Tyack, 1974; Tyack et al., 1987). While only two states required specialized credentials in 1900, nearly all states had "elaborate" (Tyack, 1974, p. 185) regulations regarding certification by 1930.

School Schooling

With the Progressive movement, reformers answered the need of industrialists for a prepared work force and addressed "internal school problems through encouraging school attendance and completion" (Edson, 1982, p. 146). A new belief that "public schools could, and indeed should, prepare youth for work" (Edson, 1982, p. 145) began to take root. The introduction of Progressive ideas into the schools was designed to improve student achievement and to meet the educational needs of "different ability groups and vocational interests" (Warren, 1990, p. 73). Troubled by a lack of standardization, inadequate rural schools, and under-prepared teachers, reformers viewed regulations and centralization as keys to school improvement. Progressives believed that by transferring school control from lay people to professionals, "a science of education might one day replace armchair wisdom or political clout in educational decision-making" (Tyack et al., 1987, p. 109).

From the 1950s through the 1980s, technological challenges and global competition spurred regulations designed to make our schools more competitive (Rippa, 1992). During the 1980s, massive education reform bills were passed by states that "detailed curriculum frameworks; teacher and student-testing programmes; homework policies; graduation requirements; no-pass no-play (e.g., football or baseball ineligibility) rules; class sizes; instructional delivery systems;

uniform mathematics, science and English requirements, and so forth" (Hanson, 1991, p. 31).

THE RISING TIDE OF DEREGULATION

With the exception of rules governing health, safety and civil rights, most public school regulations can safely be eliminated. (Washington Governor's Council on Educational Reform and Funding, 1992, p. 11)

Having examined the growth of regulation in education and the rationale behind it, we now shift our focus to the pressures behind the current deregulation movement.

Changing Political Climate

Underlying the deregulation movement is the changing political climate that has evolved since 1980. At the national level, Presidents Ronald Reagan and George Bush were at the forefront of a "New Federalism" that advocated the devolving of government power (Best, 1993). As discussed in Chapter 1, there is a renewed interest in market solutions to problems—a belief that "a bloated, parasitic public sector is blocking the bustle and growth of a more free flowing economy" (Starr, 1987, p. 124)—and that, through the utilization of market forces rather than government regulation, the economy will prosper.

The movement of the political climate to the right is in part explained by a backlash response to decades of government growth and expansion begun in the Progressive Era. Reacting to the poor performance and failures of government bureaucracy (Pirie, 1988; Savas, 1982), citizens have become increasingly discontent with inefficient and ineffective government services (Hemming & Mansoor, 1988). In addition, there is a growing concern that "government is doing more than it ought to be doing, that is, it is intruding too much into our lives" (Florestano, 1991, p. 291). With the movement of the United States into a post-industrial society, some people believe that there is less need for government (Best, 1993). According to Lewis (1993), "The monopoly of the state on service provision has been broken. The revolution is fueled by a critique of bureaucratic institutions that legitimizes the privatization of care, control, and now education" (p. 84).

School Improvement

Regulations Have Achieved All They Can

Once called "the most regulated enterprise in the United States" (Ohio Education 2000 Commission, 1989, p. 4), schools are controlled by mandates from the federal, state, and local levels. Most of these regulations are designed to provide minimal educational standards as they mandate floors rather than goals for educational practice (Campbell, Cunningham, Nystrand, & Usdan, 1975; Fuhrman & Elmore, 1992). Nonetheless, many reformers believe that extensive attempts to regulate school practice have not resulted in better schools (Consortium for Policy Research in Education [CPRE], 1992).

Faced with rules that control curriculum, mandate certification requirements, set a required number of school days, authorize certain textbooks, and specify graduation requirements (Bowers, 1990; General Accounting Office [GAO], 1994), many educators blame regulations for school failure and for their inability to improve (Carlos & Izu, 1993). The increase in regulation during the "first wave" of educational reform from the late 1970s to the mid-1980s "renewed fears about the loss of local control and led to more critical examination of the types of regulation" (CPRE, 1992, p. 1). There was a "growing awareness...that change driven primarily from the top was not effectively reaching far into the depths of the schools where teaching and learning take place" (Hanson, 1991, p. 33). In the second wave of educational reform that began in 1986, there has been a paradigm shift from a "top-down" approach to a "bottom-up" strategy of change (Murphy, 1990). Advocates of school deregulation contend that improvement can occur by granting flexibility to local schools while making them more accountable for student performance (GAO, 1994; Murphy, 1991).

Even those reformers who feel that regulations were "needed to bring schools into the twentieth century" (Fuhrman, Fry, & Elmore, 1992, p. 9) question whether it is politically feasible to use regulations to establish higher goals. In total, then, along with increasing pressures for school improvement, is the formulation of the belief that "traditional mechanisms for improvement either don't work or have reached their limits" (Mann, 1990, p. 26). In fact, regulations are now seen as barriers to good practice (Kagan, 1986). Furthermore, educators are searching for reform mechanisms that do not "depend on the prospect of more money, new legislation, or the magic of some cure-all program" (Mann, 1990, p. 26) mandated from above.

A Shift in Accountability

Deregulation is also spotlighted by a shift from a focus on process to a focus on outcomes. State regulations focus on inputs into schooling and on the educational process. Since it is difficult to measure a teacher's practice, rules have centered on regulating the process by checking compliance through subjective measures, including self-reports and visits from state agency staff. Termed "regulatory unreasonableness," the incongruence between regulatory goals and what can be measured is "characterized by formalistic, legalistic, standardized inspection processes and frequently severe paperwork burdens" (CPRE, 1992, p. 3).

Regulations are designed to set standards of good practice that schools might not otherwise meet. However, checking compliance does not reveal how much students learn but provides information such as how many hours teachers spend in certain classrooms (Bowers, 1990): "That stops far short of measuring whether students got anything out of those lessons—and of rewarding good educators and sanctioning bad ones" (Mann, 1990, p. 28). Thus accountability has been largely absent from most previous educational reform initiatives (Mann, 1990).

The move towards deregulation gained momentum in 1986 when the National Governors' Association (NGA) issued *Time for Results: The Governors' 1991 Report on Education,* which called for trading red tape for accountability. Then NGA Chairman and Tennessee Governor Lamar Alexander stated:

> The kind of horse-trading we're talking about will change dramatically the way most schools work. First, the Governors want to help establish clear goals and better report cards, ways to measure what students know and can do. Then we're ready to give up a lot of state regulatory control—even to fight for changes in the law to make that happen—*if* schools and school districts will be accountable for the results. (Alexander, 1986, p. 4)

Now, new forms of accountability make process regulations less necessary. Subjective measures of school practice are being replaced with objective indicators which allow state agencies to make greater distinctions among the performances of different schools. New assessment techniques of school outcomes have freed agency staffs from monitoring time-consuming compliance measures so they may focus their attention on the districts that need the most assistance. Furthermore, the states' focus on outcomes allows schools to concentrate on practice, thus reducing the amount of state intervention into schools (Fuhrman & Elmore, 1992).

With a transfer towards consumer (Murphy, forthcoming) and professional accountability, the focus shifts from the process to the results of education: "With accountability focused on performance, states should be able to place much less emphasis on, and perhaps even eliminate, input and process criteria used in accreditation. In theory, regulations about program and practice could be removed from the books" (Fuhrman & Elmore, 1995, p. 16). Instead, public school performance reports contain test scores, while teachers are treated more as professionals with increased autonomy and responsibility regarding instruction (Hanson, 1991; Murphy, 1990).

Flexibility Will Spur Improvement

Although the National Governors' Association was not prepared to dispense with all minimal standards, they argued that school excellence could not be "imposed from a distance," but comes from *"communities—*local school leaders, teachers, parents and citizens" (Alexander, 1986, p. 3). Thus, school deregulation "treats teachers as grownups. It gives them the flexibility to teach and the power to make decisions" (Mann, 1990, p. 26).

The theory behind increased flexibility (see Murphy & Beck, 1995, for an in-depth analysis of the theory) is stated by Natale (1990): "Give teachers and school administrators some breathing room amidst the regulations controlling schooling, and they'll be freer to do their jobs better. Students will learn more, teacher morale will pick up, education will work again" (p. 27). Unshackled from regulatory barriers, educators will be free to "design services that best meet the needs of their students" (Fuhrman & Elmore, 1995, p. 1). Kagan (1986) says: "Like the world of business, school systems are surprisingly diverse, and centrally formulated regulations that strike an appropriate definition of respon-sible behavior in one district may be unnecessary in others" (p. 74).

Having "been assigned society's most difficult tasks" without "the authority to resolve them" (Hanson, 1991, p. 34), teachers should be given the flexibility and autonomy to address problems without having their "intellect, spontaneity, insight, personal understanding, love and patience" (p. 34) constrained by rules. By providing regulatory relief, deregulation hopes to "encourage educational creativity, professionalism, and initiative" (National Governors' Association, 1990, p. 7). Thus, "those closest to the students and those with the most exper-tise—professionals at the school site" (Fuhrman & Elmore, 1995, p. 1)—can make the decisions necessary to attain the stated goals.

With established outcome goals, schools should be free to achieve them in the way most appropriate to their situations (Mann, 1990). Washington State implemented the Schools for the 21st Century Program "to determine whether increasing local decision-making authority will produce more effective learn-ing" (National Governors Association [NGA], 1990, p. 7). Hanson (1991) says, "A school trying to restructure its educational programs without changing the rules that encase it is like a sailing-boat attempting to sail into the sunset with-out casting off the lines holding it firmly to the pier" (p. 36).

Revenue Dimension

As states confront budget constraints and the unpopularity of increased taxation, deregulation provides an attractive alternative, since flexibility rather than addi-tional resources is seen as a means of school improvement: "Across the nation school systems are losing in their efforts to raise monies locally because people are reluctant to give more money without evidence of success" (Flanagan & Richardson, 1991, p. 2). Fuhrman and associates (1992) note: "Flexibility pro-grams and/or other differential treatment approaches are likely to gain popular-ity as states try to figure out how to meet growing challenges to improve education while at the same time more effectively targeting limited resources" (p. 1). If schools are given more flexibility, the prevailing belief is "that more edu-cation is possible for the same amount of money" (Hanson, 1991, p. 34).

DEREGULATION IN ACTION

In approaching educational deregulation, governmental agencies have adopted various degrees of deregulation and different approaches to selecting schools to receive flexibility. State—and federal and district—deregulation efforts provide flexibility through the elimination of regulations and by providing exemptions (Murphy, 1991).[12] In this section, we describe some of these approaches. Although we do not have a complete analysis of the types of regulations being waived, this information would be important.

Types of Deregulation

Elimination of Regulations

The first form of deregulation is the broad repeal of regulations. Arguing that the "best way to decentralize education is to start from scratch" (Lindsay, 1995a, p. 1), some states have repealed hundreds and even thousands of regulations and laws contained in the state code or enacted by state boards of education. In Minnesota, the legislature abolished "hundreds of statutes and regulations, ranging from reporting specifications to instructional time minimums to the requirement that each building have a principal, as part of the move toward more results-oriented education" (Fuhrman & Elmore, 1995, p. 16). Tennessee's State Board of Education eliminated 3,700 regulations in one effort (Lindsay, 1995a). Texas lawmakers abolished "46 years of accumulated rules and regulations" while "the state school board cut its list of rules from 490 to 230" (Harp, 1996a, p. 15). North Carolina is currently engaged in a systematic endeavor to rewrite state laws to give greatly enhanced flexibility to districts and schools (Lindsay, 1995c, 1995d). Michigan recently eliminated 30 percent of its educational code (Harp, 1996c).

Although some efforts have been less sweeping, many states have begun a process of reviewing regulations and repealing some of them for all school districts. For example, "Indiana changed the specific percent of time per subject to the number of minutes any time during the day. Arizona repealed the specified minutes per subject, and Montana removed specifications for class size and staffing ratios" (Fuhrman & Elmore, 1995, p. 17). New York is considering action to repeal the state's foreign-language requirements (Lindsay, 1995b). Georgia rescinded regulations requiring districts to purchase textbooks from a state-approved list (Diegmueller, 1995). More radically, Colorado recently debated the elimination of student attendance regulations (L. Miller, 1995), and Wisconsin legislators recently repealed legislation giving tenure to Milwaukee County teachers after three years of service (Lindsay, 1996).

Exemptions from Regulations

Rule-by-rule waivers. As an option to the repeal of state regulations, some states (e.g., Illinois and North Carolina) are allowing schools to apply for waivers from most regulations on a "rule-by-rule" (Fuhrman et al., 1992, p. 7) and "case-by-case" (GAO, 1994, p. 50) basis. In Washington State's 21st Century program, "waivers of certain state rules may be requested by schools if the rules impede implementation of a proposed program" (Fuhrman & Elmore, 1992, p. 22). Among the rules that may be waived for successful program implementation in Washington are:

> the length of the school year, teacher contact-hour requirements, program hour offerings, student to teacher ratios, salary lid compliance requirements, the commingling of funds appropriated by the legislature on a categorical basis for such programs as, but not limited to, highly capable students, transitional bilingual instruction, and learning assistance. (Washington State Senate Bill 991, 1987, cited in Fuhrman & Elmore, 1992, p. 22)

In California, a state program allows schools to "request waivers of any state education regulation if they can demonstrate that the waivers are needed to implement their restructuring plans" (GAO, 1994, p. 28).

Blanket waivers. In 1989, South Carolina became the first state to implement "a flexibility program that grants blanket waivers, or wide-scale exemptions from whole categories of education regulations, to a certain group of schools (in this case, those deemed high performing)" (Fuhrman et al., 1992, p. 1):

> The criteria for eligibility are as follows: (1) the school has been a recipient of a school-incentive reward twice since 1987 (meaning it was high performing relative to schools similar in socioeconomic statistics); (2) the school has met annual Normal Curve Equivalent (NCE) gain requirements for reading and mathematics compensatory programs; (3) the school has exhibited no recurring accreditation deficiencies in routine state department of education monitoring; and (4) the school has annually exhibited a school gain index value at or above the state average as computed in the school-incentive grant program. (p. 11)

However, the local school board can stop a school from participating in this program.

Initially given a waiver for a period of 30 months, South Carolina schools receive exemptions from most state regulations enacted in the 1970s and 1980s, including aspects of the state's Defined Minimum Program, Basic Skills Assessment Program, and the Compensatory and Remedial Education regulations (M. D. Richardson et al., 1993). Regulations concerning health and safety are not waived, but schools are freed from other rules, including the time spent on each subject and maximum class sizes. Although teachers must still be certified, they do not have to be certified in the subject area they teach. Requirements for high school graduation cannot be waived. The eligible schools are waived from state on-site monitoring visits and freed from some record keeping (Fuhrman et al., 1992). If the school district maintains high scores each year on statewide assessments, the district can continue to be free of the regulations (GAO, 1994).

In addition, South Carolina's "12 Schools Project," enacted in 1991, provides relief not only from the same state regulations as the Flexibility Through Deregulation Program but also from the annual statewide assessments. Furthermore, participating schools can "...develop their own criteria for determining (1) which children are eligible for state programs for disadvantaged children and 'gifted and talented' children and (2) which children should be promoted to the next grade level" (GAO, 1994, p. 50).

A particular type of blanket waiver is the creation of charter schools—"an independent public school of choice designed and run by teachers under contract with a public sponsor" (Williams & Buechler, 1993, p. 1). These "schools operate on contracts with sponsoring authorities (e.g., local school boards, state boards) that specify outcomes and how they will be measured" (Fuhrman & Elmore, 1995, p. 15). Under most programs, charter schools receive blanket waivers of most state regulations except those concerning issues of safety, health, and civil rights (Fuhrman & Elmore, 1995). Since charter schools are generally associated with the school choice movement, a fuller discussion is contained in the chapter on vouchers.

Eligibility

Having created varying degrees of freedom from regulations, state programs also differ in the schools that receive regulatory flexibility. Some states have granted freedom to all schools, while others have offered it to institutions selected through competitive grant programs or to high-performing schools.

All Schools

With the broad repeal of state regulations, freedom is provided to all schools. Enacted in 1990 to replace Kentucky's previous educational system, which was held by the courts to be unconstitutional, the Kentucky Education Reform Act (KERA) provides "substantial flexibility" (GAO, 1994, p. 33) to all schools. Reducing the authority of state and local school boards in daily school operations, it gave parents, teachers and administrators—through school-based decision making councils—power to "determine how the school would help students achieve the state's performance goals. School councils can make decisions on curriculum, with the state curriculum frameworks as guides; instruction; assignment of students, teachers, and space; daily schedules; discipline and classroom management; extracurricular programs and policies; and hiring of principals, teachers, and other personnel" (GAO, 1994, pp. 38-39). In addition, kindergarten through third grades were replaced by a four-year primary program: "The school councils were given the flexibility to determine how best to organize each school's primary program, although all schools were required to address certain 'critical attributes,' such as developmentally appropriate educational practices, multi-age and multiability classrooms, assessment, professional teamwork, and parental involvement" (GAO, 1994, p. 39).

Schools in Select Programs

Another means of enacting deregulation is to provide it to selected schools, often schools chosen through a competitive process. For South Carolina, the Target 2000 program provides waivers for schools chosen to participate in either a school-innovation competitive grant program or a dropout-prevention program. In these programs, "any school submitting a winning proposal, no matter the performance record, can be granted rule-by-rule waivers upon request" (Fuhrman et al., 1992, p. 9). The competitive grant program was "established to encourage innovative, comprehensive approaches to improving student development, performance, and attendance" (p. 7). Under this program, schools can request waivers from state regulations while receiving grants of up to $5,000 for a one-year planning phase and up to $90,000 for implementation (Fuhrman et al., 1992).

South Carolina's dropout-prevention program provides grants and regulatory relief to selected schools. For schools to be eligible for these grants and waivers, their programs "must incorporate one or more of the following approaches: parent training, parent involvement, mentors, enriched summer programs, interagency teams, individual plans, individual remediation, employment opportunities, and alternatives to suspension" (Fuhrman et al., 1992, p. 7).

Since the 1980s, California has been a leader in providing flexibility to schools through the School-Based Coordination Program (SBCP) and the Restructuring Grant Program. Under the SBCP program, selected schools are provided with the flexibility to be: "(1) allowed to combine resources or services or both from state categorical programs and (2) required to engage in schoolwide planning with the goal of providing all children with a high-quality curriculum" (GAO, 1994, p. 26). Categorical funds from programs for the "disadvantaged, LEP, and 'gifted and talented' students" (p. 27) can be combined. The Restructuring Grant Program provides competitive grants "to increase site-level decision making at schools in order to prompt creative and innovative local approaches to providing instruction" (p. 27). Participating schools "can request waivers of any state education regulation if they can demonstrate that the waivers are needed to implement their restructuring plans" (p. 28). Any school is allowed to apply for waivers of specific regulations as noted in the state's education code. However, "few schools in the state...had [by 1994] applied for waivers of specific regulations, according to state officials" (p. 28).

Reward for High-Performing Schools

A third means of deregulation is to provide flexibility to high-performing schools. South Carolina enacted the Flexibility Through Deregulation Program as part of a larger Target 2000 education reform act in 1989: "To reconcile the belief that controls remained necessary for some schools with the desire to foster creativity, policy makers limited the deregulation program to high-performing schools" (Fuhrman et al., 1992, p. 9). They believed that "since these were some of the best schools in the state, they were viewed least likely to abuse the flexibility given" (p. 9). Considered by some to be a pilot program, "if successful schools used flexibility in promising ways, broad-based deregulation could be extended statewide" (p. 9).

RESULTS

If you throw out the whole thing, then things that we have fought so diligently for for children over the years may go down the drain. (Lois Tinson, cited in Lindsay, 1995a, p. 17)

Having presented an overview of the various approaches to school deregulation, we now move to a discussion of the effects of increased flexibility on schools and school personnel. We then turn to a description of how schools have utilized flexibility to alter their schools. Before we begin, a cautionary note is in order. In assessing the results of deregulation programs, one must remember that many of the schools "were already successful, the kind of schools that might have been breeding grounds for innovation, regardless of the state policy that encourages it" (Fuhrman & Elmore, 1992, p. 28). Many of the programs offer deregulation only to those schools that are already high-performing on state achievement tests or that gain eligibility based upon winning applications. "Therefore, the presence of promising innovations may reflect a selection factor, not a program effect. However, it might also be argued that already successful schools have little need to change and might be wary of fixing what isn't broken or risking their successful status" (p. 28).

Researchers have found that "regulatory flexibility does appear to make a distinct contribution to school improvement, albeit in subtle ways" (Fuhrman & Elmore, 1992, p. 29). Nevertheless, only time and the expansion of deregulation programs to include more schools will reveal the true effects of increased flexibility. Expanded degrees of freedom may exacerbate problems in troubled schools. On the other hand, "it may be schools most needing improvement that most benefit from flexibility and autonomy" (p. 30).

Effects

Waivers have created a climate so that regulations are not a hindrance. We don't feel like our hands are tied; [we're] excused from DMP (Defined Minimum

Program). People here can't say we can't do it because...we can. (A South Carolina principal, quoted in Fuhrman & Elmore, 1995, pp. 7–8)

Program Design

With the many types of eligibility, it is natural to compare the effects of various designs. The blanket waiver programs, with their sweeping authorization of flexibility, appear to create "a more fertile climate for consideration of improvement efforts than rule-by-rule request programs" (Fuhrman & Elmore, 1992, p. 29; see also Murphy, 1991). Few schools in South Carolina sought waivers through an experimental program prior to the Flexibility Through Deregulation Program or through the rule-by-rule components of the Target 2000 initiative. Although this may be explained by the fact that blanket waivers do not require the investment of time and resources for waiver requests, there may be other "substantive" explanations (Murphy, 1991). Fuhrman & Elmore (1992) note:

> Automatic, sweeping deregulation may be more stimulative of change because it is not any single rule or several single rules but the intersection of many rules that constrain. Also, up-front major deregulation broadens the horizon for planning of change, removing parameters more thoroughly than waiver request programs. One might imagine that a very different change process occurs when one is told that a set or rules no longer applies than when one is told to plan an innovation and request exemption from the specific barriers identified. (p. 30)

> In states where education has traditionally been heavily regulated, deregulation appears to be a greater stimulus for schools. For example, South Carolina schools have taken greater advantage of the deregulation than Washington State, where "schools could find ways within Washington's body of statute and rule to achieve their goals without deregulation." (p. 29)

Innovation and Change

> We want to challenge school districts to improve without trying to get involved in how. (Mike Moses, Texas Education Commissioner, quoted in Harp, 1996a, p. 15)

A theme that runs throughout the literature on the deregulated schools "is the liberating effect of deregulation on school-level planning" (Fuhrman & Elmore, 1995, p. 7). In a study of deregulated schools in South Carolina by CPRE, principals reported that, as a result of the new flexibility, they could "make meaningful decisions that would affect instruction," and they found "freedom from trivial restrictions" (Flanagan & Richardson, 1991, p. 13). Furthermore, deregulation provided a reason to reexamine current school activities and programs:[13] "For many schools, it appears that the granting of deregulated status led to brainstorming and other planning activities that otherwise would not have occurred. One principal said, 'It (flexibility) gives us an opportunity to take a good look at what we're doing'" (Fuhrman et al., 1992, p. 14).

In Texas, lawmakers have provided teachers with autonomy and motivation through deregulation to improve achievement. Now, "the state is becoming a laboratory for how much freedom school districts actually want and what they will do with it" (Harp, 1996a, p. 15). Principals in the Fuhrman and associates (1992) study suggest that "horizons open up when the constraints are lifted. One reported, 'When you have a defined minimum program, there's a philosophy that the minimum becomes the maximum; you do what you're told essentially'" (p. 14). A 1991 South Carolina survey found that most principals "view(ed) themselves as agents of change who are risk-takers" (M. D. Richardson et al., 1993, p. 6). Since less time is required to fill out paperwork, more time is available for "creatively planning for instructional needs [and] an opportunity to experiment with new programs which is often a boost to teacher morale" (Flanagan & Richardson, 1991, p. 16).

Across the various state programs, schools find that their deregulated status creates a set of heightened expectations to utilize the flexibility and places them in the public spotlight (Fuhrman & Elmore, 1992, 1995): "For some principals the expectations were part of the satisfaction that comes with the opportunity to win incentive rewards and gain recognition. Said one, 'The importance of deregulation is feeling that this is something special, that others are looking at us to provide leadership'" (Fuhrman et al., 1992, p. 14). In Texas, a coordinator of the Partnership Schools believed that these schools "are basically going to be living in a fishbowl. People are going to be watching you constantly. People will be visiting your campus constantly" (Fuhrman & Elmore, 1995, p. 7). On the other hand, because principals were now asked, "What are you going to do now that you're deregulated?" (Fuhrman et al., 1992, p. 14), many found the increased expectations to be "more stressful" (p. 14).

While South Carolina's deregulated schools utilized the increased flexibility to implement many changes, a survey of principals indicated that half of the activities could have been implemented without the deregulation program. Changes could have been accomplished within the current rules or by applying for specific waivers in an experimental program that required schools to reapply annually. "Nevertheless, over 70 percent of the activities reported by principals were not begun until after deregulation," report Fuhrman and associates (1992, p. 13).

With the removal of many state rules and regulations, there are fewer excuses for poor performance. A Texas school principal stated, "'Now they [teachers] have no excuses for the lack of achievement....And so now about the only thing they can still do is to blame the home environment. And I still have a few trying to do that. Other than that, they have got to look inward'" (quoted in Fuhrman & Elmore, 1995, p. 8).

Many South Carolina principals report that deregulation allows for planning to focus on the needs of students. Increased flexibility and expectations at the local level "helped schools to restructure and become more adaptive to the needs of students," while principals can "use their professional judgment to improve the school curriculum, structure, instruction, and student morale" (Flanagan & Richardson, 1991, pp. 13–14). "A principal explained that, 'We're not doing anything directly related to deregulation, but it supports our planning, helps us move into integrated subjects without worrying'" (Fuhrman et al., 1992, p. 14).

Identification of Impediments

Sites were able to specify many factors other than regulation that hindered change efforts. (Fuhrman & Elmore, 1995, p. 8)

An important aspect of deregulation initiatives is that they help identify important impediments to change: "It makes evident what factors relate to regulation and which do not and surfaces constraints not perceived when regulation is present" (Fuhrman et al., 1992, p. 16). Fuhrman and Elmore (1995) report that "the liberation comes primarily through the removal of regulation as an excuse for traditional practice. Once the justification of rule is erased, deregulation illuminates other barriers to change, forcing schools to at least confront them, and, hopefully, to deal with them" (p. 7). In Washington State, teachers "cited the challenge of developing a consensus for change among faculty and parents as either the primary or one of the top two barriers to innovation" (p. 8).

Student Outcomes

In South Carolina, student achievement test scores did not change significantly as a result of deregulation. However, Flanagan and Richardson (1991) note, "Most schools maintained excellent student achievement scores. All schools had been experiencing high student achievement in test scores for several years prior to deregulation" (p. 16). Conversely, there was no statistically significant decrease in test scores.

The 1991 CPRE survey reported that many of South Carolina's deregulated schools "that initiated changes in the curriculum, such as extra P.E., additional extra-curricular activities, less seatwork, and increased interactive and cooperative learning experiences" (Flanagan & Richardson, 1991, p. 15) noted improved morale and attendance among students. At schools where there was no marked improvement, "students were not aware of the deregulation changes, and there was previously good student morale and high attendance" (p. 15).

How Schools Have Utilized Deregulation

Symbolically, the waivers allowed things to be turned over to the teachers, to be free to think about whatever, when developing the proposals. In my school, teachers began to think they could do anything. (A Washington 21st Century site coordinator, quoted in Fuhrman & Elmore, 1995, p. 8)

Having focused on the effects of deregulation, we now highlight how schools have utilized flexibility to alter the instructional process. According to a 1991 CPRE study, two-thirds of South Carolina schools eligible to participate in the deregulation program were, as a result, "embarking on [new] activities" (Fuhrman et al., 1992, p. 12). Many of these programs required maximum class-size waivers (GAO, 1994). "Although it is difficult to judge the depth, significance, extent and staying power of initial activities reported by principals, some of the changes (e.g., integration of subjects and ungraded primaries) are among those reformers throughout the nation currently view as promising" (Fuhrman et al., 1992, p. 16).

Multi-Age Classes

As a result of deregulation, school changes have included "developing approaches to combining children into multigrade groups so that teachers could address the needs of children on the basis of their development rather than age" (GAO, 1994, p. 9). In South Carolina, schools "were developing ungraded primary schools for grades K-3, keeping students with the same teacher or team of teachers for several years" (Fuhrman et al., 1992, p. 12). Likewise, participants in Washington State's 21st Century Program engaged in "activities, such as nongraded programs, that change traditional grade level/promotion practices" (Fuhrman & Elmore, 1992, p. 23).

Although the Kentucky Education Reform Act required schools to implement ungraded primary programs to replace grades K-3, schools were afforded wide flexibility in designing the programs and measuring student performance: "The state eliminated the age and class size restrictions for each grade level for these schools, allowing each school to determine how best to group the children in these grades" (GAO, 1994, p. 10).

One school put together several groups of first, second, and third graders, with each group having equal proportions of children at various levels of ability, children with disabilities, and boys and girls. Other schools grouped together children in kindergarten and first grade, first and second grade, and second and third grade. Schools in some districts extended the primary program to include the fourth and fifth grades. (GAO, 1994, p. 40)

Restructuring of Class Blocks

Schools have also utilized deregulation in "restructuring the school day to allow schools to schedule longer blocks of time for class periods so that some subject areas could be covered in greater depth" (GAO, 1994, p. 9). By freeing the schools from the specific time requirements to be spent on each subject during the course of the year, schools could decide to spend more time on definite subjects based upon the needs of their students. For example, one South Carolina elementary school chose to devote more time to mathematics (GAO, 1994).

In California, some high schools formed humanities courses through the combination of English and social science. Other "schools rearranged the school day to provide longer blocks of time and fewer, but more in-depth, classes or more learning experiences. For example, one school lengthened some of its class periods so that students could pursue vocational interests, such as implementing construction projects in community settings and working in local businesses" (GAO, 1994, p. 31).

New Approaches to Curriculum and Instruction

Utilizing their newfound flexibility, South Carolina teachers altered the way they taught: "New instructional approaches are being used: writing across the curriculum, manipulative math programs, cooperative learning, and peer tutoring" (Flanagan & Richardson, 1991, p. 15). Teachers in Kentucky's ungraded primary programs "were doing more hands-on instruction than lecturing and...children were more involved in group projects" (GAO, 1994, p. 41).

Creation of Thematic Units

Among the changes in deregulated schools in South Carolina were new course offerings such as "dance, drama, Latin, geography, and whole language" (Flanagan & Richardson, 1991, pp. 14–15), "additional art and music or foreign language in early grades" (Fuhrman et al., 1992, p. 12), "fine arts, vocational, foreign language, and exploratory/enrichment classes" (M. D. Richardson et al., 1993, pp. 7–8), and the "inclusion of intramural sports" (Flanagan & Richardson, 1991, p. 14).

Some schools are "combining two or more subjects into thematic units, including having some units taught by teams of teachers" (GAO, 1994, p. 9). In South Carolina, "deregulated schools were integrating subjects, for example, by blending math and science by developing thematic units of study that draw on many disciplines" (Fuhrman et al., 1992, p. 12).

One Washington State 21st Century School has integrated the curriculum to focus on international and global issues after it received "a waiver of the classroom teacher contact-hour requirement in order to release students early one day a week to permit teacher planning time" (Fuhrman & Elmore, 1992, p. 23). One Seattle school with an increasing Asian student enrollment has developed a curriculum on the Pacific Rim,

> which sets themes for each grade level and utilizes new course requirements, mini-units and interdisciplinary courses to achieve the substantive focus. For example, ninth graders, focusing on the individual as a theme, have an integrated block of English and social studies with the hope of bringing more subjects on board. In tenth grade, the theme is community; sophomore English incorporates that theme and students have a 20-hour community service requirement. Juniors will need to address the Pacific Rim theme through one of their regular subjects; each department will have at least one offering that will meet the requirement.

Seniors will have a humanities course focused on an internal theme, an adult survival skills course and a culminating senior project. (p. 23)

Utilizing flexibility in teacher credentialing requirements, California schools were able to bring artists into the classrooms. One South Carolina elementary school was able to implement a thematic unit taught by a team of teachers:

Groups of children from two different classes were combined into one large class for part of the day to read books about the weather in different parts of the world and write descriptions of it. Two regular classroom teachers teamed with an art teacher and a math teacher to teach the class. The art teacher helped the students construct models of elements of the weather, such as clouds, and the math teacher added basic math concepts to the curriculum, using weather examples, such as converting temperatures from one system of measurement to another, that is, from degrees Celsius to Fahrenheit. (GAO, 1994, p. 10)

Reallocation of Teachers' Time for Planning and Decision Making
Deregulation has allowed schools to make changes in "the school day to allow teachers more time to plan, work with other teachers, and serve on school decision making committees" (GAO, 1994, p. 9). South Carolina's program provides flexibility in scheduling to provide teachers with more planning time: "Changes that principals desire to make as a result of deregulation are: reallocation of school day time to provide biweekly or monthly release time for teacher collaboration necessary for restructuring and for parent involvement, [and] more site based management to increase teacher involvement in decision making" (Flanagan & Richardson, 1991, p. 15). Flanagan and Richardson further note that South Carolina teachers were "involved in decision-making by working on school improvement councils and shared governance committees. Representative groups of team leaders, associate schools, and restructuring teams also gave input to decision-making" (p. 16).

Likewise, in Washington State, waivers relating to "teacher hours, length of school day, length of school year, program requirements specifying time, and classroom teacher contact hours...[allowed] schools to increase teacher planning and training time during the school day" (Fuhrman & Elmore, 1995, p. 11). The GAO (1994) notes that "several schools in California lengthened the school day for 4 days a week and released the students early on the fifth day so that teachers could spend more time working together as teams to plan lessons and serve on school management councils" (p. 10).

Allowing Non-Certified People to Teach
As another result of some deregulation programs, schools are allowed to let people with unique skills or knowledge teach without meeting the usual certification requirements (Harp, 1996c): "For example, school officials in

California brought in people from the community, such as local artists, to teach classes on a few occasions" (GAO, 1994, p. 10).

Combining Programs

Deregulation programs also allow schools to combine funds from some state categorical programs or to combine their operations (GAO, 1994). Some South Carolina "elementary schools were searching for ways of eliminating or limiting pull-out programs for remedial education through block scheduling that enlarges instructional groups for regular subjects but provides every child with small group time for either remediation or enrichment" (Fuhrman et al., 1992, p. 12). Deregulation provided the solution for many of these schools.

In California, schools were allowed to combine programs or expand programs to include more children with special needs. Schools in the SBCP program were "allowed...to provide more individualized services to children with special needs by allowing the schools to focus on the needs of children, rather than providing services as defined by the categories of the state programs" (GAO, 1994, p. 29):

> For example, a child who met the criteria for more than one of the state categorical programs, such as a child who was considered LEP and also gifted and talented in math, could be provided with help to become proficient in English as well as receiving advanced instruction in math. This was made possible because state funds from the state LEP and gifted and talented programs could be combined to hire instructors with specialized skills in language and math who could teach children with special needs. (p. 29)

By combining funds from selected state programs with funds for the gifted and talented children, one school was able to expand access to its art instruction program to include children who did not meet eligibility requirements for the former program but demonstrated talent in art (GAO, 1994).

Other Results

New activities at deregulated schools were not limited to the areas described above. In Washington State, other activities included "the awarding of credit based on learner outcomes rather than seat time[,]...alternative means of student assessment[,]...year-round programs and other alterations in the length of day and year[,]...staff-designed learning environments[, and]...small learning communities in large schools" (Fuhrman & Elmore, 1992, p. 23).

BARRIERS TO DEREGULATION

In this section, we examine some of the barriers to the enactment or effective implementation of deregulation programs.

Regulations Justified by Ineffective Schools

Deregulation critics argue that the existence of perpetually poor-performing schools are justification for state regulations. Opponents of deregulation in South Carolina felt that the regulations of the state's Educational Improvement Act were "justified by the existence of persistently poor-performing, non-compliant schools and districts" (Fuhrman et al., 1992, p. 9). In these districts and especially in desegregated districts governed by white administrators, skeptics felt that "state regulations were necessary for the survival of schools" (p. 9) and to ensure "students a minimal level of education" (Fuhrman & Elmore, 1995, p. 20).

In instances where school districts perpetually fail to meet achievement objectives or to comply with state regulations, state governments find it difficult to deregulate them. In these cases, "a heavy state hand is judged to be necessary to assure that students are provided minimal services" (CPRE, 1992, pp. 4–5). Indeed, many states are implementing additional regulations or even taking over school districts which fail to perform. Merely removing regulations by itself is not likely to stimulate improvement (CPRE, 1992; Fuhrman & Elmore, 1992).

Many state regulations were implemented for important pedagogical reasons. For instance, states have limited class sizes because policymakers believe that this is fundamental to good practice (Fuhrman & Elmore, 1992). Thus, opponents argue that deregulation "inevitably means that the good laws are erased with the bad" and hard-won improvements will be lost (Lindsay, 1995b, p. 19).

Accompanying the claim that regulations are justified by persistently poor school districts is the belief that they provide leverage for local school administrators who are frequently confronted by school boards content with the status quo. Superintendents and principals often find it necessary to base requests for resources upon state mandates (Fuhrman et al., 1992). Otherwise, they may fall on deaf ears.

Inadequate Support

Lack of District-Level Support

A key barrier may be inadequate support for deregulation at the district level (Murphy, 1991; Murphy & Hallinger, 1993). Some scholars argue that "more (or possibly all) constraints should be lifted, particularly local district regulations, special education, and gifted and talented requirements" (M. D. Richardson et al., 1993, p. 7). In particular, there was "the need for district support in providing release time for planning and providing pertinent in-service" (p. 10). Schools initiating "more ambitious activities, such as restructuring their day or curriculum," note Fuhrman and Elmore (1992), "were more likely to report that their districts gave them enthusiastic support, while those schools confining their activities to more discrete changes...were more likely to cite only cautious support from their districts" (p. 20).

Still other analysts cite local schools' "unwillingness to part with past practices and a lack of knowledge about what works" (Carlos & Izu, 1993, p. 4) as barriers. Local interpretations of state regulations, district rules, and union contracts are often greater constraints than the rules themselves (CPRE, 1992; NGA, 1990). Indeed, some reviewers believe that deregulation may encourage district-level bureaucracy with increased resistance to improvement (Lindsay, 1995a).

Lack of Additional Funding

Schools that contend with scarce resources and inadequate funding will not see these problems alleviated by deregulation (Carlos & Izu, 1993). Clabaugh (1992) asks, "How would deregulation deal with that?" (p. 54). Opponents of school deregulation note that, regardless of the specific policy formulation invoked to deregulate the schools, additional school funding is noticeably absent from the proposals (Hanson, 1991). Indeed, some reformers raise the possibility that deregulation can be used by states—and the federal government—to avoid their legitimate responsibilities toward education (Murphy & Hallinger, 1993; Murphy, 1996).

In the 1991 CPRE follow-up survey of South Carolina's deregulated schools, "the most significant constraint to flexibility is the lack of additional funding" (M. D. Richardson et al., 1993, p. 6). Schools note that "additional funding should be provided for deregulated schools...[and] flexibility should be allowed for the spending of those funds" (p. 7). Although these South Carolina schools were eligible for incentive rewards, few schools applied for them. Additional funds were generally used for materials and not "seen as program support" (Fuhrman & Elmore, 1992, p. 21).

Uncertainty About Deregulation

Another confounding problem with deregulation, skeptics claim, is the uncertainty that it brings. Citing examples from the deregulation of the transportation industries (see Barlett & Steel, 1992), critics fear that teachers will pay for deregulation with the loss of jobs, pay, or benefits (Clabaugh, 1992; Murphy, 1996). In addition, prior to the implementation of deregulatory programs, school administrators want to know more about what is expected of them (Natale, 1990; Bowers, 1990).

Temporary Status

Uncertainty about the temporary nature of deregulation programs has proven to be a barrier for some schools attempting innovative programs. "For example, in several districts in South Carolina, officials were reluctant to use the flexibility available to them, they said, because the deregulation status was temporary. They did not want to make changes, such as those involved in hiring new staff, that would have to be rescinded if the school lost its eligibility" (GAO, 1994, pp. 13–14).

In the CPRE study, several South Carolina school administrators recommended that "the length of time for maintaining deregulation status should be extended, and no loss of status should occur if the school is involved in an innovative program" (M. D. Richardson et al., 1993, p. 7). Indeed, "principals expressed concern that deregulation is attached to student performance over such a short time period. They believe that five years would be a more acceptable time frame to judge deregulation status, rather than annually" (Flanagan & Richardson, 1991, p. 17).

Uncertainty About Outcome Measures

Further uncertainty stems from concerns about which accountability standards to use: "At the moment the nation is in transition between norm-referenced multiple choice tests and new, sophisticated performance assessments that are of uncertain reliability and validity" (Fuhrman & Elmore, 1995, p. 19). Opponents believe that new assessment procedures do not "accurately measure the academic progress of all students" (Carlos & Izu, 1993, p. 1). With accountability based upon standardized tests, opponents question whether teaching to the test will occur, thus detracting from other learning goals (Fuhrman & Fry, 1989; Bowers, 1990).

Satisfaction With Status Quo

Although many innovations have resulted from of deregulation legislation, the pull of the status quo prevented activity in other situations: "Schools did not always see a need to improve" (GAO, 1994, p. 12). In South Carolina, where schools received deregulation status based upon their success, some schools felt pressure to maintain the status quo, since "that is how they achieved deregulated status" (Flanagan & Richardson, 1991, p. 15). Deregulation programs do "not appear to eliminate barriers that are self-imposed or to prove sufficient stimulus for those who, for whatever reason, are hesitant to change" (Fuhrman et al., 1992, p. 16).

Non-Regulatory Constraints

Furthermore, deregulation does not address non-regulatory constraints: "Local policies, union contracts, non-educational policies, and other non-regulatory constraints on school activities, pose restrictions which make deregulation less promising, more complex and perhaps less potentially appealing" (Fuhrman & Elmore, 1995, p. 21). Schools are faced with external socioeconomic factors that affect the educational process. Children from broken, poor, impoverished and/or homeless families present pedagogical problems that are not likely to be addressed by deregulation (Clabaugh, 1992; CPRE, 1992).

CONCLUSION

In this chapter, we examined privatization via school deregulation. First, chronicling the historical growth of and rationale for educational regulation, we examined the pressures behind the shift towards deregulation as a means of educational privatization. Next, we described the various types of deregulation. We then shifted to an analysis of the results of deregulation initiatives, examining both the effects of deregulation and the ways that schools have used deregulation legislation. Finally, we examined barriers to the implementation and effectiveness of deregulatory programs.

6

Home Schooling

Reformers have championed curriculum frameworks, common cores of learning, site-based decisionmaking, total quality management, charter schools, voluntary standards, merit pay, and national certification of teachers. But, they have ignored home schooling. (Weston, 1996, p. 34)

Parents are bringing home schooling out of the underground and into the mainstream. (Stecklow, 1994, p. 32)

In the past two decades, there has been a notable increase in the number of families opting to teach their children at home rather than send them to American public and parochial schools. The rebirth of the home as the primary center of learning has been reported by Dorothy Moore (1986) to be "the fastest growing educational movement in the United States" (p. 7). By the 1970s, an estimated 10,000 to 15,000 school-aged children were being schooled at home. By 1983, 60,000 to 125,000 children were in home schools. By 1988, the numbers had increased to 150,000 to 300,000. The numbers continued to increase by about 15 percent each year, and as of 1995, there were an estimated one million school-aged children being educated at home. This growing body of people who are opting for home instruction as an alternative to the institutional schooling to which our society has been accustomed for over 100 years are sometimes referred to as "unschoolers, deschoolers, or more commonly, home schoolers" (Ray, 1986, p. 1).

In this chapter, we first examine the historical development of home schooling in the United States from the seventeenth through the twentieth centuries. Next, we review the legal developments that have affected home schoolers' rights and responsibilities to educate their children. The third section discusses the three basic rationales for home schooling: religion, socialization, and academics. Characteristics of the home school movement and the processes by which home schooling is accomplished are the focus of the fourth section. In the final section, we review the limited research on the effects of home schooling.

HISTORICAL PERSPECTIVE

Seventeenth Century

During the seventeenth century, the Southern colonies were established: the first at Jamestown, Virginia (1607), then in Maryland, North Carolina, South Carolina, and Georgia. The settlers of these colonies were primarily influenced by economic concerns (Cubberley, 1962). They were either part of the mercantile efforts of the London Company, members of proprietary colonies under royal grant, or formerly imprisoned debtors whom English philanthropists attempted to help (S. S. Cohen, 1970).

By the middle of the seventeenth century, the social structure developed into three levels (S. S. Cohen, 1970). The uppermost level lived on extensive estates and emulated the customs, dress, and habits of English rural squires. The middle level was composed of independent owners of small farms, white plantation workers, artisans, and tradesmen. The lower level of the social structure consisted of indentured servants and slaves.

The widely dispersed farms influenced the development of the educational system (Cremin, 1970). In the South, education was believed to be the responsibility not of the state but of the family. Education was considered a privilege, which was the result of both wealth and social rank. For the more affluent children, schooling was a matter usually determined by the parents (S. S. Cohen, 1970). Although some attempts were made to establish schools in the South, these efforts were rather ineffective. The Virginia Colony considered formal education relatively unimportant (Tyack, 1967). The home was the center of informal education in the South. The family was expected to provide both moral and religious training (S. S. Cohen, 1970). Parents, if they were literate, "provided a generous apprenticeship in the diverse art of living" (Cremin, 1970, p. 128). Although the father was mentor to his heirs in the wisdom of books and provided various opportunities to practice reading, tutors were often employed during much of the seventeenth century in the Southern colonies, as they were throughout the English system (Knight, 1951; Wright, 1957). Many plantation owners surrounded themselves with books in quite extensive home libraries, "and the borrowing and lending among friends and acquaintances were both frequent and spirited" (Cremin, 1970, p. 134). Reading was encouraged for information, recreation, and pleasure.

The middle colonies of New York, New Jersey, Pennsylvania, and Delaware, which were influenced both by their neighbor colonies to the north and south and by the diverse Old World countries from which their colonists had migrated (S. S. Cohen, 1970), exhibited greater diversity in their treatment of education. Some children received their education from a household, others from a church, and still others from a school (Cremin, 1970).

The first settlers of New England were Separatist Puritans who arrived in 1620 and established the Plymouth Rock Colony (Knight, 1951). Their motives for immigration to the New World were primarily religious. They came to establish churches, improve their civil life, and raise their children to worship God as they believed (S. S. Cohen, 1970). The Puritans were convinced of the necessity of Christian schools. By 1640, almost 20,000 immigrants had established the larger Massachusetts Bay Colony. The New Hampshire, Maine, and Connecticut colonies were offshoots of the original Massachusetts colony. It was in these colonies that the principle of compulsory education developed. Private benefactors were the chief financial source for funding and maintaining schools within the colonies. As a consequence, institutions such as Boston's Latin Grammar School (1635) and Harvard College (1636) were founded.

Eighteenth Century

The population of the American colonies increased approximately 34 percent per decade from 1690 to 1780, or some 45,000 to 55,000 persons per year (Cremin, 1970). As the population increased, there was a gradual development of more urban centers. Eventually, there was a change in religious thinking due to the influx of immigrants who came to America from various countries in northern Europe. Furthermore, the settlement of new frontiers required hard work rather than long sermons. Old traditions and customs that had been transplanted from Europe gave way to a rising individualism (Cubberley, 1962). Students were given either a common school education (or, if more advanced, a good English education), or a classical education in Latin school and college. Kaestle (1973) paints the educational landscape of the time as follows: "In late Colonial America schooling was plentiful but unorganized; schools were increasing in importance but still supplementary to the family, the church, and apprenticeship" (p. 12). Schools increased more rapidly than did the population, yet "the household remained the single most fundamental unit of social organization in the eighteenth century colonies, and for the vast majority of Americans, the decisive agency of deliberate cultural transmission" (Cremin, 1970, p. 480).

During the eighteenth century, tax-supported schools were difficult to establish in the South, and education was left to private institutions in the North. In Virginia, there were a few settlements with regular grammar schools like those in New England, but by 1776, there was no satisfactory system of schooling in sight (Bridenbaugh, 1981). There were three general types of educational institutions: the English (petty or common) school, the Latin grammar school, and the academy (Cremin, 1970). The English-type schools included the dame school, the elementary school, the apprenticeship, and some private schools. While the purpose of the common school was to prepare children to be clerks or tradesmen, the Latin grammar school and the academy educated students to be society's future ministers, lawyers, doctors, and scholars.

Private tutoring continued to be an important form of education for the upper class during the eighteenth century (Monroe, 1940). The prosperous planters of Virginia had an increasing concern about their children's education, and the family tutor was the answer. While tutors often taught children of less prosperous neighbors, their goal was to help wealthy planters' children fit into their privileged positions in society (S. S. Cohen, 1970).

Apprenticeship was another educational practice in the eighteenth century. By the middle of this century, laws in Virginia required that apprentices be taught reading and writing in addition to their vocational training (Monroe, 1940). Pennsylvania, New York, and all New England colonies had similar ordinances. It was the master's responsibility to provide this education, either directly or through contract. South Carolina and Georgia made the least provision for general education of apprentices, even though children in these states were often apprenticed (S. S. Cohen, 1970).

The home and family continued to be important in the eighteenth century education as the primary center of education and an important secondary center for religious life and instruction (Rossiter, 1956). Toward the end of the eighteenth century, however, the extent and kind of household education changed. Cremin (1970) identifies four significant changes that had both direct and indirect effects on schooling: (a) the marriage age in the colonies declined, and the population increased because of lower death rates and an increase in immigration; (b) schools became increasingly more accessible; (c) the American version of the traditional European extended family developed—some households had three generations under one roof—and the transmission of elements of family style and expertise was affected; and (d) the stabilization of community life, combined with the growing prevalence of churches, schools, and colleges, gradually eased the family's burden of education.

The final decades of the eighteenth century witnessed both the Revolutionary War and the beginning years of a new nation. The country needed to solve many problems, one of which was how to plan for education. Up to this time, not much progress had been made in developing a thoughtful system of public schooling, and after the war, many schools were shut down because of a lack of money for teachers or supplies. Many farmers, who made up the majority of the population, did not see the need for formal education. The years after the Revolutionary War "were a time of rapid decline in educational advantages and increasing illiteracy among the people" (Cubberley, 1962, p. 120; see also Whitehead & Crow, 1993). The Constitution had no provision for education, and, according to the 10th Amendment, states held rights not expressly given to the federal government. Education was thus, from the founding of our nation, considered to be a state rather than a national function (Meyer, 1967).

Nineteenth Century

As the nation entered the 19th century, its population was still mostly rural, forming a scattered and isolated citizenry with limited opportunity to discuss common ideas, needs, or interests (Cubberley, 1962; Whitehead & Crow, 1993). Communications were inefficient. There was no government-provided national postal service, roads were difficult to travel, and newspapers were minimally circulated—all factors contributing to the slow development of unified ideas about education (Monroe, 1940). Schools existed in isolation rather than in a system in which they articulated with the schools above or below them (Good, 1962). Well into the nineteenth century, public schools in which students started formal education between the ages of eight and 12 came into existence, but even then, students attended school only for about a half day for three months of the year. At both home and school, most of them studied primarily the *W. H. McGuffey Reader* and the Bible (R. S. Moore, 1984).

During this period, a gradual change in attitude about public support of education developed. Previously, education had been considered the responsibility of the home and "an affair of the church, somewhat akin to baptism, marriage, the administration of sacraments, and the burial of the dead" (Cubberley, 1962, p. 120). Schooling now began to be viewed as a civil or social/religious responsibility. Some schools were financed by private endowment; others from the support of caring individuals (Meyer, 1967). Some states created permanent school or literacy funds, but because these were seldom adequate, often a rate bill was created that fathers were required to pay for their children's schooling. Many philanthropic societies developed to help special classes of children who were not receiving an education, such as free Negroes and children of particular religious denominations. These societies "were formed primarily for the purpose of educating poor children" (Knight, 1951, p. 161), a practice that continued until well into the late nineteenth century. The most prominent of them was the Free Society of New York, chartered in 1805 (Meyer, 1967). Renamed the Public School Society in 1826, the Society attempted to collect fees from parents who could pay. When this failed, the system returned to a free one after six years.

Other forms of elementary education were prevalent during the nineteenth century: the Sunday School movement, the Infant School, and the Lancasterian School. The Sunday School movement, which began in England in the late 1700s for underprivileged factory children, spread rapidly and in 1785 took root in the United States in Hanover County, Virginia, in the home of Thomas Crenshaw. Poorer neighborhood children received free instruction every Sunday in reading and writing as well as in Bible stories (Drake, 1955). The infant school idea originated in England in 1799 through the efforts of a manufacturer named Robert Owen. Factory children were his apprentices from the age of five or six, so he opened a school to give children as young as three years of age moral, physical, and intellectual training. The principle of the infant school was carried over to America, modified many times, eventually became part of various city school systems, and was known as primary school (Meyer, 1967). The Lancasterian School was introduced by Joseph Lancaster, an English Quaker, in London. His method, also called the monitorial system, made it possible for one teacher to instruct 500 or more students at one time. A *Manual for Instruction* gave details for organizing and managing the school so that students could be divided into smaller groups of 10 and instruct each other (Drake, 1955). Several state legislatures in the South, Midwest, and East adopted the idea of the Lancasterian school between 1805 and 1828 (Cubberley, 1962). All of these types of education preceded the development of the public elementary school.

Although various alternative schooling movements began in the nineteenth century, many people continued to be taught at home. Many famous educators were home schooled (Fenner & Fishburn, 1968). For instance, Elizabeth Palmer Peabody, the founder of kindergarten in America, was educated by her father at home. She taught her daughters at home—Elizabeth, Mary (Mrs. Horace Mann), and Sophia (an artist and Mrs. Nathaniel Hawthorne). Other well-known, home-schooled educators of the period are Susan B. Anthony, Frances Willard, and Clara Barton. R. S. Moore (1984) lists famous people from other occupations who were home schooled during the nineteenth century, including inventors Thomas Edison and Alexander Graham Bell, industrialists Andrew Carnegie and Cyrus McCormick, scientist John Burroughs, General Stonewall Jackson, explorer Robert Peary, and Presidents Abraham Lincoln and Woodrow Wilson. Many of these individuals went to college with a home school background.

By the mid-nineteenth century, Americans had begun the "common school" crusade. Many types of people, including Daniel Webster and Edward Everett, promoted the concept of a common school for securing economic and social status, for improving social conditions, and as a point for universal reform (Whitehead & Crow, 1993). Much legislation was passed during the nineteenth century that helped establish the foundations of the common school movement. In particular, the first compulsory attendance laws were passed, beginning with Massachusetts' in 1852. Horace Mann was one of the leading proponents of common schooling. Learning to read in a school and then self-educating himself until he entered Brown University, Mann was able to convince businessmen, workers, farmers, and members of different religious denominations that public education would benefit them all. He believed that the future of the nation depended on universal public education (Cremin, 1980).

By the close of the nineteenth century, despite a decline in the illiteracy rate and an increase in the establishment of free public schools, many Americans refused to succumb to social pressure or compulsory attendance laws and to forfeit what they considered their rights and responsibilities to educate their children at home.

Twentieth Century

By 1900, compulsory attendance laws had been passed in over 30 states and in the District of Columbia. These laws generally required school attendance for a specific period of time each year for all children within certain age groups (Kotin & Aikman, 1980). Nineteen million of the nation's 25 million children were enrolled in schools (Kent, 1987). Not surprisingly, there is evidence of increased attendance in the early years of the twentieth century in both elementary and secondary schools (Knight, 1951).

The Progressive period, which reached its zenith in America during the first two decades of the twentieth century (Whitehead & Crow, 1993), had several basic themes which were reflected in education:

1. Government should regulate economic power in the public interest.
2. Expert knowledge and scientific method should be applied to solving social, political, economic, and educational problems.
3. The national environment should be conserved, and its quality enhanced.
4. Political institutions and processes should be reformed to make government more efficient.
5. The spirit of community should be revitalized in the burgeoning urban areas.
6. Educational institutions and processes should facilitate democratic participation and scientific efficiency. (p. 45)

John Dewey is the one individual most associated with the Progressive educational movement. "The complete act of thought" was a central theme in his educational philosophy (Pulliam, 1991, p. 150). In Dewey's ideal school, purposeful activities would build on common interests of children such as communication, inquiry, construction, and artistic expression (Pulliam, 1991). Children would enjoy a more varied and more flexible approach to schooling than that experienced by students in the 1800s.

During the 1930s, the Great Depression brought essentialism (Gutek, 1983), and social reconstructionists urged a return to basic skills and subjects (a focus on reading, writing, and arithmetic). The 1940s brought the expansion of the middle class in America and the relocation of many people from cities to suburbs. "Life adjustment education" then became the new movement as a response to "the social and psychological uneasiness produced by the cultural changes that followed immediately after World War II, such as rising divorce rates, increases in juvenile delinquency, and living in communities which were evolving" (Gutek, 1983, p. 279). During the 1950s, a number of educational critics appeared, the most notable of whom were Arthur E. Bestor, Jr., Admiral Hyman Rickover, Max Rafferty, and Robert Hutchins. These critics attacked life adjustment and progressive education as pedagogically weak, creating academics inferior to European schools, and promoting an overly permissive attitude that had lowered America's civic and moral standards (Pulliam, 1991). As a result of the Soviet Union's orbiting of a space satellite around the earth in October, 1957, widespread demands were made for more rigorous academic standards and programs, especially in mathematics and science (Gutek, 1983).

The 1960s brought the civil consciousness of Americans to the forefront. Many special programs were designed to be culturally sensitive, and many acts were passed to rectify language deficiencies. The Civil Rights Act of 1964 and the Bilingual Education Act of 1968 were passed. Early childhood programs, such as Operation Head Start and Follow Through, were developed. Attempts were also made to revise curricula in schools to include a stronger emphasis on mathematics and science (Gutek, 1983).

In the 1970s, the bleak economy greatly affected the financial resources available to public schools. The energy crisis, precipitated by the OPEC oil embargo, inspired educators to focus on "energy education" and "energy conservation programs" (Gutek, 1983). Special education legislation was enacted to benefit handicapped students between the ages of three and 21.

The 1980s were a period in which public education was much more critically examined than ever before in a variety of well-publicized reports such as *A Nation At Risk: The Imperative for Educational Reform* by the National Commission on Excellence in Education. The Commission recommended a "return to the basic subjects," which it defined as: English, mathematics, social studies, computer science, and foreign language (National Commission on Excellence in Education, 1983).

During the twentieth century, the relationship of the family to schools changed dramatically. Parental control of education was significantly weakened (Murphy & Beck, 1995). Parents began to be viewed as "presumptively incompetent in the area of education as schooling became less an issue of individual development and...more an issue of social needs and group value" (Arons, 1981, p. 6). Not surprisingly, by the 1960s, the public began to lose confidence in the schools (Tyack, 1974)—confidence that has continued to erode over the last quarter century (see Chapter 1). Some parents have become convinced that "little children *are* better taught at home than in school, but also better socialized by parental example and sharing than by other little people" (R. Moore & Moore, 1984, p. 240). The home schooling movement has grown from a minority of 10,000 to 15,000 in the 1970s to one million home schooled in 1995. This strength in numbers has enhanced the movement's ability to negotiate for its own advantages and protection.

As a result of the exodus of so many children from public schools, compulsory attendance laws have been challenged in almost every state, and hundreds of court cases have been fought over various rights of home schoolers to educate their children as they see fit. We turn in the next section to a review of these legal aspects of the home schooling movement.

LEGAL DEVELOPMENTS

Support for home schools is growing in legal circles as well. (Weston, 1996, p. 34)

During the first 250 years of the United States, education was not subject to the myriad regulations that presently conflict with parents' rights to control the process of their children's education. Parental liberty was held inviolate. Neither was education primarily a governmental responsibility (Klicka, 1995).

Courts

To illustrate how strongly early American case law favored parental rights, consider the case of *Commonwealth v. Armstrong* (1842), which shows many courts in early America not only protected parental rights but also incorporated Judeo-Christian principles directly into their opinions. Although this case involves a church-related issue of whether a minister had violated parental rights over a child by baptizing the child without the permission or even the knowledge of the parent, the judge's decision speaks to broader issues of the times. Judge Lewis, speaking for the court, said:

> The authority of the father results from his duties. He is charged with the duties of maintenance and education. These cannot be performed without authority to command and to enforce obedience. The term *education* is not limited to the ordinary instruction of the child in the pursuits of literature. It comprehends a proper attention to the moral and religious sentiments of the child. In the discharge of this duty, it is the undoubted right of the father to designate such teachers, either in morals, religion, or literature, as he shall deem best calculated to give correct instruction to the child. No teacher, either in religion or any other branch of education, has any authority over the child, except what he derives from its parents or guardian. (p. 33)

Even though the Constitution does not specifically mention the right of parents to educate their children, that right is derived from the Fourteenth Amendment and covered under the First Amendment. The Fourteenth Amendment guarantees that all citizens have the right to "liberty," which cannot be taken away without due process. The United States Supreme Court has determined that this guarantee includes "parental liberty." The Supreme Court has consistently held that parents have the "fundamental right" to direct the upbringing and education of their children (*Pierce v. Society of Sisters*, 1925; *Wisconsin v. Yoder*, 1972). The First Amendment guarantees all citizens the right to freely exercise their religious beliefs. Because the majority of home schooling occurs for religious reasons (Ray, 1990), the courts have held that these families are protected by the First Amendment. For example, if a home school family is being prosecuted for not complying with local restrictions, such as the requirement of a college degree or teaching certificate for the parent-teacher, it may use the First

Amendment as a defense, as long as it proves the particular restriction violates its religious beliefs.

However, at the same time the United States Supreme Court has asserted parents' rights to educate their children it has also created a state "interest" in education. Consequently, government controls have been initiated and continue to be promoted based on the U.S. Supreme Court's rulings that children must grow up to be "literate" and "self-sufficient" (*Plyer v. Doe*, 1982; *Wisconsin v. Yoder*, 1972). In order to further protect its interests in education, the state consistently tries to impose restrictive regulations—such as teacher certification requirements, curriculum guidelines, home visits, standardized testing requirements, and countless other controls—on parents who are home schooling (Klicka, 1995).

Whenever the rights of parents to educate their children under either the First or Fourteenth Amendment are at issue, a specific legal test must be applied (Klicka, 1995). This test, made up of four parts, is often referred to as the "compelling interest test" (*Sherbert v. Verner*, 1963; *Wisconsin v. Yoder*, 1972). This standard of review requires home schoolers who are asserting a religious belief to prove two parts of the test and the state to prove the other two parts. The burden of proof is on the home school family first to demonstrate that their belief which opposes a particular state requirement is both "sincere" and "religious" (*Wisconsin v. Yoder*, 1972). Second, the home school family must prove that their sincere religious belief is "burdened." Then the burden of proof shifts to the state. First, the state must prove that its requirement is "essential" or "necessary" "to accomplish an overriding governmental interest" in education (*Lee v. U.S.*, 1982). Second, the state must show that its requirement "is the least restrictive means of achieving some compelling state interest" (*Thomas v. Review Board*, 1981, p. 718). If the state can prove that its interest necessitates the creation of a particular regulation and that the regulation is the least restrictive means of enforcing that interest, then the religious belief of the home schooler must give way.

This raises the question: What is the state's legitimate interest in education? According to U.S. Supreme Court precedents in *Wisconsin v. Yoder* (1972), *Plyer v. Doe* (1982), and *Life Baptist Church v. Town of East Longmeadow* (1987), the state's interest is two-fold: civic and economic. Children must both acquire the necessary reading and writing skills to be able to vote and participate in our democratic system and be able eventually to provide for themselves so they will not become a burden on the state.

The case of *Wisconsin v. Yoder* (1972) established a framework for determining whether someone's beliefs are religious rather than merely philosophical. The Supreme Court discussion revolves around which types of beliefs are protected and which are not:

> A way of life, however virtuous and admirable, may not be interpreted as a barrier to a reasonable state of education if it is based on purely secular considerations; to have the protection of the Religious Clauses, the claims must be rooted in reli-

gious belief....Thus, if the Amish asserted their claims because of their subjective evaluation and rejection of the contemporary secular values accepted by the majority, much as Thoreau rejected the social values of his time and isolated himself at Walden Pond, their claims would not rest on a religious base. Thoreau's choice was philosophical and personal rather than religious, and such belief does not rise to the demands of the Religious Clauses. (p. 216)

In 1965, the U.S. Supreme Court had defined "religious training and belief" as a "sincere and meaningful belief which occupies in the life of its possessor a place parallel to that filled by God" (*Seeger v. United States,* 1965). The Court also explained that a belief is not religious if it is predominantly political, sociological, or philosophical or if it is based merely on a personal moral code. A particular family's beliefs are, in fact, religious when their belief system is dependent upon a supreme being—a supernatural God and His revelation (Klicka, 1995).

The U.S. Supreme Court has offered some guidelines on determining whether an individual's religious beliefs are sincere. In *Thomas v. Review Board* (1981), the Court stated, "Religious beliefs need not be acceptable, logical, consistent, or comprehensible to others in order to merit First Amendment protection." The Court continued:

The guarantee of free exercise is not limited to beliefs which are shared by all of the members of a religious sect. Particularly in this sensitive area, it is not within judicial function and competence to inquire whether the petitioner or his fellow worker more correctly perceived the commands of their common faith. Courts are not arbiters of scriptural interpretation. (pp. 715–716)

The issue of whether the home school family's religious beliefs are being burdened or violated by the state is fairly easy to prove in a court of law. In *Wisconsin v. Yoder* (1972), Jonas Yoder was prosecuted for truancy for keeping his children at home in obedience to his sincerely held religious beliefs. The U.S. Supreme Court emphasized the fact that because of the threat of criminal prosecution, Yoder was "burdened," thus satisfying the second part of the test. This proof of "burden" was again defined in the case of *Lyng v. Northwest Indian Cemetery Protection Association* (1988), when the court concurrred with the *Wisconsin v. Yoder* (1972) case in which it had been ruled that "the statute directly compelled the Amish to send their children to public high schools contrary to the Amish religion and way of life" (p. 217).

The United States Supreme Court has made it clear that the state, not the parents, has the burden of proving that its particular regulation, which is in conflict with the home schoolers' religious beliefs, is "essential" for children to be educated. In the cases of both *Thomas v. Review Board* (1980) and *Sherbert v. Verner* (1963), the Court held that such infringements must be subjected to strict scrutiny and could be justified only by state proof of a compelling interest. The Supreme Court has made it clear in *U.S. v. Lee* (1982) that, as a part of the compelling interest test, there must be a showing of "essentiality" of the particular requirement: "The state may justify a limitation on a religious liberty by showing that it is essential to accomplish an overriding governmental interest" (p. 257). Furthermore, in *Sheridan Road Baptist Church v. Department of Education* (1986), the demand was on the state to prove that its regulation was essential:

> In order to justify averring plaintiff's fundamental First and Fourteenth Amendment rights, the state must establish that enforcing the certification requirement, without exception, is essential to ensure the adequate "secular" education required by the compulsory attendance law. (pp. 59, 140)

The fourth part of the "compelling interest test" demands that, even if the state could establish that a particular regulation is compelling, it must still demonstrate with evidence that no alternative form of regulation exists which would be less restrictive to the First Amendment rights involved (*Sherbert v. Verner*, 1963). The United States Supreme Court held in *Wisconsin v. Yoder* (1972) that Wisconsin's interest in compulsory education was "otherwise served" by the Amish program of informal, home training in the practical and occupational skills of living and working given by their parents and the whole Amish community. Virtually all regulations on education could be justified as "reasonable," but many cannot be proven "essential." A federal district court ruling on *Jeffrey v. O'Donnell*, 702 F.Supp. 513 (1988), struck down a compulsory attendance law in Pennsylvania that was being abused by school districts as they were disapproving and prosecuting home schoolers based on arbitrary standards created by school superintendents. The federal district court realized that free exercise rights were involved and a stricter scrutiny had to be applied. The court stated, "The threat to sensitive First Amendment freedoms mandates judicial intrusion in the form of declaring the particular provision of the law unconstitutional for vagueness" (pp. 519, 521).

One of the most recent cases, *Michigan v. DeJonge* (1993), which was brought before the Michigan Supreme Court, applied "strict scrutiny" and the four-pronged "compelling interest test" to protect home schools. The DeJonge case involved home school parents who had been criminally prosecuted and convicted for teaching their children without appropriate teacher certification as required by law. The Michigan Supreme Court ruled that the DeJonges easily met the first two parts of the "compelling interest test":

> The DeJonges believe that the Word of God commands them to educate their children without state certification. Any regulation interfering with that commandment is state regulation of religion....Our rights are meaningless if they do not permit an individual to challenge and be free from those abridgments of liberty that are otherwise vital to society. (p. 137)

The Court further ruled that the state had failed to provide one scintilla of evidence that the DeJonge children have suffered for the want of certified teachers and, therefore, that teacher certification was not essential. In reaching this conclusion, the Supreme Court relied on studies supplied by the Home School Legal Defense Association (HSLDA), in which no positive correlations between the student's performance and the teacher's qualifications were found. The Court also relied on information supplied by the HSLDA which demonstrated that Michigan was the last state still to require teacher certification of home schoolers.

Statutes

Home schooling nearly died with the advent of public schools and subsequent compulsory attendance laws. In the 1980s, however, home schooling experienced a rebirth in popularity as hundreds of thousands of families began teaching their children at home. In 1980, only three states in the entire country—Utah, Ohio, and Nevada—officially recognized the right to home school in their state statutes. In most states, home school families were often prosecuted under criminal truancy laws and educational neglect charges (Klicka, 1995). Due primarily to the efforts of the Home School Legal Defense Association, founded in 1983, and the willingness of many families to stand on their convictions, home schooling is now legal in all 50 states.

As of March, 1995, 34 states, by statute, specifically allowed "home instruction" or "home schooling" provided certain requirements were met (Klicka, 1994). At least five of these 34 statutes merely require home schoolers to submit an annual notice of intent verifying that instruction will be given in certain core subjects for the same number of days as in the public schools. According to home schooling advocates, the states of Montana, Wyoming, Mississippi, Wisconsin, and Missouri tend to have "model laws" based on the "honor system," which protects parental liberty and greatly reduces the monitoring power of state authorities. Colorado and Georgia have similar laws, but parents are required to have their children tested every year. In Virginia, Maryland, Vermont, and Tennessee, home school laws include options for families to obtain religious exemptions from various compulsory attendance requirements (Maryland Regulations Code; Tennessee Code Annotated; Vermont Statutes Annotated; Virginia Code). In Maryland and Tennessee, home schools can choose to be supervised by churches or church schools instead of local public school authorities.

In several states where home schools are recognized as private schools, parents who are home schooling for religious reasons are properly protected. For example, in 1983, Alabama amended its compulsory attendance law, exempting all schools operated as a ministry of a church or denomination from teacher certification and accreditation requirements (Alabama Code). In 1984, Alaska and Nebraska followed suit. Presently, in at least 12 states, home schools may be operated as private schools (Klicka, 1994). The remaining states require that home schools be approved by the local school superintendent or school board.

Oklahoma is the only state with a constitutional amendment protecting home schools; it grants no real authority to the state legislature to regulate home schooling. In Article 13, section 4, the Oklahoma Constitution declares:

> The legislature shall provide for the compulsory attendance at some public or other school, unless other means of education are provided, of all children in the State who are sound in mind and body, between the ages of eight and sixteen, for at least three months each year. (in Klicka, 1995, p. 161)

Because neither the Constitution nor the statutes define "other school," parents educating their children could possibly qualify as an "other school." In 1907, during the Oklahoma Constitutional Convention, one of the delegates, Mr. Buchanan, proposed that the phrase "unless other means of education be provided" be added to Article 13, section 4. Mr. Buchanan's proposal was supported by another delegate, Mr. Baker, who confessed his own children were home schooled. Thus the framers of the Oklahoma Constitution specifically intended to preserve the right of parents to educate their own children at home.

All the cases and amended statutes mentioned, and many dozens more, point to a trend in the courts and legislatures for less state control of home education. In particular, the courts have found compulsory attendance laws to be overly restrictive concerning home schooling (Klicka, 1995). A new set of issues currently reaching the courts has to do with the ability of home schooled students to selectively access public school offerings, whether academic classes or co-curricular activities.

THE RATIONALE FOR HOME SCHOOLING

> Home schooling has become popular for various reasons, but most people involved in the movement believe that traditional schools have failed in key areas. Concerns about violence, lack of discipline, and content curricula are common, as is the notion that specific needs can better be met in the personal setting of the home. (Robertson, 1994, p. 24)

The growth of the home schooling movement can be traced to a variety of factors—factors that emanate in the larger environment around schooling and conditions of the educational enterprise itself. In Chapter 1, we examined some of the environmental factors that influence privatization strategies in general. Here, we review the educationally grounded rationale that supports the home schooling movement. We organize that discussion around three issues: religion, socialization, and academics.

Religion

According to studies conducted by Shepherd (1986), many parents choose home education in search of religious liberties for their families. Rather than "following secular modes of thought, many of the overtly religious parents who instruct their own children are more interested in indoctrinating their sons and daughters in truths already known, namely the truths of the Bible" (p. 59). In a pamphlet published by *Teaching Home Magazine*, editor Sue Welch (1991) answers "Home School Questions and Answers" with a biblical scripture followed by the comment: "The underlying motivation for educating children at home is the concern for their spiritual and character development, that this is God's will for them" (p. 1). Anderson (1994) states, "Homeschooling allows us to teach our children the whole view of our world. We encourage our children to embrace the reality of God in past history and present daily life. We discuss biblical history and apply what we learn (from the tragedies and victories) to our lives today" (p. 1). Adventists, Amish, Methodists, and many fundamentalists try to apply the biblical injunction to "be not conformed to this world" (Romans 12:2, King James Version) by avoiding public schools.

Many Christian home educators home-teach their children not only to inculcate religious values but also to reinforce the wife's homemaking role, citing the biblical injunction to the wife "to bring them [her children] up in the discipline and instruction of the Lord" (Ephesians 6:4) (Shepherd, 1986).

Socialization

Opponents of home schooling argue that, even if children do receive a good grounding in the academics at home, they will lack the proper socialization skills needed to be functional members of society (Whitehead & Crow, 1993). Most home school parents, however, decry the socialization their children would receive at school. D. Moore (1986), in particular, distinguishes between "positive socialization, based on a stable family life" (p. 7) and "negative socialization, a me-first attitude, peer dependency, and rejection of family values" (Oregon Department of Education, 1988, p. 1). John Holt suggests that peer groups in schools have a negative effect on children—"that children learn from peers that it is 'smart' to smoke cigarettes, drink alcohol, and turn to drugs" (cited in Whitehead & Crow, 1993, p. 134). These parents view home schooling as a means of protecting their young from the rivalry, ridicule, competition, and conflicting moral values they believe are associated with much of the socialization that takes place in schools. As one parent in an Oregon study remarked, "We want our children to be peer-independent" (Oregon Department of Education, 1988, p. 1).

In their book *Home Schooling for Excellence*, Colfax and Colfax (1988) address the issue of the socialization of home schoolers:

> In the first place, homeschooled children are seldom, if ever, socially isolated. Indeed, precisely because they have more opportunities to interact with a wide range of people, they tend to become socially competent and socially responsible

at an earlier age than most of their conventionally schooled peers. The argument that socialization is the primary function of the schools—and educators are increasingly claiming just that as their failure to develop the intellect becomes more and more obvious—ignores evidence that peer group pressure in the schools, except in some very special contexts, does little to foster intellectual growth or the acquisition of desirable social values. (p. 101)

David Guterson, home school father, public school teacher, and author of *Family Matters: Why Homeschooling Makes Sense* (1992), says:

Homeschooling is certainly no cure-all for our social ills, and if practiced without vision or without sensitivity to the nation's social needs, may, in fact, do great social harm. Homeschooling can be a social danger when it is chiefly a strategy for narrowing the child's experience for political, social, or religious purposes. (pp. 61–62)

Guterson goes on to elaborate, however, upon the potential for home schooling to "nurture the kind of independent-minded, critical electorate our republic now desperately needs" and to "generate a new respect for diversity in values, pursuits, and principles, while inspiring a broader commitment to community service." (p. 63)

Academics

Home schooling has also become popular because some parents are becoming increasingly frustrated with the quality of education their children are receiving. They believe that "they can do a better job of teaching their children themselves" (Stecklow, 1994, p. 32). Robertson (1994) tells the story of an Alexandria, Virginia, mother who had a child "falling through the cracks." As the boy fell further and further behind his public school classmates, school administrators told the mother not to worry, that her son was just a slow learner. She said, "They didn't want to recognize what the problem was." After two years of home study, the child's performance had improved to where he was several years ahead in science, and ahead of his grade in social studies. The mother proclaimed that at home she could "take him at his level and go at his own pace." The mother took control of the curriculum in order to use it to her child's advantage (p. 6).

Riemer (1994) explains, in "Perspectives From a Home Schooling Educator": "I have always believed in being a lifelong learner, and I would like to pass down this passion for learning to my children" (p. 53). Riemer believes, along with other home schoolers, that parents are, and should be, the essential influence in a child's life. He and his wife have had the flexibility to design a very eclectic curriculum which includes reading, writing, mathematics, science, geography, social studies, literature, Spanish, art, music, physical education, religious studies, and citizenship. Parents who home school often plan for their children to be involved in organized sports (soccer, baseball, and basketball), drama presentations, science fairs, band and orchestra practice and recitals, technological training on computers, Boy and Girl Scouts, 4H, dance, and many other activities that extend beyond the academic practice and preparation offered in the public schools preparation. Montgomery (1989) has concluded that the broad spectrum of involvement of home schoolers may nurture leadership better than the curricula of conventional schools.

WHAT DO WE KNOW ABOUT THE HOME SCHOOLING MOVEMENT?

As the home school population grows and gains credence, it is also becoming more divergent in nature. (Weston, 1996, p. 34)

Personal Statistics

As noted earlier, the Home School Legal Defense Association estimates that one million students are being home schooled. According to the Home Education Research Institute's (HERI) first report, *A Nationwide Study of Home Education: Family Characteristics, Legal Matters, and Student Achievement* (Ray, 1990), which uses 1988 statistics, the following picture emerges of the demographic and educational characteristics and religious preferences of those home schooled in the United States.

The average educational level of the fathers studied was 15.0 years of formal training (or about 3 years of college), with 14.1 years (or about 2 years of college) reported for the mothers. For comparative purposes, Ray notes that, in 1988, 20.3 percent of those at least 25 years of age in the United States had four or more years of college. In this study of home education, 42.7 percent of the parents had four or more years of college. In another study of home school parents as educators, Mayberry (1995) reports the percentage of home schoolers with a college degree at a slightly higher 45 percent.

The average family in the HERI study consisted of father, mother, and 3.2 children, for a family size of 5.2. The average United States family size was 3.2 in 1988. Thus the home school families studied were about 64 percent larger than average. A nearly equal number of male (50.9%) and female (49.1%) students were home schooled. Their mean age was 8.24 years. On average, the children had been taught at home for three years, since age five.

Fifty-five percent of the home education families were within the $25,000 to $49,999 range for total annual income. The median income category for them was $35,000 to $49,999. The median family income in the United States in 1987 was $30,850.

The overwhelming majority of home school parents in the study characterize themselves as Christian, with 93.8 percent of fathers and 96.4 percent of mothers describing themselves as "born-again." About 40 percent of the fathers and

41 percent of the mothers considered themselves Independent Charismatic or Independent Fundamental/Evangelical. The category of Baptist included 18.4 percent of the fathers and 17.6 percent of the mothers. Catholics represented 3.4 percent of the fathers and 3.2 percent of the mothers. There were extremely few parents in the following categories: Muslim, Jewish, Mormon, or New Age. Ray (1990) and Wartes (1990) report consistent findings and confirm the high percentage of Protestant home schoolers.

The Home Schooling Movement

Home schoolers network and socialize through many different organizations and "circles of associates." Many national organizations exist for the benefit and support of home schoolers, such as: the Moore Foundation, Washington State; Homeschooling Information Clearinghouse (HIC), California; the Alliance for Parental Involvement in Education (ALLPIE), New York; Home Education League of Parents (HELP), California; Alternative Education Resource Organization (AERO), New York; the American Homeschool Association (AHA), Washington State; the National Association of Catholic Educators (NACHE), California; the Jewish Home Educators Network (JHEN), Maine; and the National Association for Mormon Home Educators (NAMHE), Utah. These organizations, seemingly the most prominent, welcome membership from home schoolers seeking information and support. Multiple other, often parallel, organizations exist at the state level as well.

In 1983, the Home School Legal Defense Association (HSLDA) was founded to bring together a large number of home school families so that each could have a low-cost method of obtaining quality legal defense. At present, there are more than 45,000 members of HSLDA in various states. The Association is located in Purcellville, Virginia, 50 miles west of Washington, D.C. Six attorneys preside over legal matters with a staff of 33 aides. At a cost of $100 per year per family, "experienced legal counsel and representation by qualified attorneys" are available for every member family if challenged in the area of home schooling. Although HSLDA considers itself to be a Christian organization with a Christian board and staff, "We believe it is our duty to advocate the right of all to home school" (Home School, n.d., p. 8). All six of HSLDA's attorneys are home school fathers. Among the current staff, 32 of their children are participating in or have finished home schooling. In the fall of 1991, HSLDA of Canada was launched as a sister organization due to public demand. The HSLDA publishes and distributes voluminous information about research studies that favor home schooling, as well as about current arbitration activity and results from court cases, national home school statistics (from the Home School Research Institute), and warnings about progressive education.

The National Homeschool Association (NHA) is a nationwide, nonprofit organization incorporated in 1988 (inception: 1986) whose primary aims are to advocate individual freedom and choice in education, to serve families who home school, and to inform the general public about home education. The NHA operates with an elected council which acts by consensus. The NHA communicates with a large number of national, regional, state, and local groups and uses its national perspective to monitor developments within the home schooling movement and to identify issues that affect home school families. An NHA national conference with workshops and activities for the entire family is held each year. Benefits of the 15 dollar annual membership include a subscription to the NHA quarterly journal, voting privileges for all elections, and access to NHA network and referral services. Included in the "welcome packet" is a one-page letter of addresses, an application brochure, a two-page resource list, and a question and answer section, plus a copy of the quarterly journal, *Forum*.

A recent issue of *Forum* contains 30 pages of "Why NHA?", as well as articles written by parents and a student on socialization, academic advice, the college quest, and information about how to get more politically involved in defense of home schooling. The motto for the NHA organization, printed on its stationery and its newsletter, reads: "To advocate individual choice and freedom in education, to serve those families who choose to home school, and to inform the general public about home education."

Two thousand members nationwide now subscribe to NHA, and the numbers are growing. Since the NHA is considered to be a service-oriented network for exchanging information, each year 30,000 to 40,000 inquirers are referred to state and local support groups in their areas for assistance. According to one of the council members we interviewed, NHA leaders spend much of their time reading and extrapolating information regarding state home school organizations and disseminating information to others.

THE HOME SCHOOLING PROCESS

Over the last decade, researchers have provided considerable insights into the educational process that unfolds in home schools. We examine those findings in the paragraphs below.

Curriculum

Home schoolers use a variety of materials when instructing their children. According to the National Home Education Research Institute study (Ray, 1990), 67.4 percent of parents reported that they hand-picked the major curriculum components for their students. A satellite school curriculum was used by 5.1 percent of the parents. A home education program provided by a local private

school was used by another 1.3 percent. Finally, 31.4 percent of parents reported they used a complete curricular package (including language, mathematics,
social studies, and science materials for the full year). The remaining parents in
the study reported using a combination or multiple options. The study also indicated that home school families visited libraries about three times per month.
Slightly more than half (57.8%) of the home school families reported having
computers in their homes.

After years of reviewing materials of all kinds that were brought to their attention by publishers, educators, and home schoolers and that were variously
described to them as "unique," "innovative," and "creative," Colfax and Colfax
(1988) concluded that:

1. Most of the early reading and early math products are overpriced, gimmicky,
   and of relatively little value.
2. Reading, writing, and arithmetic workbooks are designed to meet classroom
   and teacher needs rather than the needs of children, and as such are more concerned with occupying time than with providing real skills in an efficient manner.
3. Far less time and effort are needed to provide children with the basics than
   educators and schoolbook publishers are inclined to admit.
4. A few readily available books and projects will ordinarily suffice to provide the
   child with a firm grounding in the basics that will, in turn, allow him or her to
   get on with the business of higher-order learning and thinking. (p. 69)

The Colfaxes go on to list their favorite materials for home schooling:
Sullivan Associates reading workbooks, creative writing projects, and jour-
nals; Spectrum Mathematics workbooks; Golden Step Ahead math, reading,
science, and social studies books from the publishers of the highly regarded
Golden Books (Western Publishing Company); the Honor Roll Achievement
Books (Harbor House); and the School Zone series. They suggest that a
"basics potpourri" approach be utilized with these "over-the-counter" materials found in markets. In addition, they argue for the use of more "hands-on"
and "exploratory" methods.

In the *Middle Tennessee Home Education Association Handbook (MTHEA
Handbook)* (Middle Tennessee, 1995), several suggestions are given for methods
and materials to be used in home schooling a child:

1. Textbook curriculum should be adapted to the child using an integrated and
   linear approach .
2. Use workbooks from publishers such as Alpha Omega, Accelerated Christian
   Education (ACE), and Christian Light Education.
3. Read John Holt's *Teach Your Own* and *Learning All The Time* to gain an understanding of the "unschooling approach" to learning from real life experiences
   through natural curiosity.

4. Read Susan Schaeffer Macaulay's *For The Children's Sake* to gain an understanding of the Charlotte Mason Approach of using living books and narration to help students comprehend the need for cooperation and self-discipline. Special emphasis is given to the humanities.
5. Correspondence schools are suggested for those who want an independent study program, as offered through Christian Liberty Academy or Calvert.
6. Unit studies are suggested for making sure every subject relates to every other subject, with the use of varied resources, especially library books. Examples of materials are: Advanced Training Institute of America (ATIA), Weaver, KONOS, and Alta Vista. (p. 17)

Teaching

Although control over what is taught and when may be the prime concern of most home school parents, how children are taught is of equal concern to many (Colfax & Colfax, 1988). Home schooling permits parents to choose from a wide variety of methods of teaching, to use and adapt those that work best for their children, and to vary techniques as circumstances demand. Unlike teachers and administrators, who "sometimes seem to have a trained susceptibility to commercially promoted educational gimmickry" (p. 44), parents can be skeptically eclectic in their choice of and commitment to methods and materials. The Colfaxes explain how home school parents have a great advantage by also being able to:

1. control the scheduling and timing (flow) of accomplishing lessons
2. control the personnel the child encounters (protection from teachers with serious intellectual, personality, and character defects)
3. [enhance] efficiency in on-task activities and time for extra-curricular activities
4. [promote] student autonomy. (p. 45)

Guterson (1992) claims that "the majority of homeschooling families are far better attuned than public schools to the revelations of learning theory—that subdivision of educational psychology devoted to discovering how people learn" (p. 169). As a public school educator and home school father, he maintains that educational institutions are thoroughly at odds with what science tells us about how people should learn. Guterson advocates individual learning and the "empowerment" of each student. His discussion in Chapter 9 of *Family Matters: Why Home Schooling Makes Sense* revolves around the lack of success humanists and learning and behavioral theorists have had in seeing their theories applied successfully to the classroom. He points out that massive educational institutions are, by definition, incapable of sophisticated responsiveness to individual students, as recommended by Gardner's theory of multiple intelligences. Guterson blames his own failure in inspiring public high school students to generate creative writing, research projects, and dramatic presentations upon his "forgetting the central learning theory and that each child learns differently" (p. 181). He testifies that the success he and his wife have had teaching their children at home is due in part to their ability to provide their children with the freedom to learn in their own unique ways.

Time

According to the National Home Education Research Institute (Ray, 1990), 88 percent of the time spent in home schooling is done by mothers. The father does 10 percent of the teaching, while 2 percent of the teaching is done by some other person. The majority of home schoolers spend five to six hours per day on academics and schedule fine arts, physical education, and extra curricular activities for later afternoon. The *MTHEA Handbook* (Middle Tennessee, 1995) suggests that "adding four hours of teaching to your schedule will be an adjustment. It will be easier if you organize your home, divide the chores, delegate, and plan your meals, days and activities" (p. 12). Most states' laws require home schooled students to be taught a minimum of four hours per day, 180 days per year.

Costs

Costs vary for home schooling a child, depending on the types of materials used and the extent to which field trips and attendance at special events are an extension of the curriculum. The *MTHEA Handbook* (Middle Tennessee, 1995) suggests that families spend what they have and use creativity to supply the rest. It is suggested that libraries and used-book fairs, along with home-made charts and visual aids, can help to keep costs down (p. 12). According to *A Nationwide Study of Home Education: Family Characteristics, Legal Matters, and Student Achievement* (Ray, 1990), the average home education family spent $488 per student per year. In comparison, the average per student cost in public elementary and secondary schools for the same year was reported as $3,987, although this includes the cost of instruction, which the home school figure does not. In the July 1993 edition of *Kiplinger's Personal Finance Magazine,* an estimate of $350 to $400 per student each year was given as a home-based curriculum cost by Davis and Quillen. They suggested that "designing your own curriculum" and buying the textbooks separately can cut costs to about $150 but takes more time. Add the costs of field trips, extracurricular projects, and school supplies, and the total cost is anywhere from several hundred to several thousand dollars. Of course, one parent usually stays home to do the teaching (Davis & Quillen, 1993), and extra financial burdens may be placed on the family in terms of the opportunity costs of foregone income.

RESEARCH ON THE EFFECTS OF HOME SCHOOLING

We are just beginning to develop an understanding of the effects of the current trend of home schooling on students. Aggregating early findings is difficult for a variety of reasons, some of which have to do with the quality of the studies themselves and some of which can be attributed to the fact that much of the work in this area has a strong advocacy perspective. Nonetheless, initial clues are emerging. We discuss these findings below under two headings: socialization and academic performance.

Socialization

Multiple investigations in recent years have examined the socialization of home schooled children. Some studies have dealt with self-esteem and self-concept, while others have looked at the interactive behaviors of home schoolers. Wesley Taylor (1986) studied 224 home schooled students in grades four to 12 throughout the United States and found that the self-concept of home schooled students was significantly higher than that of public schooled students for both the global scale and all six subscales of the Piers-Harris Children's Self-Concept Scale (PHCSCS). Hedin (1991) also examined the self-concept of home schooled children using the PHCSCS. He compared those who were educated in public, Christian, and home schools and found no difference in self-concept among the groups. However, the self-concept of all of them as a group was higher than that of the public school population that was used to develop the self-concept test.

One of the most recent investigations in the general area of "socialization" was completed by Smedley (1992). He used the Vineland Adaptive Behavior Scales to evaluate the communication skills, socialization, and daily living skills of demographically matched public schooled and home educated students. The scores were combined into one composite which reflected the general maturity of each subject. Smedley's data revealed that "home-educated children in this sample were significantly better socialized and more mature than those in public school" (p. 1).

Shyers (1992) has completed another of the most recent and widely disseminated reports comparing the social adjustment of home schooled and traditionally schooled students. He studied students who were either solely home educated solely classroom educated. The children were observed and videotaped in free play and group interaction activities and were evaluated by trained observers who did not know their schooling background. Classroom-educated children received significantly higher problem behavior scores than did their home educated agemates. The traditionally schooled students tended to be considerably more aggressive, loud, and competitive than were the home educated children. These findings are supported by Bronfenbrenner's (cited in R. Moore & Moore, 1994) claim that, until fifth or sixth grade, children who spend more time with peers will become peer dependent and, to the extent they are pressured by peer values, will lose self-worth optimism, respect for parents, and trust in their peers. Indeed, research has shown home schooled children to be remarkably self-reliant and less susceptible to peer pressure than the average American student (Ray & Wartes, 1991). Conservatively, the evidence to date suggests that the self-concept of home schooled children is not negatively impacted by home schooling. A more aggressive interpretation would lead one to claim that the self-concept of home schooled children is actually higher than that of the conventionally schooled population.

Montgomery (1989) investigated the extent to which home schooled students were experiencing conditions which foster leadership in children and adolescents ages 10 to 21. Her findings suggest that the home educated are not isolated from social and group activities with other youth and adults. They are quite involved in church youth groups and other church activities, jobs, sports, summer camps, music lessons and recitals, and 4H. Montgomery concluded that home schooling may nurture leadership as well as or better than conventional schooling does. These findings are supported by studies by R. Moore & Moore (1984) indicating "that parents who provide reasonably responsive home environments during those years, without wholesale interference from peers, produce children who display confidence and a sense of direction, often becoming leaders" (p. 62). Separate studies by K. C. Johnson (1991), Rakestraw (1988), Reynolds (1985), Schemmer (1985), and Wartes (1987) have all established that home schooled children are actively involved in myriad activities outside the home with peers, children of different ages, and adults. The data from this research suggest that, as a group, home schoolers are not being socially isolated nor are they emotionally maladjusted.

Academic Performance

Qualifications of Parents to Teach
Opponents of home schooling argue that parents may not be qualified to teach their children because they lack advanced degrees and because most do not have an education degree or certification. According to Gross (1991), "More so than other youngsters, homeschooled children are limited by their parents' expertise and knowledge" (p. 120). As noted earlier, studies show that most home school parents have an average of only about 14 years of education. Gross discusses the potential for home schooled students to outgrow their parents' expertise beyond the basic skills needed in earlier years.

In an interview for *Mothering Magazine,* John Holt (1981) addresses the critique that parents without backgrounds in education or teaching experience are at a disadvantage in a home school situation. Holt replies, "I'd say parents have a great advantage....I wouldn't say that a person was disqualified from doing it because they had had training in education, but I would say that practically everything they taught you at that school of education is just plain wrong. You have to unlearn it" (p. 91).

The Colfaxes, who began home schooling their children in 1973 during a time of resurgence of home education, also question the necessity of teacher education and state certification. As their eldest son, Grant, was admitted to Harvard University in 1983, they found themselves "being cast into the role of experts" (Colfax & Colfax, 1988, p. xiii). They question the claim that parents cannot be trusted to decide what their children will learn. They argue that parents who have assumed the task of educating their children at home have been, almost without exception, successful in imparting important skills. The Colfaxes claim that parents are more qualified than professional educators to assess their children's learning styles and needs, to manage time wisely, and to empower their children with "real life" responsibility.

Test Scores

How do home schoolers fare on standardized achievement tests? While the absence of appropriate controls means that the data must be viewed skeptically, it is still worth noting that, generally speaking, children who are taught by their parents have repeatedly scored above national averages on standardized achievement tests. For example, Wartes (1987, 1988, 1989, 1990), a public high school counselor, has studied the Stanford Achievement Test (SAT) scores of hundreds of home educated students, grades K–12, in Washington State for several years. He has found that these students consistently score above the national average in reading, language, math, and science, with the median score at about the 67th percentile.

The largest nationwide study to date examined the achievement of home educated children whose families were members of the HSLDA. Ray (1990) gathered data on approximately 1,500 families and 4,600 children. He found that these home educated students averaged at or above the 80th percentile on standardized achievement tests in all subject areas. Scores in reading (84th percentile), language (80th percentile), and mathematics (81st percentile) were quite high. In addition, Ray found that the home educated did quite well in areas that skeptics often consider to be too difficult for the untrained to teach or in subject areas in which home educators might be less interested. For example, these students scored, on average, at the 84th percentile in science and the 83rd percentile in social studies (Ray, 1990).

According to test results provided by the Riverside Publishing Company and analyzed by Ray (1994), the nationwide average for home schooled students is at the 77th percentile on the Basic Battery of the Iowa Test of Basic Skills. Across all grade levels (K-12), 54.7 percent of home schooled students scored in the top quartile, more than double the number of conventionally schooled students.

What these studies reveal, primarily, is a need for better research on the effects of home schooling on the academic achievement of home schooled students. Research that controls for entry-level achievement is particularly needed.

Graduation and Higher Education

Many private colleges and universities now have a home educated student application form for students who may not have a transcript. Indeed, many institutions are aggressively recruiting home schoolers. The *MTHEA Handbook* (Middle Tennessee, 1995) claims that one application has been available since 1988 (p. 19). In the article "Charity Begins at Home" (1995), Jennie Ethell of HSLDA is quoted as saying, "A great number of colleges are waking up to the fact that homeschoolers are out there, doing well and are eager to go on to higher education" (p. C2). From the list compiled in February, 1995, by HSLDA of approximately 250 colleges and universities that have accepted home schoolers in the United States, Oral Roberts University's student body shows the impact of home schooling. Two hundred twelve home schooled students from 35 states and 10 different denominations are currently enrolled. Fifty-nine percent are female. Their average ACT and SAT scores are considerably above the national average. Other colleges listed which have accepted home schoolers with success include: The Citadel (South Carolina), U.S. Air Force Academy (Colorado), U.S. Naval Academy (Maryland), Harvard University (Massachusetts), MIT (Massachusetts), Oxford University (England), Princeton University (New Jersey), Yale University (Connecticut), and Moody Bible Institute (Illinois). Home schooler Grant Colfax (one by one his brothers followed suit) is a testimony to the acclaimed success of home schoolers in higher education. Grant graduated magna cum laude from Harvard, became a Fulbright scholar, and graduated from Harvard Medical School after being entirely home schooled by his parents (Gibbs, 1994).

CONCLUSION

In this chapter, we discussed the historical development of home schooling in the United States. We also reviewed the legal foundations of the home schooling movement. The characteristics and processes of home schooling were also examined, with attention centered on the important issues of curriculum employed and teaching methods utilized. The final section of the chapter provided the reader with an overview of the limited research conducted to date on home schooling in the areas of socialization and academic achievement. While it is premature to make any well-grounded claims about the advantages of home schooling based on the quality and quantity of research conducted to date, there are indications that home schooling may be more effective than its critics contend.

7
Volunteerism

The participation of volunteers in furthering the education process is both perceived and believed to be good and to contribute to the welfare of America's students. (Michael, 1990, p. 1)

Americans need to guard against overestimating what volunteers can be expected to accomplish. Volunteers are not a substitute for trained teachers and staff. (Sewall, 1990, p. 22)

I n this chapter, we examine volunteerism as a strategy for privatization in education. As we saw in Chapter 1, as a form of privatization, volunteerism moves both the financing and delivery of educational services from the public to the private domain. Although the use of volunteers in schools is not new, schools are increasing their reliance on them by creating organized volunteer programs. Expanding the volunteer list to include students, senior citizens, corporate partners, and others in the community, schools are finding new ways to put volunteers to work in the educational enterprise. We begin this chapter with an examination of the pressures fueling the volunteer movement. Then, we turn to an analysis of who is volunteering and how schools utilize them. Effects of volunteerism on schools, students, and volunteers are then described. Finally, we review strategies for overcoming barriers to creating successful volunteer programs.

THE VOLUNTEER MOVEMENT

Public interest and involvement in volunteer work in education is not new. In fact, the informal education of many primitive societies is much more akin to such an approach than it is to our own highly structured system of formal education. (Janowitz, 1965, introduction)

Traditional Role of Volunteers

The increase in school volunteerism is part of an "increased emphasis on volunteerism in general" (Tierce & Seelbach, 1987, p. 33) across the nation. Since the Kennedy Administration, the nation's Presidents have encouraged Americans to volunteer in their communities. Faced with fiscal constraints, they have called upon volunteers to step in to address unmet needs. Brudney (1990) notes, "As a relatively inexpensive form of labor, volunteers offer governments the potential to maintain or even enhance the amount and quality of services with a minimal investment of public resources" (p. 11). Volunteers have answered the challenge to meet governmental and public needs. Furthermore, "many consider volunteerism interwoven with the very fabric of American democracy and culture" (p. 2).

Since the beginning of the public schools, volunteers have played an important role. Volunteers "have helped raise funds for extras (and sometimes essentials) to supplement school budgets. Parents ran school parties, took children on field trips, chaperoned, decorated, baked, and were usually available when called" (Carter & Greisdorf, 1982, p. 16). However, "these volunteers were for the most part parents of children in a particular school, parents of former pupils or interested neighbors. No formal recruiting or training was involved and principals carried on such programs on a local option basis" (Jamer, 1961, p. 2). Therefore, "parental involvement has often been constrained to professionally acceptable roles within the school. Enlisting parents as sponsors of field trips and partners in fundraising via candy sales, bakery goods exchanges, and holiday bazaars has for years marked the limits of parental intrusion into the curriculum of the school" (Crowson, 1992, pp. 185–186).

Growth of Organized Volunteer Programs

As early as the 1950s, there were efforts to organize school volunteer programs (Merenda, 1989; Michael, 1990). In 1956, New York City's Public Education Association (PEA) created the School Volunteer Program. Noting the importance of volunteers in hospitals and social services and the success of a similar program in London, organizers believed that "volunteers can be equally useful in the schools" (Jamer, 1961, p. xv). Foreshadowing the current interest in volunteerism, Jamer (1961) further noted, "Though such use of lay people has been limited in the past we are entering upon a period of change and experimentation in education and the volunteers' role in the schools may well assume increasing importance" (p. xv).

Aiming to create "a more structured and accountable volunteer activity that would recruit volunteers, provide training, and consult teachers about whether they wished to have volunteers in their classrooms" (Michael, 1990, p. 6), the goals of the New York program were to have parents perform routine tasks, assist teachers in individual instruction, and provide unique experiences and services. Initially, 20 volunteers were recruited to tutor children in reading. With funds from the Ford Foundation and other groups, the volunteer program was expanded "to improve recruitment, training, and utilization of volunteers" (p. 6), with the school system increasing its share of funding for the program over a three-year period.

The success experienced by the school volunteer program led to the PEA in New York City being inundated by requests from all over the nation for information about the program. Unable to handle the response, the PEA established the National School Volunteer Program (NSVP, now the National Association of Partners in Education). The program provided citizens in 17 cities with consultation, advice, and training materials for establishing their own volunteer programs (Michael, 1990). "Sparked by interest and enthusiasm on the part of an individual parent, teacher, or school principal" (p. 9), school volunteer programs expanded rapidly during the 1970s and 1980s. A 1988 report by the NSVP determined that volunteer programs were operating in every U.S. state and territory as well as the District of Columbia.

During the past two decades, the surge in volunteerism has been "a revolution sweeping the country" (Carter & Greisdorf, 1982, p. 16). Government's "conception of volunteers has changed from nonessential frill to valuable human resource. And the idea of a volunteer program has evolved from haphazard initiative to systematic strategy for providing services" (Brudney, 1990, p. 20). Thus, parents and other volunteers are "employed in paraprofessional capacities—often with close-to-instruction duties as teachers' aides" (Crowson, 1992, p. 186). The use of volunteers "is decidedly on the upswing and is heavily encouraged in most locales" (p. 14). Indeed, "the trend today is toward the development of a comprehensive, systemwide volunteer program and the employment of a professional person to coordinate the various aspects of the program" (Decker & Decker, 1988, p. 4).

Despite the interest in volunteerism, a complete statistical profile of volunteers and their activities does not exist (see Michael, 1990, Chap. 3). Most of the existing data were collected in the 1980s as parts of other surveys. According to the National Center for Education Statistics (NCES), schools expected to have over 1.3 million people serve as volunteers in the 1987–1988 school year. Of these, about one million were in public schools, with the remainder serving in private institutions. Volunteers were serving in 47,300, or 60 percent, of public elementary and secondary schools. Typically, volunteers were more common in larger schools, elementary schools, suburban areas, and schools with low minority enrollments (unpublished data from NCES, cited in Michael, 1990).

Although the NSVP notes that "school volunteers" were synonymous with "parents" (cited in Lipson, 1994, p. 1) in the 1960s and 1970s, the term has grown to encompass many other groups of people. In particular, as mothers have entered the work force, schools have found others interested in volunteering, including students, senior citizens, retired teachers, and members of the business community. Moreover, the role of volunteers has expanded to include participation in more areas of schooling and greater scope of involvement.

In general, school volunteers are considered to be those "persons who work without pay, usually under the direction of an authorized teacher or other school employee, in support of school objectives to enhance the education of students. It includes people who participate in some aspect of instruction as well as those who help with clerical or other support activities" (Michael, 1990, p. 3). With the growth of community and corporate partnerships, Gray (1982) considers volunteers to be "any resource made available to the school system that the school system does not pay for" (p. 1). This definition includes people who may volunteer at schools while being paid by their employer.

RATIONALE FOR VOLUNTEERISM

As violence and student failures continue to escalate, parent and community involvement is emerging as the vital "missing link" to reaching educational goals in many school communities. (Batey, 1996, p. xiii)

In order to enhance and enrich the quality of education for students, it is imperative that the many talents of volunteers be channeled and utilized. Volunteers can be a school's most valuable resource if they are used effectively. (South Carolina State Department of Education, 1987, p. 1)

Although volunteerism is not new, "in the late 1970s and throughout the 1980s, ... several forces combined not only to increase reliance on volunteers but also to change the way in which scholars and practitioners conceive of this practice" (Brudney, 1990, p. 7). These include the heightened pressures of limited resources in the wake of increasing demands, teacher professionalization and increasing demands for school improvement, and a rising tide of parental and community involvement in schools.

Limited Resources

At the forefront of schools' efforts to increase their number of volunteers are the limited resources they have available to confront increasing demands and expectations. Hansen and Mackey (1993) note, "Schools can always use another hand, and some desperately need as many as they can get" (p. 28).

Fiscal Constraints

Today, school districts are often "caught between the rock of spiraling costs and declining revenues and the hard place of student/faculty need" (Armengol, 1992, p. 467). Resistance to tax increases, depleted revenue streams, other demands on state budgets, and efficiency drives have limited the availability of budget increases. With a large percentage of school funds designated for personnel, "budget cuts often create a shortage of classroom aides and specialists, who add to the richness of the curriculum and provide vital assistance to overburdened teachers" (Lipson, 1994, p. 1). Thus, "the primary catalyst to increased governmental interest in volunteer involvement is a serious, long-term erosion in fiscal capacity" (Brudney, 1990, p. 7).

Through the use of volunteers, schools hope to "alleviate some of the economic pressures" (Tierce & Seelbach, 1987, p. 33) and "achieve greater productivity through increased non-salaried resources" (Utah State Office of Education, 1988, p. 1). This can be accomplished by using "resources that can be provided to paid staff by unpaid staff" (p. 1). The effects of inadequate funding can be mitigated if volunteers "provide resources from the community for enrichment of the school program" (South Carolina State Department of Education, 1987, p. 1). Thus, schools "have learned to tap those riches through volunteer programs, with the happy result of high returns for negligible costs" (Armengol, 1992, p. 468) and with "the potential to maintain or even enhance the amount and quality of services with a minimal investment of public resources" (Brudney, 1990, p. 11).

Increasing Demands

The increasing demands placed upon schools further stretch the limited resources: " 'I just can't get it all done!' It is the classic lament of the teacher stretched too thin by the demands of the classroom" (Angelis, 1990, p. 19). Therefore, another force behind volunteerism is the call to "recognize the changes in society and in today's family structure, and redirect the flow of volunteer resources and activities accordingly" (Utah State Office of Education, 1988, p. 1). With the increase in the number of women in the work force and single-parent households, parents have less time to spend with their children and education (Burns, 1993). By bringing members of the community into the schools, volunteers "provide positive role models for students" (South Carolina State Department of Education, 1987, p. 1).

In addition, as schools are asked to take ever more responsibility for children and their families, "busy classroom...teachers are unable to provide the help some children need. Volunteers can fill in the gap" (Criscuolo, 1985, p. 9). Mainstreaming handicapped children places additional demands on teachers (Cuninggim, 1980). There are those students who "have special educational needs: hearing, visually, or speech impaired; orthopedically handicapped; mentally retarded; learning disabled; emotionally disturbed; and gifted students" (Buffer, 1980, p. 113).

Inequalities

Organized volunteer programs like the early one in New York City often seek to address inequalities in the educational system:

> Growing out of the civil rights movement and the war on poverty, and closely associated with new hopes for cognitive intervention in early childhood, these volunteer programs are expected to compensate for the inequalities in educational opportunity that remain a part of the American school system. (Janowitz, 1965, introduction)

Inequalities "include such contributing factors as underprivileged and ambitionless homes, crowded classrooms, overworked and sometimes poorly trained teachers, and in New York and some of our other big cities, great numbers of children wholly or largely unfamiliar with the English language" (Nichols, 1961, p. ix). However, volunteer program organizers realize the need to assist not only inner-city children but also rural children from low socioeconomic backgrounds (Janowitz, 1965).

School Improvement

Another rationale for volunteer programs in the school is to "strengthen education" (South Carolina State Department of Education, 1987, p. 1) and to "enhance and enrich the quality of education for students" (p. 1). Utah's Master Plan for Implementing a Statewide Volunteer System includes a mission statement "to increase student achievement through the more effective use of volunteers" (Utah State Office of Education, 1988, p. 1). Taranto and Johnson (1984) state, "With increased emphasis on accountability and an equally strong emphasis on individualized instruction, school systems are viewing the volunteer as a viable element in improving the quality of education" (p. 3).

Volunteer programs are often designed to "enhance the role of the teacher" (Utah State Office of Education, 1988, p. 1) "by allowing teachers and other school staff more time for professional instruction" (South Carolina State Department of Education, 1987, p. 1). For instance, "a large part of a teacher's classroom time is taken up by routine duties, unrelated to teaching, which can be satisfactorily performed, with a minimum of practice, by an intelligent volunteer. Relieved of such chores a teacher has more time for teaching" (Nichols, 1961, p. x). Thus, "the volunteer can help free the teacher so that more children can get individual assistance and, hopefully, improve upon basic, social, and other needs" (Taranto & Johnson, 1984, p. 3).

With teachers overburdened, volunteers are sometimes sought to "provide additional individualized instruction through one on one contact with students"

(South Carolina State Department of Education, 1987, p. 1). Furthermore, volunteer programs can "increase the levels of knowledge, experiences, and resources within the classroom through volunteers from all sectors of the community" (Utah State Office of Education, 1988, p. 1).

Labeled by Taranto and Johnson (1984) as "the most important advantage to be obtained from an effective volunteer program" (p. 6), another improvement rationale for creating volunteer organizations is to enhance a school's public image. Therefore, "a well-organized program in a school, or district, usually tells the students that educators, parents, business people, politicians, and others are working toward the best educational institution possible" (p. 6).

Parent and Community Involvement

Volunteer programs are also often created for "promoting community relations" (South Carolina State Department of Education, 1987, p. 1) by allowing volunteers to "serve as bridges to the community and...supportive spokespersons for the school's programs" (Cuninggim, 1980, p. 108). Thus, volunteer programs are part of the "new press toward parent involvement in education and a strengthening of school-community relations" (Crowson, 1992, p. 1). Indeed, this empowerment movement "springs from frustration with past modes of participation to provide genuine channels for influence in policy making, and from a concomitant desire of citizens to play a larger role in determining the quantity and quality of services they receive and the policies that affect them" (Brudney, 1990, p. 14). Now, "more than ever, schools are looking for ways to involve the community in the planning and decision-making process involved in school programming. Two important and doable vehicles for getting this involvement are advisory committees and volunteer programs" (Decker et al., 1994, p. 51). Thus, all stakeholders are included in determining a school's destiny (Fisher, 1994).

Crowson (1992) notes, "Declining public confidence in schooling, perceptions of a crisis in school quality, and a lessening faith in the inviolability of professional expertise have led to a reform movement that is currently rediscovering the power of the parent" (p. 8). By bringing volunteers, especially parents, into the schools, educators hope to "focus on the home as the base for learning" (Utah State Office of Education, 1988, p. 1) and to "broaden parents' understanding of the total educational process" (South Carolina State Department of Education, 1987, p. 1).

By involving volunteers, schools also hope to "increase community understanding of the problems facing public schools and enlist the support of citizens in an effort to improve education" (South Carolina State Department of Education, 1987, p. 1). In addition, the aim is to "provide an exchange of ideas, concerns, and proposals between school personnel and citizens of the community" (p. 1).

Although schools at times have been reluctant to involve parents, community support is increasingly seen as essential for schools. Crowson (1992) states,

"Few educators do not recognize that tax revenues, the construction of new schools, a favorable board majority, and their own jobs fundamentally depend on the maintenance of support from the community and parents" (p. 10). In some areas, "school budget increases...have gone down to defeat at the hands of the older segment of the population, which sees no reason to support a system it neither needs nor wants and from which it derives no benefits" (Armengol, 1992, p. 467). Therefore, "to maintain support, the most common administrative strategy is the *facilitative* act of opening channels of communication between the school and the home or community" (Crowson, 1992, p. 11).

VOLUNTEERS IN ACTION

We must all work together if our children are to acquire the knowledge, skills, and character they will need. (Benjamin, 1996, p. ix)

All community partners are potential lifesavers in children's learning. (Batey, 1996, p. 12)

Today, volunteers are recruited both on an individual basis and through partnerships with corporations and community groups.

Individuals

Today's volunteers include parents, senior citizens, other students, and many other adults. Indeed, South Carolina encourages "cross-sectional representation of the entire community...in effective recruitment techniques for school volunteers" (South Carolina State Department of Education, 1987, p. 7). With the increase in the number of single parent and two-income households, "schools that are serious about increasing volunteer involvement are looking to other sources [than parents] of volunteer support" (Decker et al., 1994, p. 51).

Parents

Although the demographics of volunteers are changing, parents still remain a vital part of the volunteer effort. Hunter (1989) states, "Parents' aid to education has become a full-blown 'Par-aide' as thousands of willing collaborators, without professional training, are recruited into the classroom" (p. 36). In fact, "most parents want to give something to the school, and school service is an excellent avenue to do so" (Powell, 1986, p. 32). According to the NSVP study cited by Michael (1990), 33 percent of school volunteers are parents.

Senior Citizens

Today, "the need for older volunteers is increasing as numbers of women who traditionally have been the core of community volunteers are dropping out of the volunteer sector to join the work force" (Tierce & Seelbach, 1987, p. 33). With life expectancy rising, "seniors now remain healthier longer, and productivity and community contributions continue well beyond traditional boundaries" (Carter, 1992, p. 373). To meet growing demands, "more and more schools are discovering that there is a wealth of experience and expertise available in their communities' senior populations" (Armengol, 1992, p. 468). The benefits of senior volunteers are numerous. They "have more discretionary time, are more available, and are generally very enthusiastic about volunteering" (Tierce & Seelbach, 1987, p. 35). Thus, "properly utilized—the wisdom and skills of retirees have the potential to relieve many strains now burdening our society" ("Helping Hands," 1993, p. 25). According to the NSVP survey (cited in Michael, 1990), older citizens comprise 24 percent of all school volunteers.

Students

The use of other students as volunteers in the schools has been advocated for some time (Hedges, cited in Arkell, 1975). They may be students in the upper grades of the K-12 system or college students. The popularity of service-learning programs in high schools and colleges has expanded the number of students volunteering. Twenty-one percent of volunteers are students (NSVP, cited in Michael, 1990).

Others

Besides the parents, senior citizens, and students who volunteer their time in schools, numerous other individuals share their time with schools. These include retired teachers, other professionals, and non-parents. The availability of volunteers is largely dependent upon the population base in the community. For example, volunteers from Chicago's Great Lakes Naval Base spend Saturdays "as tutors for students in grades 4-6 who are identified by their teachers as needing help" (Michael, 1990, p. 53).

Corporate and Community Partnerships

Because of the time and cost that may be required to recruit individual volunteers in sufficient numbers, "a number of school districts have turned to a relatively newer concept—partnerships—to reach out to the larger community" (Decker & Decker, 1988, p. 12). In contrast to volunteer programs that focus on the use of individuals, corporate and community partnerships "bring support to education by involving *groups* or *organizations*" (Decker et al., 1994, p. 51) such as businesses, industrial firms, civic groups, educational institutions, and social service agencies. "Achieving rapid popularity during the past decade" (Crowson, 1992, p. 14), school partnerships are "a special, formalized approach to community involvement" (p. 14) that "draws on its combined resources to develop a program uniquely fitted to the needs of students" (Michael, 1990, p. 56).

With no set blueprint for their organization, tremendous variety exists in partnership programs. Many focus upon the individual school. For example, the Adopt-a-School program "is an exclusive one-to-to-one partnership in which a business adopts one school and provides all the resources needed to supplement the curriculum" (O'Connell, 1985, p. 9). In contrast, more structured and formalized programs involve entire school districts and many partners. Typically, smaller and less structured programs occur in rural areas, while formalized partnerships predominate in urban areas (Mann, 1987b). In many partnerships, businesses release their employees to volunteer in the schools (Baas, 1990). In addition, partners may offer direct financial or material support for school projects (Trachtman, 1988a).

Another major type of partnership program focuses upon collaboration between the private sector and the public schools to initiate changes in public policy or to implement systemic educational reform. Taking a larger programmatic or policy approach, these partnerships seek to influence the public debate over schools and to engender long-term educational reforms. Other partnerships provide technical and managerial assistance to improve the operation and efficiency of schools (Mann, 1987a; Merenda, 1989; see also Trachtman, 1988b, 1988c).

The National Association of Partners in Education (NAPE) (1997) conservatively estimates that there are 400,000 school/business partnerships in the United States.[14] In the 1989–1990 academic year, 51 percent of school districts had partnership programs involving 2.6 million volunteers. Approximately 29.7 million students (65 percent of the total) were enrolled in school districts with active partnership programs. During 1989–1990, educational partners donated almost $1 billion in goods and services. Parent organizations were the most common sponsors of partnership programs.

HOW SCHOOLS UTILIZE VOLUNTEERS

Although the uses of volunteers may be "as varied as the needs of the student participants" (Michael, 1990, p. 56), their activities are broadly grouped into three areas: instructional activities, support functions, and advisory and advocacy activities. Data from NCES (as cited in Michael, 1990)[15] regarding activities of school volunteers found 40 percent participating in instructional activities, 30 percent in extracurricular activities, 15 percent involved in management or advisory support, 10 percent offering clerical support, 10 percent engaged in monitoring of school grounds or the cafeteria, and less than 5 percent in counseling support.

Instructional Activities

In regard to teaching and learning, "volunteers can add new dimensions to classroom learning while supplementing increasingly scarce instructional resources"

(Tierce & Seelbach, 1987, p. 34). Today, "it's no longer unusual to find parents and other adults in the classroom, assisting the teacher through a volunteer program" (Miller & Wilmshurst, 1984, p. 1). At one Oklahoma elementary school, "volunteers are an integral part of kindergarten every day" (Michael, 1990, p. 84). In their study of this program, Michael and fellow researchers found:

> It [was] hard to tell which of the adults in the three kindergarten sections were staff and which were volunteers. The volunteers are essential to the teacher's program, in which children are busy with many different activities at the same time. Volunteers were clearly comfortable with their roles, helping with paints, pinning up artwork, smiling with approval, or clearing up spills. (pp. 84-85)

Tutoring and Mentoring

One of the most common functions performed by volunteers is tutoring (Michael, 1990). A volunteer can "reinforce and supplement the academic endeavors of a child" (Batey, 1996, p. 49) by "work[ing] with individual children on mastery and practice" (Michael, 1990, pp. 46-47). Tutoring may involve "reading, math, English as a second language, writing, and computer use" (Michael, 1990, p. 49). Other "assignments that call for interacting with individual students include listening to a child read, giving corrective feedback on arithmetic exercises, reviewing spelling words, going over lessons that took place during a child's absence, and monitoring vocabulary practice" (Strom & Strom, 1994, p. 330). Carter (1992) notes:

> Mentors help pupils "stay on task" by providing one-on-one instruction. They tutor and serve as teaching assistants. Seniors work individually with children suffering from developmental delays in both cognitive and motor-skill areas. They hold special study sessions after school and on weekends in preparation for SAT and exit competency exams. Older adults visit, teach, and reassure "home-bound" and handicapped youngsters, and they give all students ideal adult role models. (p. 374)

Tutoring programs take place during the school day, after school, or during the summer.

Often, volunteers tutor students who have special needs. For example, they work with special education and emotionally disturbed students. In one Florida program, volunteers assist "self-motivated students in grades 1-6 to develop problem-solving skills and creative thinking" (Michael, 1990, p. 62).

Curriculum Enrichment

Experts can bring valuable insight into the classroom from their experience in the field. For example, schools "recruit working and retired scientists and engineers, most of whom are not certified as teachers, to volunteer in science and math classrooms or in after-school activities—usually on a part time or one time basis" (Fox, 1986, p. 5). Volunteers share "ballet, music, weaving, crochet, theater, painting, pottery, sculpting, and other specialized arts, crafts, and hobbies" (Carter, 1992, p. 374). Through presentations and discussions, schools use volunteers to share their travel experiences and knowledge of foreign languages. Furthermore, volunteers "work with students on poetry, short stories, and letters, to supplement the creative writing curriculum" (Michael, 1990, p. 62). For example, "one volunteer, 'Story-teller Bob,' combines books with unique costumes to spark interest in young listeners and readers, thereby inspiring improved reading and verbal skills" (p. 374). In Milton, Massachusetts, Collicot School organized "Read Aloud Week" where 100 community volunteers "gave more than 50 enthusiastic hours so that each classroom would have at least one visiting reader every day" (Griffin, 1988, p. 57).

In addition, "older volunteers can enliven a classroom by offering new and unique perspectives to traditional topics" (Lipson, 1994, p. 1). For instance, "elders can bring a wide range of life experiences along with a longer and broader historical perspective to the classroom" (Tierce & Seelbach, 1987, p. 35). In fact, they

> can be a living history lesson. What was it like to live through the Depression or the Holocaust, to participate in civil rights marches or anti-war demonstrations, to fight in Vietnam, to visit a divided Berlin, to watch the Watergate investigation unfolding, to live through a major event in your town's history? (Hansen & Mackey, 1993, p. 30)

On a more basic level, volunteers "train students in study techniques, such as organizing, planning, alphabetizing, and locating information; test taking; and memory devices" (Michael, 1990, p. 62). They are used to monitor students using computers and provide "drill and practice using flash cards" (Strom & Strom, 1994, p. 330). In a Washington, DC, school, a federal judge visits weekly to quiz fifth graders on "general-knowledge questions" (Michael, 1990, p. 88). Meanwhile, "a brokerage firm has developed a stock market program using math and reading skills; children follow the progress of stocks in daily newspapers, plan investment strategies, and make or lose 'money.' At the end of the year, the firm provides each child one share of stock" (p. 88).

Vocational and Technical Programs

Through in-class demonstrations, visits to construction sites, and internships, students learn from volunteer carpenters, painters, plumbers, brick masons, mechanics, and electricians. In some instances, students participate in year-long projects where houses are built or cars are restored (Carter, 1992).

With the focus on school-to-work, many partnership programs involve schools forming alliances with businesses. For example, career academies train students for specific occupations such as electrical science, computers, health care, and financial services (Dayton, Raby, Stern, & Weisberg, 1992).

Businesses provide mentors and summer internships for these academies' students, opportunities for teachers to keep their skills current, and equipment. In addition, companies may help manage the career academies (Pauly, Kopp, & Haimson, 1994).

Career Exploration

By explaining and discussing their careers, volunteers can provide students with information on opportunities and prerequisites for entering their chosen fields. Through presentations and demonstrations, volunteers are called upon to provide students with information on the skills required, the benefits and liabilities of the career choice, and the potential opportunities in the field (Hunter, 1989). For example, "retired physicians, dentists, nurses, engineers, researchers, teachers, and professors share their wisdom and expertise in classrooms as daily visitors, guest lecturers, substitutes, or mentors. One retired horticulturalist teaches science and, together with a retired contractor, builds greenhouses for schools" (Carter, 1992, p. 374). Likewise, "a chemist can provide fascinating, 'real-world' information for chemistry students, an editor for English students, and so forth. At the high-school level, you might also give students tips on preparing resumes and interviewing for entry-level jobs" (Hansen & Mackey, 1993, p. 28). Furthermore, volunteers offer internships to students or opportunities for teachers to learn more about the areas they teach through job "shadowing" (p. 31).

Cultural Awareness

By sharing their unique cultures, volunteers can bring a heightened sense of cultural awareness to the classroom. Through presentations and activities, volunteers can teach about their culture's history, customs, art, music, and contributions to society (Hunter, 1989). Volunteers are called upon to "share a foreign language or discuss another country" (Batey, 1996, p. 49). Furthermore, "by employing a common theme—for example, the native American—history, geography, science, anthropology, and archaeology can be intertwined with dance, music, art, and culture" (Carter, 1992, p. 374). With volunteers as chaperones, "history and geography are exciting, thanks to field trips to museums, monuments, displays, ships, trains, planes, and battlefields" (p. 374).

Intergenerational Exposure

A benefit of older volunteers is the exposure that it provides children to senior citizens. Lipson (1994) notes, "An intergenerational program can also fill a personal gap left by the decline of the extended family" (p. 1). An Ann Arbor, Michigan, "program emphasizes development of relationships across generations, with the major goal of enhancing the self-esteem of both volunteers and students. The major focus is on working with youths who are at risk of dropping out" (Michael, 1990, p. 46).

Counseling

Through counseling and guidance programs, volunteers "spend time listening to and communicating with young people" (Carter, 1992, p. 374). They serve as "adult friends, typically spending 30 minutes a week with students, one to one" (Michael, 1990, p. 62), "offering encouragement to troubled children" (Strom & Strom, 1994, p. 330). Volunteers "provide college, career, and vocational counseling and assist students and families with scholarship and loan applications" (Carter, 1992, p. 374). In Contra Costa County, California, students in detention centers or under court jurisdiction receive special attention from volunteers when they need "someone to listen, to care, and to help" (Michael, 1990, p. 57). At one Oklahoma elementary school where the working middle-class parents do not have as much time as they might like to spend with their children, a partnership has been formed with a local college. College students walk over to the school "to talk with their young friends, walk with them on the school grounds, or help with a school project" (p. 84).

Homework Assistance

For many volunteers, their involvement in education begins when the school day ends and students need assistance with their homework. In Chicago, the public schools in conjunction with a local newspaper operate the *Homework Hotline* on which "volunteers answer students' telephone questions about homework on all subjects, [with] the majority of calls concern[ing] language arts and mathematics" (Michael, 1990, p. 53). Operating the line Monday through Thursday evenings, volunteers include current and retired teachers and professionals who come by after leaving work. Meanwhile, Dade County, Florida, "volunteers provide after-school enrichment in math, science, social studies, communication, physical education, and computers" (Michael, 1990, p. 62).

Extracurricular Activities

Schools also often call upon volunteers to assist with extracurricular activities. Besides serving as an assistant coach or staff member to a sports team, they "sponsor or help with a special interest club, such as making videos, puppetry, needlework, computers, stamp or coin collecting, chess, poetry, doll making, carpentry, gardening, rocks and minerals, photography, or dance" (Hansen & Mackey, 1993, p. 29). Volunteers "provide advice to students working on a school newspaper, literary magazine, or yearbook" (p. 32). In addition, "volunteers accompany students to cultural events, as well as advise drama clubs, bands, singers, musicians, and artists. Behind-the-scenes production, direction, lighting, makeup, and wardrobe design require time, patience, and special technical skills" (Carter, 1992, p. 374).

Support Functions

Volunteers play a vital role in supplementing the efforts of staff and administrators. They assist teachers and staff with clerical duties, care for the school facility, provide technological expertise, provide safety and health services, and donate supplies.

Instructional Support

Volunteers "can be a part-time or full-time classroom aide and assist teachers by preparing and organizing class materials, checking tests, keeping records, collecting papers, distributing materials, giving make-up tests, and working with student's projects" (Hansen & Mackey, 1993, p. 29). They grade papers, serve as room parents and chaperones, supervise the lunchroom and playground, prepare bulletin boards (Michael, 1990).

Clerical Work

Through clerical support, volunteers can assist the school staff. Thus, "burgeoning clerical tasks in the school office, classroom, and library are eased, and volunteers perform labor-intensive work with name-tag preparation, displays, and bulletin boards" (Carter, 1992, p. 374). Volunteers may interpret for parents who do not speak English, provide orientation for new students, or phone parents to inform them of school activities. Furthermore, they assist in monitoring the cafeteria, "enrollment and pre-enrollment work, answering telephones, attendance monitoring, high school registration, filing, typing, [and] duplication" (Michael, 1990, p. 66).

Physical Plant

With many of the nation's school facilities in need of repair, volunteers are a ready source of labor. For example, "after a hurricane destroyed playground facilities at one school, a grandfather and his son donated time and materials to build a new and improved structure. Landscaping and planting around neighborhood schools is often done *gratis* by older and more experienced gardeners" (Carter, 1992, p. 374). In addition, volunteers enhance the interior of school buildings by providing decorations and painting murals.

Library Staff

Many schools are expanding their library services through volunteer support. For example, a Bloomington, Indiana, school library's half-time paid librarian is supported by ten mothers who volunteer their time and efforts (DiSilvestro & DiSilvestro, 1985b). Elsewhere, volunteers process and shelve books, create bulletin boards, and organize reading and story-telling programs (Michael, 1990).

Technological Expertise

Faced with the rapid rise of technology, schools are turning to volunteers to provide computer and technical experience. With many teachers and administrators lacking computer expertise, proficient volunteers "can provide computer instruction for students or teachers, help the school decide what hardware and software to buy, or help set up systems" (Hansen & Mackey, 1993, p. 29). Widely publicized, NetDay96 prepared many of California's schools for accessing the internet. Parents, engineers and politicians were among the more than 20,000 people who volunteered to lay six million feet of cable in 5,000 schools (West, 1996). With similar programs now in more than 30 states, schools are realizing economic benefits. In Maryland, a three-day Net Weekend attracted 8,000 volunteers to install wiring in over 500 public schools. If the schools had paid for these services, it would have cost an estimated $5 million (Trotter, 1996).

Security
   To address concerns about violence and crime, schools are turning to volunteers "to help students feel more secure during school hours" (Rowicki & Martin, 1994, p. 4). A Florida volunteer program uses audiovisual materials to help primary and elementary school students learn how to react to strangers. Volunteers assist with "safety patrol meetings, monitoring on buses, assisting with loading and unloading buses" (Michael, 1990, p. 67), "patrolling parking lots, and providing supervision at before- and after-school activities" (Stephens, 1996, pp. 17-18). In addition, volunteers are used to control crowds during athletic events (Thorne, 1983).

Health Programs
   Volunteers also provide assistance in school clinics and work with health screenings (Michael, 1990). Health care professionals can teach CPR or "give talks on sex education, nutrition, and other health-related topics" (Hansen & Mackey, 1993, p. 30). At Dallas's Health Special High School, "five different sets of volunteers provide a variety of support services to the school and its pregnant students. Volunteers help with intake interviews and clinic and child care services and help the girls resolve problems so they can continue their education after the birth of their babies" (Michael, 1990, p. 67). With schools looking to combat drugs, volunteers "help by assisting school personnel to set up and run a drug and alcohol awareness program" (Hansen & Mackey, 1993, p. 30).

Advisory and Advocacy Activities

Although parents have long been involved in parent-teacher organizations, volunteers are becoming increasingly involved in advisory and advocacy functions. These include opportunities to make school decisions, perform public relations tasks, raise funds, and coordinate other volunteers.

Decision Making
   An expanding area of volunteer involvement, focused primarily on parents,

is site-based decision making (see Murphy & Beck, 1995). Volunteers "serve on participatory management team[s], parent-teacher advisory board[s], or school improvement team[s]" (Batey, 1996, p. 50). They sit on school committees and organizations or "stand up for students' rights in appropriate meetings and forums" (p. 50). In addition, "parents help evaluate how well school programs work, help decide on school budget expenditures, and assist in the development of school and district policies and programs" (Burns, 1993, p. 18).

Public Relations

Volunteers build bridges between the school, the community, and business-es. They may be recruited to publicize activities, prepare and edit newsletters, and to "act as host or hostess to guests visiting the school" (Batey, 1996, p. 50). In Dade County, Florida, *"Ambassadors for Public Education* volunteers serve as a communication link between the principal and the community by keeping local businesses and organizations abreast of school activities" (Michael, 1990, p. 62). Meanwhile, Positive Parents of Dallas, a PTA subgroup, "concentrates on pro-viding information to the media" (p. 17).

Fund Raising and Donation of Supplies

Constantly searching for new sources of funds, many schools are delegating responsibility for fund raising to volunteers. They organize bake sales, car wash-es, general stores, and special events. Increasingly, volunteers request donations and grants on behalf of the school (Batey, 1996). As an alternative means of par-ticipation, volunteers can "provide money for students who aren't able to afford field trips" (p. 50).

With limited budgets, schools always need additional supplies not provided for in their budgets. Thus, volunteers "save supplies for math, science, art, or social studies (such as buttons, fabric, yarns, pop bottles, socks, rocks, and tooth picks)" (Batey, 1996, p. 49). Furthermore, they can "sew curtains, chair covers, and so on—make things that may be needed in the school" (p. 49). Frequently, business and industry have surplus products and goods that they are unable to use or sell. Thus, the National Association for the Exchange of Industrial Resources matches excess equipment and supplies held by corporations with schools that can utilize them. In the past 20 years, they have redistributed over $500 million worth of goods to schools and other nonprofit organizations ("The Secret Behind Donated Supplies," 1995).

Volunteer Coordination

With the growth of organized programs, volunteers serve as organizers of vol-unteer efforts. They are involved in "recruitment, placement, volunteer record-keeping, [and] recognition" (Michael, 1990, p. 67). This may include communicating with volunteers and assisting with volunteer program activities. Furthermore, volunteers can provide transportation for "other people in your community, especially senior citizens, who would be glad to help out in the schools if they only had some way to get there" (Hansen & Mackey, 1993, p. 32).

EFFECTS

While the effects of volunteer programs are widely chronicled through anecdotal evidence that is mostly speculative in nature, there is limited empirical research on outcomes (Michael, 1990). In part, this may be expected because "good evaluation is expensive, and few local school systems have the staff or resources to conduct research. It is usually difficult to justify evaluation expenditures for a 'free' or 'low-cost' activity such as a volunteer program" (p. 37). Of the existing studies, many relate to tutoring and are limited in scope and design. However, in a review of the literature, the Committee on the Use of Volunteers in Schools "was impressed that findings about the effects of school volunteers in the reported research were almost uniformly positive. Conversely, almost nothing indicated negative effects resulting from volunteer use in the schools" (p. 40).

Schools

Although the use of volunteers in non-instructional areas apparently has not been studied, "data on school volunteerism suggest that it accounts for many thousands of volunteer hours each year" (Michael, 1990, p. 37). Burns (1993) notes, "Although children, families, teachers, and schools benefit individually, their partnership enhances the entire process of education" (p. 9). Through the efforts of volunteers, the school climate is improved. As "schools reach out to involve parents, family attitudes toward the school become more positive" (p. 10). The safety of the school as a place of learning is enhanced, because "most times the sight of an adult will be sufficient deterrence for a child contemplating some type of misbehavior" (Michael, 1990, p. 4).

Volunteers often leave schools with "a deep and profound respect for the professional competence required to teach in a way to accelerate learning" (Hunter, 1989, p. 41). From a public relations perspective, "a spirit of cooperation and involvement grows at a time when many citizens might feel alienated from the public schools" (Otterbourg, cited in Decker & Decker, 1988, p. 19). As their involvement and concern for public schools increase, better communication is fostered among citizens, students, schools, and business. In addition, "community members' awareness increases, especially concerning the needs of schools and, more specifically, concerning the support and community resources available and necessary to help meet those needs" (p. 19). Older volunteers have the opportunity to influence the political environment for education in a given community. With more retirees than younger voters in some areas, "the impressions older adults have about the state of education often determine whether school bond issues pass or fail. Grandparent volunteers who observe the hard work and success of students and teachers can be influential in informing their peers about school needs and achievements" (Strom & Strom, 1994, p. 334).

For schools, "opportunities arise to access previously unknown but available resources from the private sector and community organizations" (Otterbourg, cited in Decker & Decker, 1988, p. 18). With community and business partnership programs, "schools are gaining much-needed pragmatic support as businesses come forward to donate or loan equipment and supplies and share employees and executives to help with school management" (Baas, 1990, p. 1).

Nevertheless, volunteer programs are not a cure-all for school problems. Sewall (1990) notes that "well-meaning people outside education—including policymakers—often assume that volunteers provide magical added benefits to schools and thereby ensure school improvement" (p. 22). However, "volunteers act at the margin of the curriculum, and they have no formal disciplinary power" (p. 22). Instead, by assisting with the instructional process and relieving the teacher from time-consuming clerical tasks, they can be a resource for teachers.

Teachers

A volunteer program "positively affects the structure and operation of classrooms...[and] the teaching practices of teachers" (Michael, 1990, p. 36). Among the benefits of school volunteer programs, "teachers and staff perceive increased 'caring' in people and organizations outside the schools, and increased communication and trust between education and the private sector" (Otterbourg, cited in Decker & Decker, 1988, p. 18). As one means of relieving teachers of burdensome tasks, volunteers have an opportunity "to improve teacher morale and create a positive climate for teaching" (Potter, 1995, p. 1). Thus, "the time that teachers do not have to devote to supervising students outside the classroom can be spent planning and preparing" (p. 1). Thus, teachers are freed to develop new curricula and tailor instruction to student needs. Streit (cited in Michael, 1990) found that a Michigan volunteer program resulted in improved teacher effectiveness. As one junior high teacher said after a volunteer program relieved her of routine tasks, "They have helped me to be a more effective teacher" (Powell, 1986, p. 33). Furthermore, partnership programs enable businesses to "help teachers upgrade or develop new skills and learn about the labor market in their fields" (Baas, 1990, p. 1).

Another benefit for teachers is a better understanding of their students and families. When parents volunteer, "teachers gain an understanding of families' cultures, needs, goals, and capabilities. They also learn that parents can offer valuable resources, skills, talents, and creativity that can enrich teaching and learning" (Burns, 1993, p. 10).

Students

As the focus of most volunteer programs, students have been found to benefit in numerous ways.

> Most valuable of all, perhaps, has been the individual help which volunteers have been able to give to children who were dropping behind in reading or other subjects. In these cases the regular time and continuing interest and encouragement given to the individual child by the volunteer—a friendly adult—have supplied what the teacher of a large class could not possibly give and have over and over again changed the attitude of the child from apathy, discouragement and rebellion to interest, self-confidence and enthusiasm. (Nichols, 1961, pp. x–xi)

Research indicates that volunteer tutoring programs lead to improved academic performance. In a review of studies on tutoring, Michael (1990) reports:

> Almost all reported academic gains for tutored students greater than those for students who were not tutored or greater than would otherwise have been expected for the tutored students. In no instance did researchers report negative effects on academic performance. (p. 32)

In a study involving 147 students receiving tutoring from older citizens matched with a control group from the same classrooms not receiving tutoring, Cooledge and Wurster (1985) found "that those students tutored by retirees made significantly greater gains in reading than similar students who did not have the extra assistance" (p. 345). Hedin (1987) reports that peer or cross-age tutors may be more effective than adult tutors. In 45 of 52 studies, Cohen, Kulik, and Kulik (1982) found that students tutored by other students demonstrated higher academic achievement than control students. Moreover, volunteer programs appear to be effective in improving language arts and problem-solving skills and foreign-language proficiency (Michael, 1990).

Besides academic benefits, tutoring results in "increased confidence and self-esteem on the part of students. In the case of peer and cross-age tutoring, both academic and psychological benefits were reported for the tutors as well" (Michael, 1990, p. 32). For example, "students' learning horizons are expanded, particularly in their awareness of the worlds of work, science, technology, and the arts as well as in their awareness of the relationship of school work to employment" (Otterbourg, cited in Decker & Decker, 1988, p. 18). In addition, "students learn that adults care, develop increased self-confidence, and receive important encouragement to stay in school, seek training after high school, and secure employment after graduation" (p. 18). With seniors as volunteers, students benefit from "individual attention, getting to know people outside their age group, and learning that older people care about them" (Strom & Strom, 1994, p. 333). In addition, "elderly school volunteers can help dispel many pathological myths surrounding aging, later life, and the elderly" (Tierce & Seelbach, 1987, p. 35). For handicapped students, volunteer programs have recorded improved academic skills, greater self-esteem, improved gross motor abilities from an exercise program, and the chance to be mainstreamed (Michael, 1990).

Other "effects include attitudinal changes in students, measured in terms of classroom behavior, attendance, or staying in school" (Michael, 1990, p. 35). A Washington, DC, program designed to bring mathematicians and scientists into the classroom resulted in students reporting an increased interest in studying math and science and pursuing a career in those fields (Federal City Council, 1987, in Michael, 1990). Stephens (1996) notes, "Recent studies show that most young people believe adults play a major role in counseling and encouraging kids toward non-violence" (p. 17).

Volunteers

Research on the effects of volunteerism on volunteers themselves is mixed: "A number of studies have linked volunteering with better health, improved life satisfaction, and increased social ties. Other studies, however, have failed to demonstrate such effects from volunteering. Taken together, *the research on the benefits to volunteers is inconclusive*" (Fischer & Schaffer, 1993, p. 186).

Some research has "shown that participation in meaningful parent-involvement programs can improve parents' self-image, increase their respect for teachers and schools, and give them increased confidence in their ability to help their children succeed in school" (Burns, 1993, p. 10). In a random sample of volunteers and adults who wanted to volunteer but had not been given the opportunity, Harty (1984) reported that volunteers exhibit a higher self-concept and "a greater internal locus of control (more self-motivating) than did non-volunteers" (p. 15). Typical volunteer reactions are: "When I'm typing exams, I find myself answering the questions. I'm really amazed at how many I'm able to answer. It's funny, but I've gained confidence in myself and I find myself taking on things I would not have done before doing volunteer work" (a parent volunteer, cited in Powell, 1986, p. 32). "I have a master's in math and have taught school. However, since the birth of my children, I have stayed home. Now that they are in school, I felt a need to do something useful, but did not want a full-time job. I now tutor students in math and really enjoy it" (a parent tutor, cited in Powell, 1986, pp. 32-33). Parents' "involvement in and positive attitudes toward public education increase as they see their children benefiting from partnership programs" (Otterbourg, cited in Decker & Decker, 1988, p. 19).

For senior citizens, "volunteering allows them to help others, remain productive, and feel useful" (Bruner et al., 1992, cited in Strom & Strom, 1994, p. 334; see also Okun, 1994). Volunteering may be helpful for people experiencing changes in their lives as they grow older: "It appears that an important, direct benefit from volunteering is generativity: a feeling of fulfillment because someone else is benefiting, a sense of connectedness to others, and a sense of meaning and purpose" (Fischer & Schaffer, 1993, p. 192). For example, "talking with students promotes new ideas, encourages optimism, and reduces loneliness. The mental stimulation of an academic environment can also improve memory. Since failures in memory are closely associated with growing old, people usually assume that nothing can be done about it" (Strom & Strom, 1994, p. 334).

Regarding students as volunteers, the research indicates that they may not benefit. For example, Arkell (1975) reported that the "student-helper roles of tutor, clerical worker, and audio-visual operator [were] ineffective in changing students' self-esteem, attitude toward school, performance in spelling and achievement in arithmetic" (p. 115).

As a result of school partnership programs, businesses are often "portrayed in a more favorable light, and the publicity they receive reinforces corporate and organizational efforts in the area of community relations, particularly community service" (Otterbourg, cited in Decker & Decker, 1988, p. 18). Furthermore, "as awareness of educational problems increases, businesses gain a greater appreciation of schools' strengths and weaknesses and, in some cases, experience the satisfaction of successfully addressing problems through combined efforts" (p. 18).

OVERCOMING BARRIERS

Putting volunteers into classrooms to help teachers sounds good, but as administrators might well tell you, not everyone will welcome the idea. (Goetter, 1987, p. 34)

Barriers to the creation and sustained success of organized school volunteer programs may come from all sides. These include internal and external pressures.

Schools

Resistance From Administrators
Without support from administrators, the long-term survival of a volunteer program is in doubt. Indeed, "support from 'the top down' sustains success in most corporate structures" (Goetter et al., 1987, p. 56). However, "principals aren't always thrilled at the idea of extra supervisory duties" (Goetter, 1987, p. 34). Support can be demonstrated through written documents, regulations, and public pronouncements (Michael, 1990). Even when administrators may be supportive of volunteer programs, they may place heavy restrictions on them. In Washington, DC, the school board enacted specific rules regarding the utilization of school volunteers. They are prohibited from performing:

"Any function or service that is currently being performed by an employee" and voluntary services or their availability are not [to be] used as a basis for "reduction

in force" of school personnel. Volunteers are required to sign a statement acknowledging that they have been informed of the nature and scope of the voluntary services to be performed and of the board's regulations, especially those concerning
confidentiality, conflict of interest, liability protection, and political activity.
(Michael, 1990, p. 87)

District funding and support are essential to the sustained success of a school
volunteer program. For instance, in addition to funding a district-level volunteer
coordinator, the Spokane school system provides public relations for the program and funds for volunteer training workshops. However, administrative support should not necessitate a highly centralized program. In diverse urban areas,
it is important that schools have a high degree of flexibility to adapt programs to
the needs of their students (Goetter et al., 1987). The school coordinators recruit
volunteers and are "responsible for orienting, training, and placing volunteers in
that building, as well as collecting and forwarding data on hours worked and services performed and working with teachers to evaluate the program" (Michael,
1990, p. 93).

Resistance From Teachers

Although more cordial towards volunteers than in the past, "the typical
school remains warily protective of its professional prerogatives and maintains a
careful (often subtle) distancing between parental involvement and teachers'
work roles" (Crowson, 1992, p. 186). Indeed, "some teachers consider volunteers [to be] classroom intruders" (Goetter, 1987, p. 34) or spies (Goetter et al.,
1987). Sometimes, "well-meaning administrators impose volunteers on teachers,
who feel the burden of yet another task assigned to them. Involving teachers
early in the process and at appropriate stages, will help relieve that burden"
(Lipson, 1994, p. 1). A volunteer program "may represent a threat to many staff
members. [However,] if it does not create a level of discomfort, then it probably
is not a substantive change effort" (Fisher, 1994, p. 73). Furthermore, "care must
be taken not to dominate this [volunteer] movement, but to provide collaboration in reaching a destination" (Fisher, 1994, p. 72). Michael (1990) "notes that
teachers are more likely to welcome and use volunteers when the principal's
support is clear and enthusiastic" (p. 93). To avoid fears and to provide reassur-
ance, teachers "who are directly affected by school volunteers must have a voice
in program decisions from the start" (Gray, 1982, p. 5).

A participant in the NEA School Renewal Network noted, "A lot of excuses
can be given for not wanting parents in the classroom, but I have to believe that
the real reason in most cases is the teachers' lack of belief in themselves" (cited
in Burns, 1993, p. 11).

Some teachers are concerned that parents will encroach upon their areas of
responsibility and will not follow instructions and school regulations, particularly

in regard to their confidentiality. They are afraid parents will cause confusion and disrupt the classroom. Others fear that parents may cause trouble if they see something in the classroom they don't like. (p. 12)

Teachers need training and support to involve parents effectively. Although teachers may be resistant to outsiders in the classroom, organizers should help them "realize how much more individual attention can be given to the children with just one more adult there to help. Activities no longer have to be limited to the classroom, and the variety of skills and experiences that parents can bring to the children are limited [only] by the number of parents [and other volunteers]" (Miller & Wilmshurst, 1984, p. 1). Cuninggim (1980) notes:

School volunteer programs succeed when teachers really want the help of volunteers and when they and the volunteers become coworkers and effective partners on the educational team. Since volunteers work at the request of a teacher and under the direction of a teacher or school staff member, much of the thinking and planning that makes the teacher-volunteer partnership effective must be done by the teacher. (p. 110)

Closely working with teachers, "successful volunteer programs try to deal with the issue of teacher participation by providing orientation to the objectives and potential of a volunteer program, not only by volunteers but also for teachers and other school staff" (Michael, 1990, p. 95).

As long as volunteers remain under the supervision of teachers and do not replace staff, national teacher unions appear to be receptive to volunteers. However, local union leaders may have dissenting opinions (Michael, 1990).

Inadequate Preparation for Use of Volunteers

A major inhibitor of volunteer programs is "poor coordination or sloppy management, lack of adequate orientation and screening, and confusion over objectives" (Michael, 1990, p. 99). For schools, "knowing how to involve parents remains a big puzzle" (Batey, 1996, p. xiii). As Goetter (1987) notes, "Even if you overcome objections, you might find it difficult to keep volunteers coming back" (p. 34). If people volunteer their time and services, "it's crucial that good use be made of their time" (Katz, 1983, p. 29). It is important to prepare the school for volunteers. As with most programs, successful school programs begin "on a limited basis" (Schreter, 1991, p. 36). The success of a program will generate interest among others through "word-of-mouth recommendations by teachers and principals" (Goetter et al., 1987, p. 58). In addition, volunteers can be recruited through brochures, signs, and local media.

Before a school initiates an organized volunteer program, an assessment should be conducted to determine the school's needs and what the program should try to accomplish (DiSilvestro & DiSilvestro, 1985a). Thus, "key administrators and other decision makers, whose influence and support can make the program successful, should be identified, informed of the project, and involved as much as possible in order to build institutional support" (Lipson, 1994, p. 1). Indeed, "for volunteers to be properly utilized in the school, they must be assigned to teachers who have requested their services" (Taranto & Johnson, 1984, p. 53).

In small programs, responsibility for volunteers may be assigned to the principal or a volunteer coordinator. However, large programs require additional planning and supervision. Unless there is a paid coordinator or director, "the program lacks direction" (Criscuolo, 1985, p. 9). Successful programs have a manager with access to the school principal or superintendent. With organized school volunteer programs, "the coordination responsibilities are often part of the duties of a systemwide director of community relations or community education when such a position exists" (Decker & Decker, 1988, p. 4). This "volunteer coordinator acts as a liaison among the administrators, teachers, and volunteers and relieves teachers of some of the responsibilities inherent in the operation of a volunteer program" (p. 4). In some cases, nonprofit organizations organize and manage volunteer programs (Michael, 1990).

For a clearer understanding between volunteers and school officials, it is important that volunteers have a written job description. It should include where they will work, their duties, schedule, and any other considerations that may be involved (Buffer, 1980; Lipson, 1994). Volunteers' skills, psychological needs, and motivations can be matched with school needs (Clary, Snyder, & Ridge, 1992). To foster effectiveness and feedback, it is important that volunteer programs be evaluated on a regular basis (Fisher, 1994; Taranto & Johnson, 1984). Evaluation "must be built in from the start and put to use" (Gray, 1982, p. 6). Procedures should be in place to resolve conflicts.

Possible Negative Consequences

The use of volunteers is sometimes inhibited in schools and school systems because of three potential negative consequences: inequities, costs, and legal problems. One barrier to the increased use of volunteers is the inequities that may be created within a school system. Since many volunteer programs are organized not at a district basis but at the school level, "it is possible that some schools in well-to-do areas, possibly those with well-informed or knowledgeable parents, are more likely to use volunteers than schools in poorer areas. If so, how expanded use of volunteers could be implemented so that it does not increase inequity between schools is a question for research" (Michael, 1990, p. 40).

Although by their very nature, "it is assumed that school volunteers are a low-cost, even free resource, little attention has been paid to the 'cost-benefit ratio' of volunteer programs. Generally, it is assumed that the value of volunteer services far exceeds the administrative and other costs associated with such programs" (Michael, 1990, p. 41). Nevertheless, there is little evidence to support this. Large programs require a paid volunteer coordinator and more administrative attention. These programs, indeed, mean greater costs, but these are funds "that are repaid in many ways several times over, but hard dollars nevertheless" (Gray, 1982, p. 3).

In today's litigious climate, it is necessary for volunteers to be covered by liability insurance. In some cases, state laws extend coverage to volunteers as it does to teachers and staff. Otherwise, school systems obtain the same coverage from their insurance companies (Lipson, 1994). Likewise, volunteers may need to be tested for tuberculosis. The local health department may be willing to visit the schools to screen for this disease (Lipson, 1994).

Volunteers

As important as the barriers within the schools to organized volunteer programs, there are also numerous roadblocks on the participants' side. Despite a desire to be involved in the school, many parents and other interested individuals are reluctant to volunteer unless invited by the school.

Previous School Experiences

For many parents and other potential volunteers, remembering their own school experiences makes them reluctant to become involved. In fact, "schools sometimes contribute to these negative responses by calling on parents only when their children have problems. If parents faced similar difficulties when they were in school, the negative feelings are reinforced" (Burns, 1993, p. 12). In low socioeconomic areas, these problems may be exacerbated by extended families, frequent relocations, and lack of telephones. These "mental barriers must be addressed before schools can expect to reach out" (Jennings, 1992, p. 65). Still others feel that they do not have the necessary skills or knowledge to become involved. Thus, schools should demonstrate to potential volunteers "that their involvement and support make a great deal of difference, and that they need not be highly educated or have large amounts of free time for their involvement to be beneficial" (Burns, 1993, p. 13). Principals and teachers must extend a warm welcome to volunteers (Batey, 1996).

Successful programs offer volunteers a wide range of options for involvement (Gray, 1982). They "need to be able to choose from a continuum of activities that accommodate different schedules, preferences, and capabilities" (Burns, 1993, p. 17). Care needs to be taken not to overburden volunteers (Goetter et al., 1987). Furthermore, they "won't continue to volunteer if they can't find a parking space at school, aren't recognized by teachers when they enter school, or are made to wait in the principal's office until someone can identify why they're there. Worse: A parent arrives to find the teacher didn't expect him at that time" (DiSilvestro & DiSilvestro, 1985a, p. 27). Periodically, assignments should be assessed to insure that volunteers and teachers are compatible (Tierce & Seelbach, 1987, p. 40). Clary and associates (1992) note, "Functional theory suggests that volunteers will be satisfied with their involvement precisely to the extent that it meets their needs, goals, and motivations" (p. 345). Thus, periodic reassignments may be necessary.

Lack of Preparation

Volunteers may lack preparation for the tasks they are expected to perform. Thus, orientation and inservice programs are important (see Taranto & Johnson, 1984). School leaders, community agency workers, and post secondary institutions may be available to work with volunteers. Since participants are giving up their own time, lengthy lectures with technical jargon should be avoided in favor of brief sessions that include audiovisuals or field trips and volunteer handbooks (Buffer, 1980; Criscuolo, 1985; DiSilvestro & DiSilvestro, 1985a). Other inservice programs may focus on planning and delivering presentations (Hunter, 1989).

The establishment of professional standards can be critical to a volunteer program's sustained success. Spokane's Volunteer Program "requires and nurtures professionalism among volunteers. Professionalism builds trust and credibility, leads to increased referrals, honors the work of the volunteer, insures the health and safety of students and enhances the overall work environment" (Goetter et al., 1987, p. 58). Thus, volunteers apply for a position. If found inappropriate, they are not allowed to volunteer. They are expected to keep their time commitments and follow the teacher's guidelines. For volunteers who have not been employed, the Spokane program provides essential job skills training (Goetter et al., 1987).

Lack of Ownership

In a study of the Spokane Volunteer Program, Goetter and associates (1987) cite neighborhood ownership as crucial to the continuing success of volunteer efforts. With the expansion of volunteer programs, "a cadre of supportive educators, volunteers and former volunteers" (p. 57) develop. In each school, a volunteer coordinator serves as a liaison between the district's paid coordinator and the school and between the school and volunteers. As a mediator, this volunteer coordinator pairs volunteers' abilities and skills with the needs of teachers, in addition to resolving complaints and problems (Goetter et al., 1987). Volunteers should be involved in a program's steering committee (DiSilvestro & DiSilvestro, 1985a).

Lack of Rewards

Volunteer programs may falter if benefits accrue only to the school and to students. It is important to recognize and foster rewards that benefit volunteers. Recognition for volunteer efforts may be as simple as cards or notes from children, small gifts, or an appreciation banquet. In addition, programs should provide opportunities for volunteers to acquire new skills and develop their talents. Educational offerings might include computer training and invitations to professional inservice programs. For those who have been out of the work force for some time, volunteering allows them to "ease" back in (Goetter et al., 1987).

Lack of Transportation

For senior citizens and lower socioeconomic volunteers, a lack of transportation can be a major barrier to school involvement. With limited incomes, the cost of bus fare, if available, and lunch may be too expensive. Thus, some volunteer programs recruit other volunteers to provide transportation, use school buses, or provide a mileage allowance or bus fare (Lipson, 1994).

CONCLUSION

In this chapter, we examined volunteerism as a means of privatization in education. Through organized volunteer programs, unpaid workers perform school tasks that relieve the burden on teachers, administrators, and staff. Assessing the forces behind the volunteer movement, we then described the sources of volunteers and the roles that they are filling in schools. The effects of volunteerism on the schools, teachers, students, volunteers, and community partners were discussed. Finally, we provided strategies for overcoming barriers to successful volunteer programs.

Notes

[1] Parts of Chapters 1 and 2 were originally presented as the Division A Vice-Presidential invited address—*Privatization Policy: Framing the School Reform Debate Around Contracting Out*—at the 1996 meeting of the American Educational Research Association.

[2] Recently a number of analysts have begun to call into question the accuracy of claims that America's public schools are seriously troubled. See, for example, Berliner (1993), Berliner and Biddle (1995), and Jaeger (1992).

[3] Blaschke (1972) reminds us that an aborted attempt at performance contracting was first attempted in Gainesville, Georgia, in the late 1960s.

[4] While the National School Boards Association is keeping an open mind on the issue of contracting out educational services (Olson, 1994; Shannon, 1995), other educators and educational associations are less than enamored with the idea. A recent survey conducted by the National Association of Elementary School Principals found, for example, that 64 percent of the principals sampled disapproved of the strategy of private for-profit firms to help them educate students and operate schools (Miller, 1995, p. 7). Teacher unions, especially the National Educational Association, have also taken a dim view of contracting by EMOs (see Geiger, 1995; Shanker, 1994).

[5] AAEPP is located at N7425 Switzke Road, Watertown, WI 53094. The president of the Association is Chris Yelich. She can be reached by phone at (800) 252-3280 or FAX at (414) 699-8280.

[6] John McLaughlin can be reached by mail at The Education Investor, P.O. Box 6234, St. Cloud, MN 56302 or by phone or FAX at (612) 259-9319.

[7] None of the test data for the first year on the Turner initiative had been released when this chapter was written (phone discussion with William DeLoache, August 9, 1996).

[8] As noted earlier, a number of thoughtful analysts argue that claims about the massive failure of public education are overdrawn at best and inaccurate at worst (see especially Berliner & Biddle, 1995).

[9] The reader should not confuse the alternative "free schools" movement with the "freedom of choice" laws used by Southern states to avoid desegregation (See History, Court Cases, in this chapter).

[10] In an end note in *Politics, Markets, and America's Schools*, Chubb and Moe (1990) acknowledge that "the decline in SAT scores has, in fact, never been adequately explained" (p. 280).

[11] The multilingual choice program is a seven-year program in foreign language instruction that begins in sixth grade.

[12] It is important to note that deregulation is often accompanied by efforts to reduce the power and influence of federal agencies and district offices (Gursky, 1992; Pitsch, 1995; Schmidt, 1994a, 1995c) and state educational agencies (Harp, 1995a, 1995b; Lawton, 1995; Lindsay, 1995a, 1995c, 1995e; J. Richardson, 1995). At the federal level, in particular, but also at the state and local levels, deregulation is sometimes promoted through the use of block grants.

[13] Johnson (1994) studying the same phenomenon in South Carolina reached the opposite conclusion. In her study, deregulation led to changes on the margin at best.

[14] NAPE's figures are based on school districts having an average of 50 partnership programs per district. Its member districts report having 20 to 500 partnerships. Thus, if 51 percent of public school districts have partnership programs, the resulting product (7,650 districts with an average of 50 partners) would be 382,500 partnerships.

[15] Since volunteers may participate in more than one area, the numbers sum to more than 100 percent.

References

Achilles, C. M., & DuVall, L. (1994, August). *Society's tectonic plates will move: Will education's?* Paper presented at the annual conference of Professors of Educational Administration, Indian Wells, CA.

Alabama Code, § 16-28-1.2 et seq.

Alexander, L. (1986). Chairman's summary. In *Time for results: The governors' 1991 report on education* (pp. 2–7). Washington, DC: National Governors' Association.

American Enterprise Institute for Public Policy Research. (1970). *U.S. government finances: A 22-year perspective, 1950–1971.* Washington, DC: Author

American Federation of Teachers. (1994a). *The private management of public schools: An analysis of the EAI experience in Baltimore.* Washington, DC: Author.

American Federation of Teachers. (1994b). *EAI's mismanagement of federal education programs: The special education and Chapter I track records in Baltimore.* Washington, DC: Author.

American Federation of Teachers. (1995). *How private managers make money in public schools: Update on the EAI experiment in Baltimore.* Washington, DC: Author.

American Federation of Teachers. (1996). *Setting the record straight: Wrapup on the EAI experiment in Baltimore.* Washington, DC: Author.

Anderson, M. (1994, September). Homeschooling. In *Nashville Kids & Parents* (p. 1) [Pamphlet]. Nashville, TN: The Tennessean.

Angelis, J. (1990). Bringing old and young together. *Vocational Educational Journal, 65*(2), 19, 21.

Applebome, P. (1994a). Edison seeks distance from Whittle. *Network News and Views, 13*(12), 83–84. (Reprinted from *The New York Times*).

Applebome, P. (1994b). Class notes. *Network News and Views, 13*(12), 86. (Reprinted from *The New York Times*).

Applebome, P. (1995). New breed of teachers become entrepreneurs and roving innovators. *Network News & Views, 14*(7), 73–74. (reprinted from the *New York Times*, May 31, 1995).

Arkell, R. N. (1975). Are student-helpers helped? *Psychology in the Schools, 12*(1), 113–115.

Armengol, R. (1992). Getting older and getting better. *Phi Delta Kappan, 73*(6), 467–470.

Arons, S. (1981). *Value conflict between American families and American schools.* Amherst: Massachusetts University, National Institute of Education. (ERIC Document Reproduction Service No. ED 210 786).

Aronson, J. R., & Hilley, J. L. (1986). *Financing state and local government* (4th ed.). Washington, DC: Brookings Institution.

Ascher, K. (1991). The business of local government. In R. L. Kemp (Ed.), *Privatization: The provision of public services by the private sector* (pp. 297–304). Jefferson, NC: McFarland.

Association for Supervision and Curriculum Development. (1986, September). *School reform policy: A call for reason.* Alexandria, VA: Author.

Astuto, T. A. (1990, September). *Reinventing school leadership* (Working memo prepared for the Reinventing School Leadership Conference, pp. 1–5). Cambridge, MA: National Center for Educational Leadership.

Avenoso, K. (1995, April). Education Inc. *Network News and Views, 14*(4), 79–80.

Baas, A. (1990). The role of business in education. *ERIC Digest Series, 47.* (ERIC Document Reproduction Service No. ED 321 344).

Baber, W. F. (1987). Privatizing public management: The Grace Commission and its critics. In S. H. Hanke (Ed.), *Prospects for privatization. Proceedings of the Academy of Political Science* (Vol. 36, No. 3, pp. 153–163). Montpelier, VT: Capital City Press.

Bahl, R. (1984). *Financing state and local government in the 1980s.* New York: Oxford University Press.

Bailey, R. L. (1995). Macomb school has a new lesson plan: The corporate-run Edison project. *Network News & Views, 14*(11), 59–63.

Bailey, R. W. (1987). Uses and misuses of privatization. In S. H. Hanke (Ed.), *Prospects for privatization. Proceedings of the Academy of Political Science* (Vol. 36, No. 3, pp. 138–152). Montpelier, VT: Capital City Press.

Bailey, R. W. (1991). Uses and misuses. In R. L. Kemp (Ed.), *Privatization: The provision of public services by the private sector* (pp. 233–249). Jefferson, NC: McFarland.

Banathy, B. H. (1988). An outside-in approach to design inquiry in education. In Far West Laboratory for Educational Research and Development (Ed.), *The redesign of education: A collection of papers concerned with comprehensive educational reform* (Vol. 1, pp. 51–71). San Francisco: Far West Laboratory.

Barth, R. S. (1986). On sheep and goats and school reform. *Phi Delta Kappan, 68*(4), 293–296.

Barlett, D. L., & Steel, J. B. (1992). *America: What went wrong.* Kansas City, MO: Andrews & McNeel.

Batey, C. S. (1996). *Parents are lifesavers: A handbook for parent involvement in schools.* Thousand Oaks, CA: Corwin Press.

Bauman, P. C. (1996). *Governing education: Public sector reform or privatization.* Boston: Allyn and Bacon.

Beales, J. R. (1994). *Teachers, Inc.: A private-practice option for educators.* Los Angeles: Reason Foundation.

Beales, J. R., & O'Leary, J. O. (1993, November). *Making schools work: Contracting options for better management.* Los Angeles: Reason Foundation.

Beales, J. R., & Wahl, M. (1995). Private vouchers in Milwaukee: The PAVE program. In T. M. Moe (Ed.), *Private vouchers* (pp. 41–73). Stanford, CA: Hoover Institution Press.

Beare, H. (1989, September). *Educational administration in the 1990s.* Paper presented at the national conference of the Australian Council for Educational Administration, Armidale, New South Wales, Australia.

Beck, L. G., & Murphy, J. (1993). *Understanding the principalship: A metaphorical analysis, 1920–1990.* New York: Teachers College Press.

Becker, G. S. (1983). A theory of competition among pressure groups for political influence. *The Quarterly Journal of Economics, 98*(3), 371–400.

Beers, D., & Ellig, J. (1994). An economic view of the effectiveness of public and private schools. In S. Hakim, P. Seidenstat, & G. W. Bowman (Eds.), *Privatizing education and educational choice: Concepts, plans, and experiences* (pp. 19–38). Westport, CT: Praeger.

Bell, P., & Cloke, P. (1990). Concepts of privatisation and deregulation. In P. Bell & P. Cloke (Eds.), *Deregulation and transport: Market forces in the modern world* (pp. 3–27). London: David Fulton.

Benjamin, R. C. (1996). Forward. In C. S. Batey, *Parents are lifesavers: A handbook for parent involvement in schools* (p. ix). Thousand Oaks, CA: Corwin Press.

Bennett, D. (1994). Entrepreneurship: The road to salvation for public schools. *Education Leadership, 52*(1), 76–77.

Bennett, D. A. (1990). Choice and desegregation. In W. H. Clune & J. F. Witte (Eds.), *Choice and control in American education: Vol. 2. The practice of choice, decentralization and school restructuring* (pp. 125–152). London: Falmer Press.

Bennett, J. T., & DiLorenzo, T. J. (1987). In S. H. Hanke (Ed.), *Prospects for privatization. Proceedings of the Academy of Political Science* (Vol. 36, No. 3, pp. 14–23). Montpelier, VT: Capital City Press.

Bennett, J. T., & Johnson, M. H. (1980, October). Tax reduction without sacrifice: Private-public production of public services. *Public Finance Quarterly, 8*(4), 363–396.

Berliner, D. C. (1993, April). Mythology and the American system of education. *Phi Delta Kappan, 74*(8), 632–640.

Berliner, D. C., & Biddle, B. J. (1995). *The manufactured crisis: Myth, fraud, and the attack on America's public schools.* Reading, MA: Addison-Wesley.

Bernas, T. G. (1992, April). *Documenting the implementation of school based management/shared decision making in a non-Chapter 1 elementary school.* Paper presented at the annual meeting of the American Educational Research Association, San Francisco.

Berry, W. D., & Lowery, D. L. (1987). *Understanding United States government growth: An empirical analysis of postwar growth.* New York: Praeger.

Berube, M. R. (1994). *American school reform: Progressive, equity, and excellence movements, 1883–1983.* Westport, CT: Praeger.

Best, J. H. (1993). Perspectives on deregulation of schooling in America. *British Journal of Educational Studies, 41*(2), 122–133.

Bingham, J. (1996). The Edison Project: Reinventing school. *Network News & Views, 15*(6), 87–89.

Blaschke, C. (1972). *Performance contracting: Who profits most?* Bloomington, IN: The Phi Delta Kappa Educational Foundation.

Blumberg, A. (1985). *The school superintendent: Living with conflict.* New York: Teachers College Press.

Bolin, F. S. (1989, Fall). Empowering leadership. *Teachers College Record, 19*(1), 81–96.

Borcherding, T. E. (1977a). One hundred years of public spending, 1870–1970. In T. E. Borcherding (Ed.), *Budgets and bureaucrats: The sources of government growth* (pp. 19–44). Durham, NC: Duke University Press.

Borcherding, T. E. (1977b). The sources of growth of public expenditures in the United States, 1902–1970. In T. E. Borcherding (Ed.), *Budgets and bureaucrats: The sources of government growth* (pp. 45–70). Durham, NC: Duke University Press.

Bowers, B. C. (1990). *State efforts to deregulate education* (ERIC Digest Series No. EA 51). Eugene, OR: ERIC Clearinghouse on Educational Management.

Bowler, M. (1994). Sylvan project reaps results in pupil scores. *Network News & Views, 13*(10), 56.

Boyd, W. L. (1987, Summer). Public education's last hurrah? Schizophrenia, amnesia, and ignorance in school politics. *Educational Evaluation and Policy Analysis, 9*(2), 85–100.

Boyer, E. L. (1992). Forward. In Carnegie Foundation for the Advancement of Teaching, *School choice* (pp. xv-svii). Princeton NJ: Author.

Bradford, M. A., Malt, R. A., & Oates, E. (1969, June). The rising cost of local public service. *National Tax Journal, 22,* 185–202.

Bradley, A. (1995a). Heavy artillery weighs in as battle over control of Pa. district escalates. *Education Week, 14*(29), 6.

Bradley, A. (1995b). Public backing for schools is called tenuous. *Education Week, 15*(7), 1, 13.

Brazer, H. E. (1981). On tax limitation. In N. Walzer & D. L. Chicoine (Eds.), *Financing state and local governments in the 1980s.* Cambridge, MA: Oelgeschlager, Gunn & Hain.

Bridenbaugh, C. (1981). *Early America.* New York: Oxford University Press.

Brodinsky, B. (1993). How 'new' will the 'new' Whittle American school be? *Phi Delta Kappan, 74*(7), 540–547.

Brown, B. W. (1992). Why governments run schools. *Economics of Education Review, 11*(4), 287–300.

Brown, F. (1995) Privatization of public education: Themes and concepts. *Education and Urban Society, 27*(2), 114–126.

Brown, F., & Hunter, R. C. (1995). Introduction: Privatization of public school services. *Education and Urban Society, 27*(2), 107–113.

Brown, S. (1991). A cautionary note. In R. L. Kemp (Ed.), *Privatization: The provision of public services by the private sector* (pp. 272–275). Jefferson, NC: McFarland.

Brown v. Board of Education of Topeka, 347 U.S. 483 (1954).

Brudney, J. L. (1990). *Fostering volunteer programs in the public sector: Planning, initiating, and managing voluntary activities.* San Francisco: Jossey-Bass.

Buchanan, J. M. (1977). Why does government grow? In T. E. Borcherding (Ed.), *Budgets and bureaucrats: The sources of government growth* (pp. 3–18). Durham, NC: Duke University Press.

Buchanan, J. M. (1987). *Economics: Between predictive science and moral philosophy.* College Station, TX: Texas A&M University Press.

Buchanan, J. M. (1989). *Essays on the political economy.* Honolulu: University of Hawaii Press.

Buchanan, J. M., & Tullock, G. (1962). *The calculus of consent: Logical foundations of constitutional democracy.* Ann Arbor: University of Michigan Press.

Buckeye Institute (1996). *Competitive contracting in Ohio public schools.* Dayton, OH: Author.

Buffer, L. C. (1980). Recruit retired adults as volunteers in special education. *Teaching Exceptional Children, 12*(3), 113–115.

Burke, C. (1992). Devolution of responsibility to Queensland schools: Clarifying the rhetoric critiquing the reality. *Journal of Educational Administration, 30*(4), 33–52.

Burns, R. C. (Ed.). (1993). *Parents and schools: From visitors to partners* (NEA School Restructuring Series). Washington, DC: National Education Association.

Bush, W. C., & Denzau, A. T. (1977). The voting behavior of bureaucrats and public sector growth. In T. E. Borcherding (Ed.), *Budgets and bureaucrats: The sources of government growth* (pp. 90–99). Durham, NC: Duke University Press.

Butler, S. M. (1987). Changing the political dynamics of government. In S. H. Hanke (Ed.), *Prospects for privatization. Proceedings of the Academy of Political Science* (Vol. 36, No. 3, pp. 4–13). Montpelier, VT: Capital City Press.

Butler, S. (1991). Privatization for public purposes. In W. T. Gormley (Ed.), *Privatization and its alternatives* (pp. 17–24). Madison: The University of Wisconsin Press.

Caldwell, B. (1990). School-based decision-making and management: International developments. In J. Chapman (Ed.), *School-based decision-making and management* (pp. 3–26). London: Falmer Press.

Callahan, D. E. (1962). *Education and the cult of efficiency: A study of the social forces that have shaped the administration of the public schools.* Chicago: University of Chicago Press.

Campbell, R. F., Cunningham, L. L., Nystrand, R. O., & Usdan, M. D. (1975). *The organization and control of American schools* (3rd. ed.). Columbus, OH: Merrill.

Campbell, R. F., Fleming, T., Newell, L., & Bennion, J. W. (1987). *A history of thought and practice in educational administration.* New York: Teachers College Press.

Candoli, I. C. (1991). *School system administration: A strategic plan for site-based management.* Lancaster, PA: Technomic.

Candoy-Sekse, R. (1988). *Techniques of privatization of state-owned enterprises: Vol. 3. Inventory of country experiences and reference materials.* Washington, DC: The World Bank.

Carlos, L., & Izu, J. A. (1993). *Deregulating categorical programs: Will it work?* San Francisco: Far West Laboratory for Educational Research and Development (ERIC Document Reproduction Service No. ED 370 248)

Carnegie Council on Adolescent Development. (1989). *Turning points.* Washington, DC: Author.

Carnegie Forum on Education and the Economy. (1986, May). *A nation prepared: Teachers for the 21st century.* Washington, DC: Author.

Carnegie Foundation for the Advancement of Teaching. (1992). *School choice.* Princeton, NJ: Author.

Carroll, B. J., Conant, R. W., & Easton, T. A. (1987). Introduction. In B. J. Carroll, R. W. Conant, & T. A. Easton (Eds.), *Private means, public ends: Private business in social service delivery* (pp. ix-xiii). New York: Praeger.

Carter, J. K., & Greisdorf, C. (1982). Volunteers in public schools. *School Business Affairs, 48*(10), 16–17, 28–29.

Carter, J. S. (1992). Bridging education's generation gap. *Clearing House, 65*(6), 373–375.

Chapman, J. (1990). School-based decision-making and management: Implications for school personnel. In C. Chapman (Ed.), *School-based decision-making and management* (pp. 221–244). London: Falmer.

Charity begins at home. (1995, January 8). *The Tennessean,* p. C2.

Chubb, J. E., & Moe, T. M. (1990). *Politics, markets, and America's schools.* Washington DC: The Brookings Institution.

Clabaugh, G. K. (1992). Deregulation and schooling: What can go wrong? *Educational Horizons, 70*(2), 53–54.

Clark, D. L. (1990, September). *Reinventing school leadership* (Working memo prepared for the Reinventing School Leadership Conference, pp. 25–29). Cambridge, MA: National Center for Educational Leadership.

Clark, D. L. (1996, May). *The challenge to the survival of the common school.* Unpublished manuscript, University of North Carolina at Chapel Hill, School of Education.

Clark, D. L., & Meloy, J. M. (1989). Renouncing bureaucracy: A democratic structure for leadership in schools: In T. J. Sergiovanni & J. A. Moore (Eds.), *Schooling for tomorrow: Directing reform to issues that count* (pp. 272–294). Boston: Allyn & Bacon.

Clarkson, K. W. (1989). Privatization at the state and local level. In P. W. MacAvoy, W. T. Stanbury, G. Yarrow, & R. J. Zeckhauser (Eds.), *Privatization and state-owned enterprises: Lessons from the United States, Great Britain and Canada* (pp. 143–194). Boston: Kluwer.

Clary, E. G., Snyder, M., & Ridge, R. (1992). Volunteers' motivation: A functional strategy for the recruitment, placement, and retention of volunteers. *Nonprofit Management and Leadership, 2*(4), 333–350.

Clowse, B. B. (1981). *Brainpower for the cold war.* Westport, CT: Greenwood Press.

Cobb, C. W. (1992). *Responsive schools, renewed communities.* San Francisco: Institute for Contemporary Studies (ICS) Press. (ERIC Document Reproduction Service No. ED 378 688).

Cohen, D. L. (1992a). Children without "traditional family" support seen posing complex challenge for schools. *Education Week, 12*(8), 5.

Cohen, D. L. (1992b). Nation found losing ground on measures of child well-being. *Education Week, 12*(28), 14.

Cohen, D. L. (1993). Half of Black, Hispanic children may be poor by 2010. *Education Week, 8*(9), 11.

Cohen, D. L. (1994). "Distressed" communities jeopardize children's well-being, report says. *Education Week, 13*(31), 5.

Cohen, M. D., March, J. G., & Olsen, J. P. (1972). A garbage can model of organizational choice. *Administrative Science Quarterly, 17*(1), 1–26.

Cohen, P. A., Kulik, J. A., & Kulik, C. C. (1982). Educational outcomes of tutoring: A meta-analysis of findings. *American Educational Research Journal, 19*(2), 237–248.

Cohen, S. S. (1970). *A history of Colonial education, 1607–1776.* New York: Harper & Row.

Coleman, J. S. (1990). Preface: Choice, community and future schools. In W. H. Clune & J. F. Witte (Eds.), *Choice and control in American education: Vol. 1. The theory of choice and control in education* (pp. ix-xxii). New York: The Falmer Press.

Colfax, D., & Colfax, M. (1988). *Home schooling for excellence.* New York: Warner.

Combs, A. W. (1988, February). New assumptions for educational reform. *Educational Leadership, 45*(5), 38–40.

Committee on the Judiciary, House of Representatives. (1986). *Privatization of corrections: Hearing before the Subcommittee on Courts, Civil Liberties, and the Administration of Justice* (Serial No. 40). Washington, DC: U.S. Government Printing Office.

Commonwealth v. Armstrong, 1 PA. L. J. 393 (Pa. 1842).

Conley, S. C. (1989, March). *Who's on first? School reform, teacher participation, and the decision-making process.* Paper presented at the annual meeting of the American Educational Research Association, San Francisco.

Consortium for Policy Research in Education. (1992, June). Ten lessons about regulation and schooling. *CPRE Policy Briefs: Reporting on Issues and Research in Education Policy and Finance.* Brunswick, NJ: Author. (ERIC Document Reproduction Service No. ED 348 729).

Cookson, Jr., P. W. (1992). Preface. In P. W. Cookson, Jr. (Ed.). *The choice controversy* (pp. vii-xi). Newbury Park, CA: Corwin Press.

Cooledge, N. J., & Wurster, S. R. (1985). Intergenerational tutoring and student achievement. *The Reading Teacher, 39*(3), 343–346.

Coons, J. E., & Sugarman, S. D. (1978). *Education by choice: The case for family control.* Berkeley, CA: University of California Press.

Cooper, B. S., & Doyle, D. P. (1996). Education supply: Will it create demand? *Education Week, 15*(26), 48, 37.

Cremin, L. A. (1970). *American education: The Colonial experience, 1607–1783.* New York: Harper & Row.

Cremin, L. A. (1980). *American education: The national experience, 1783–1896.* New York: Harper & Row.

Criscuolo, N. P. (1985). Implementing an exemplary volunteer program in reading. *Catalyst for Change, 15*(1), 9–11.

Cronin, J. M. (1973). *The control of urban schools: Perspectives on the power of educational reformers.* New York: The Free Press.

Crowson, R. L. (1992). *School-community relations, under reform.* Berkeley, CA: McCutchan.

Cuban, L. (1984). *How teachers taught: Constancy and change in American classrooms, 1890–1980.* New York: Longman.

Cuban, L. (1984). School reform by remote control: SB813 in California. *Phi Delta Kappan, 66*(3), 213–215.

Cuban, L. (1989). The "at-risk" label and the problem of urban school reform. *Phi Delta Kappan, 70*(10), 780–84, 799.

Cubberley, E. P. (1962). *Public education in the United States.* Cambridge, MA: Houghton Miflin.

Cuninggim, W. (1980). Citizen volunteers: A growing resource for teachers and students. *Teaching Exceptional Students, 12*(3), 108–112.

Darr, T. B. (1991). Privatization may be good for your government. In R. L. Kemp (Ed.), *Privatization: The provision of public services by the private sector* (pp. 60–68). Jefferson, NC: McFarland.

David, A. (1992). *Public-private partnerships. The private sector and innovation in education.* Santa Monica, CA: Reason Foundation.

Davis, K., & Quillen, K. (1993, July). Your family finances: The economics of teaching your kids at home. *Kiplinger's Personal Finance Magazine,* p. 30.

Dayton, C., Raby, M., Stern, D., & Weisberg, A. (1992). The California partnership academies: Remembering the 'forgotten half.' *Phi Delta Kappan, 73*(7), 539–545.

D.C. school system to hire private firm for tutoring. (1994). *Education Week, 13*(34), p. 4.

De Alessi, L. (1987). Property rights and privatization. In S. H. Hanke (Ed.), *Prospects for privatization. Proceedings of the Academy of Political Science* (Vol. 36, No. 3, pp. 24–35). Montpelier, VT: Capital City Press.

Decker, L. E., & Decker, V. A. (1988). *Home/school/community involvement.* Arlington, VA: American Association of School Administrators. (ERIC Document Reproduction Service No. ED 298 610).

Decker, L. E. (1994). *Home-school-community relations: Trainers manual and study guide.* Charlottesville, VA: University of Virginia, Mid-Atlantic Center for Community Education. (ERIC Document Reproduction Service No. ED 371 822).

De Hoog, R. H. (1984). *Contracting out for human services: Economic, political, and organizational perspectives.* Albany: State University of New York Press.

Dellar, G. B. (1992, April). *Connections between macro and micro implementation of educational policy: A study of school restructuring in Western Australia.* Paper presented at the annual meeting of the American Educational Research Association, San Francisco.

Diegmueller, K. (1995). Texas debates "open market" for textbooks. *Education Week, 14*(26), 1, 8–9.

DiSilvestro, F., & DiSilvestro, R. (1985a). Before signing up recruits, figure out how they can help. *American School Board Journal, 172*(10), 27.

DiSilvestro, F., & DiSilvestro, R. (1985b). Room mothers are great, but today's parent volunteers can do so much more. *American School Board Journal, 172*(10), 26–27.

Donahue, J. D. (1989). *The privatization decision: Public ends, private means.* New York: Basic Books.

Downs, A. (1967). *Inside bureaucracy.* Boston: Little, Brown.

Doyle, D. P. (1994a). The reform agenda: Private management and school reform. *Network News & Views, 13*(6), 41–43.

Doyle, D. P. (1994b). The role of private sector management in public education. *Network News and Views, 13*(11), 51–54.

Doyle, D. P., & Hartle, T. W. (1985). Leadership in education: Governors, legislators and teachers. *Phi Delta Kappan, 67*(1), 21–27.

Drake, W. E. (1955). *The American school in transition.* Englewood Cliffs, NJ: Prentice Hall.

Dudek & Company. (1989). *Privatization and public employees: The impact of city and county contracting out on government works.* (Report No. NCEP-RR-88-07). Washington, DC: U.S. National Commission for Employment Policy.

Edison Project to run two Dade County schools. (1996). *Education Week, 15*(16), 4.

Edison Project's core team named. (1992, February 27). *Whittle News* [Press release].

Editorial Projects in Education. (1996). Vouchers: Cure or poison. *Education Week* [Online]. Available: http://www.edweek.org/context/election/vouchers.html [1997, April 5].

Edson, C. H. (1982). Schooling for work and working at school: Perspectives on immigrant and working-class education in urban America, 1880–1920. In R. B. Everhart (Ed.), *The public school monopoly: A critical analysis of education and the state in American society* (pp. 145–188). Cambridge, MA: Ballinger.

Education, Inc.: Perspectives on private management of public schools. (1994). *Network News & Views, 13*(9), 55.

Education Industry Conference. (1996, March). *Enterprising Educators*, p. 1. (Newsletter of the American Association of Educators in Private Practice)

Elkin, N. (1987). Privatization in perspective. In B. J. Carroll, R. W. Conant, & T. A. Easton (Eds.), *Private means, public ends: Private business in social service delivery* (pp. 171–177). New York: Praeger.

Elmore, R. F. (1990). Choice as an instrument of public policy: Evidence from education and health care. In W. H. Clune & J. F. Witte (Eds.), *Choice and control in American education: Vol. 1. The theory of choice and control in education* (pp. 285–318). New York: The Falmer Press.

Elmore, R. (1990). Introduction: On changing the structure of public schools. In R. Elmore & Associates (Eds.), *Restructuring schools: The next generation of educational reforms* (pp. 1–29). San Francisco: Jossey-Bass.

Elmore, R. F. (1993). School decentralization: Who gains? Who loses? In J. Hannaway & M. Carnoy (Eds.), *Decentralization and school improvement* (pp. 33–54). San Francisco: Jossey-Bass.

Elmore, R. F. (1996, February). *Education policy research: Where we've been, where we are, where we should go* (Paper commissioned by the National Institute on Governance, Finance, Policy-Making, and Management). Washington, DC: United States Department of Education, Office of Educational Research and Improvement (OERI).

Evans, K., & Carroll, T. (1995). Why we did it. *Network News & Views, 14*(4), 74.

Farrell, W. C., Johnson, J. H., Jones, C. K., & Sapp, M. (1994) Will privatizing schools really help inner-city students of color? *Educational Leadership, 52*(1), 72–75.

Fenner, M. S., & Fishburn, E. C. (1968). *Pioneer American educators.* Port Washington, NY: Kennikat Press. p.73–98.

Fine, M. (1993, Winter). A diary on privatization and on public possibilities. *Educational Theory, 43*(1), 33–39.

Fischer, L. R., & Schaffer, K. B. (1993). *Older volunteers: A guide to research and practice.* Newbury Park, CA: Sage.

Fisher, S. (1994). Preparing for change: Parental involvement at Mt. Carmel High School. *NASSP Bulletin, 78*(560), 69–74.

Fitzgerald, R. (1988). *When government goes private: Successful alternatives to public services.* New York: Universe Books.

Fitzgerald, M. R., Lyons, W., & Cory, F. C. (1990). From administration to oversight: Privatization and its aftermath in a southern city. In R. C. Hula (Ed.), *Market-based public policy* (pp. 69–83). New York: St. Martin's Press.

Fixler, F. L., & Poole, R. W. (1987). Status of state and local privatization. In S. H. Hanke (Ed.), *Prospects for privatization. Proceedings of the Academy of Political Science* (Vol. 36, No. 3, pp. 164–178). Montpelier, VT: Capital City Press.

Fixler, P. E. (1991). Service shedding—a new option. In R. L. Kemp (Ed.), *Privatization: The provision of public services by the private sector* (pp. 39–52). Jefferson, NC: McFarland.

Fixler, P. E., & Poole, R. W. (1991). Status of local privatization. In R. L. Kemp (Ed.), *Privatization: The provision of public services by the private sector* (pp. 69–84). Jefferson, NC: McFarland.

Flanagan, J. L., & Richardson, M. D. (1991, August). *Deregulated schools: A research study.* Paper presented at the annual meeting of the National Conference of Professors of Educational Administration, Fargo, ND. (ERIC Document Reproduction Service No. ED 341 151).

A flawed experiment. (1995, September 20). *Philadelphia Inquirer* [Editorial], p. A10.

Florestano, P. S. (1991). Considerations for the future. In R. L. Kemp (Ed.), *Privatization: The provision of public services by the private sector* (pp. 291–296). Jefferson, NC: McFarland.

Foner, P. S. (Ed.). (1945). *The complete writings of Thomas Paine.* New York: The Citadel Press.

Fox, S. R. (1986). *Science in the classroom: Two strategies.* Washington, DC: National Institute for Work and Learning. (ERIC Document Reproduction Service No. ED 337 357).

Friedman, M. (1995, April). Public schools: Make them private. *Network News and Views, 14*(4), 69–71.

Frug, J. (1991). The choice between privatization and publicazation. In R. L. Kemp (Ed.), *Privatization: The provision of public services by the private sector* (pp. 305–310). Jefferson, NC: McFarland.

Fuhrman, S. (1994). Politics and systemic education reform. *CPRE Policy Briefs,* RB-12–04/94, pp. 1–7.

Fuhrman, S. H., & Elmore, R. F. (1992). *Takeover and deregulation: Working models of new state and local regulatory relationships.* New Brunswick, NJ: Consortium for Policy Research in Education. (ERIC Document Reproduction Service No. ED 345 368).

Fuhrman, S. H., & Elmore, R. F. (1995). *Ruling out rules: The evolution of deregulation in state education policy.* New Brunswick, NJ: Consortium for Policy Research in Education.

Fuhrman, S. H., & Fry, P. (1989). *Diversity amidst standardization: State differential treatment of districts.* Brunswick, NJ: Consortium for Policy Research in Education (ERIC Document Reproduction Service No. ED 315 903).

Fuhrman, S. H., Fry, P., & Elmore, R. F. (1992). *South Carolina's flexibility through deregulation program: A case study.* New Brunswick, NJ: Consortium for Policy Research in Education (ERIC Document Reproduction Service No. ED 345 371).

Fusarelli, L. D., & Scribner, J. D. (1993, October). *Site-based management and critical democratic pluralism: An analysis of promises, problems, and possibilities.* Paper presented at the annual conference of the University Council for Educational Administration, Houston.

Gamble, C. (1996). Hartford officials agree to pay EAI $3 million. *Education Week, 15*(16), 7.

Garms, W. I., Guthrie, J. W., & Pierce, L. C. (1978). *School finance: The economics and politics of public education.* Englewood Cliffs, NJ: Prentice-Hall.

Geiger, K. (1995). Privatization: An interim report card. *Education Week, 14*(27), 34, 39.

General Accounting Office. (1994). *Regulatory flexibility in schools: What happens when schools are allowed to change the rules?* (GAO/HEHS-94-102). Washington, DC: Author. (ERIC Document Reproduction Service No. ED 373 388).

General Accounting Office. (1996). *Private management of public schools: Early experiences in four school districts.* Washington, DC: Author.

Gibbs, N. (1994, October) Home sweet home. *Time Magazine,* pp. 62–63.

Goetter, W. G. J. (1987). When you create ideal conditions, your fledgling volunteer program will fly. *The American School Board Journal, 174*(6), 34, 37.

Goetter, W. G. J., Shreeve, W., Norby, J. R., Midgley, T. K., de Michele, B. (1987). The professional volunteer: A new concept—Time-tested. *Canadian Vocational Journal, 23*(1), 56–58.

Goetz, C. J. (1977). Fiscal illusion in state and local finance. In T. E. Borcherding (Ed.) *Budgets and bureaucrats: The sources of government growth* (pp. 176–187). Durham, NC: Duke University Press.

Goldman, H., & Mokuvos, S. (1991). Dividing the pie between public and private. In R. L. Kemp (Ed.), *Privatization: The provision of public services by the private sector* (pp. 25–28). Jefferson, NC: McFarland.

Goldring, E. B., & Sullivan, A. V. S. (1995). Privatization: Integrating private services in public schools. In P. W. Cookson & B. Schneider (Eds.), *Transforming schools* (pp. 539–562). New York: Garland.

Golle, J. T. (1994). You must take care of your customer. *Network News & Views, 13*(9), 59–60.

Gomez-Ibanez, J. A., Meyer, J. R., & Luberoff, D. E. (1990). In A. H. Munnell (Ed.), *Is there a shortfall in public capital investment?* (pp. 143–174). Boston: Federal Reserve Bank of Boston.

Good, H. G. (1962). *A history of American education.* New York: Macmillan.

Goodlad, J. I. (1984). *A place called school: Prospects for the future.* New York: McGraw-Hill.

Gormley, W. T. (1991a). The privatization controversy. In W. T. Gormley (Ed.), *Privatization and its alternatives* (pp. 3–16). Madison: The University of Wisconsin Press.

Gormley, W. T. (1991b). Two cheers for privatization. In W. T. Gormley (Ed.), *Privatization and its alternatives* (pp. 307–318). Madison: The University of Wisconsin Press.

Gramlich, E. M., & Koshel, P. P. (1975). *Educational performance contracting: An evaluation of an experiment.* Washington, DC: The Brookings Institution.

Gray, S. T. (1982, July). Managing school volunteers—Eight keys to success. Paper presented at the International Conference for Parent/Citizen Involvement in Schools, Salt Lake City, UT. (ERIC Document Reproduction Service No. ED 226 463).

Griffin, W. M. (1988). Read aloud week at Collicot School. *Educational Leadership, 45*(8), 57.

Gross, R. E. (1991). *Social science perspectives on citizenship education.* New York: Teachers College Press.

Gursky, D. (1992). Cincinnati cuts more than half of central office. *Education Week, 11*(35), 1, 13.

Gutek, G. L. (1983). *Education and schooling in America.* Englewood Cliffs, NJ: Prentice-Hall.

Guterson, D. (1992). *Family matters: Why homeschooling makes sense.* San Diego, CA: Harcourt Brace.

Guthrie, J. W. (1986, December). School-based management: The next needed education reform. *Phi Delta Kappan, 68*(4), 305–309.

Guthrie, J. W. (1996a, March). *Reinventing educational governance and the R&D agenda it implies.* (Paper commissioned by the National Institute on Governance, Finance, Policy-Making, and Management). Washington, DC: United States Department of Education, Office of Educational Research and Improvement (OERI).

Guthrie, J. W. (1996b, May). *Consortium on renewing education: High performing and newly productive schools—a proposal to the Ball Foundation.* Nashville, TN: Vanderbilt University, Peabody College, Peabody Center for Education Policy.

Hakim, S., Seidenstat, P., & Bowman, G. W. (1994). Introduction. In S. Hakim, P. Seidenstat, & G. W. Bowman (Eds.), *Privatizing education and educational choice: Concepts, plans, and experiences* (pp. 1–15). Westport, CT: Praeger.

Hancock, L. N. (1995). A Sylvan invasion. *Network News & Views, 14*(1), 70.

Hanke, S. H. (1985). The theory of privatization. In S. M. Butler (Ed.), *The privatization option: A strategy to shrink the size of government* (pp. 1–14). Washington, DC: The Heritage Foundation.

Hanke, S. H. (1987). Privatization versus nationalization. In S. H. Hanke (Ed.), *Prospects for privatization. Proceedings of the Academy of Political Science,* (Vol. 36, No. 3, pp. 1–3). Montpelier, VT: Capital City Press.

Hanke, S. H. (1989). Privatization at the state and local level: Comment. In P. W. MacAvoy, W. T. Stanburg, G. Yarrow, & R. J. Zeckhauser (Eds.), *Privatization and state-owned enterprises* (pp. 195–202). Boston: Kluwer.

Hanke, S. H., & Dowdle, B. (1987). Privatizing the public domain. In S. H. Hanke (Ed.), *Prospects for privatization. Proceedings of the Academy of Political Science* (Vol. 36, No. 3, pp. 114–123). Montpelier, VT: Capital City Press.

Hanke, S. H., & Walters, S. J. K. (1987). Privatizing waterworks. In S. H. Hanke (Ed.), *Prospects for privatization. Proceedings of the Academy of Political Science* (Vol. 36, No. 3, pp. 104–113). Montpelier, VT: Capital City Press.

Hansen, B. J., & Mackey, P. E. (1993). *Your public schools: What you can do to help them.* North Haven, CT: Catbird Press.

Hanson, E. M. (1991). Educational restructuring in the USA: Movements of the 1980s. *Journal of Educational Administration, 29*(4), 30–38.

Hardin, H. (1989). *The privatization putsch.* Halifax, Nova Scotia: The Institute for Research on Public Policy.

Harp, L. (1993). Engler's choice plan includes student grants. *Education Week, 13*(6), 1, 18.

Harp, L. (1995a). Fervor spreads to overhaul state agencies. *Education Week, 14*(24), 1, 13.

Harp, L. (1995b). Texas lawmakers reach accord on overhaul of education laws. *Education Week, 14*(36), 19.

Harp, L. (1996a). Code revisions spur change in Texas climate. *Education Week, 15*(17), 1, 15.

Harp, L. (1996b). Getting down to business at next week's summit. *Education Week, 15*(26), 1, 22.

Harp. L. (1996c). Michigan education-code overhaul shifts power. *Education Week, 15*(16), 20.

Harty, H. (1984). Influence of a school volunteer program on the personal and psychological growth of community adults. *Catalyst for Change, 13*(2), 15–18.

Hatry, H. P. (1991). Problems. In R. L. Kemp (Ed.), *Privatization: The provision of public services by the private sector* (pp. 262–266). Jefferson, NC: McFarland.

Hawley, W. D. (1995). The false premises and false promises of the movement to privatize public education. *Teachers College Record, 96*(4), 735–742.

Haynes, M. L. (1995). Educational experiment. *Network News & Views, 14*(10), 80–81.

Heaviside, S., & Farris, E. (1989). *Education partnerships in public elementary and secondary schools. Survey Report.* Washington, DC: National Center for Education Statistics.

Hedin, D. (1987, Winter). Students as teachers: A tool for improving school climate and productivity. *Social Policy,* 42–47.

Hedin, N. S. (1991). Self-concept of baptist children in three dimensional settings. *Home School Researcher, 7*(3), 1–5.

Heise, M., Colburn, K. D., Jr., & Lamberti, J. F. (1995). Private vouchers in Indianapolis: The Golden Rule program. In T. M. Moe (Ed.), *Private vouchers* (pp. 100–119). Stanford, CA: Hoover Institution Press.

Helping hands. (1993). *NEA Today, 11*(6), 25.

Hemming, R., & Mansoor, A. M. (1988). *Privatization and public enterprises.* (Occasional Paper No. 56). Washington, DC: International Monetary Fund.

Henderson, K. (1994). Free-lance teachers sell talents to schools with special needs. *Network News & Views, 13*(11), 57–58.

Henig, J. R. (1994). *Rethinking school choice: Limits of the market metaphor.* Princeton, NJ: Princeton University Press.

Heritage Foundation. (1997). *Educational choice in the United States* [Online]. Available: http://www.heritage.org/heritage/schools/intro.html [1997, January 21].

Hilke, J. C. (1992). *Competition in government-financed services.* New York: Quorum Books.

Hill, P., Pierce, L. C., & Guthrie, J. W. (in press). *Private provision in the public interest.* Chicago: University of Chicago.

Hirsch, W. Z. (1991). *Privatizing government services: An economic analysis of contracting out by local governments.* Los Angeles: University of California, Institute of Industrial Relations.

Holt, J. (1981, Spring). Mothering interviews. *Mothering Magazine,* p. 91.

Home School Legal Defense Assocation. (n.d.) p. 8.

Hudgins, E. L., & Utt, R. D. (1992). Introduction. In E. L. Hudgins & R. D. Utt (Eds.), *How privatization can solve America's infrastructure crisis.* Washington, DC: The Heritage Foundation and The National Chamber Foundation.

Hula, R. C. (1990a). Preface. In R. C. Hula (Ed.), *Market-based public policy* (pp. xiii-xiv). New York: St. Martins Press.

Hula, R. C. (1990b). Using markets to implement public policy. In R. C. Hula (Ed.), *Market-based public policy* (pp. 3-18). New York: St. Martin's Press.

Hunter, M. (1989). Join the "Par-aide" in Education. *Educational Leadership, 47*(2), 36-41.

Hunter, R. C. (1995a). Private procurement in the public sector in education. *Education and Urban Review, 27*(2), 136-153.

Hunter, R. C. (1995b). Privatization of instruction in public education. *Education and Urban Society, 27*(2), 168-194.

Innerst, C. (1994). Hartford schools turned over to a for-profit firm. *Network News & Views, 13*(11), 58-59. (Reprinted from *The Washington Times,* October 5, 1994).

Ismael, J. S. (1988). Privatization of social services: A heuristic approach. In J. S. Ismael & Y. Vaillancourt (Eds.), *Privatization and provincial social services in Canada* (pp. 1-11). Edmonton, Canada: The University of Alberta Press.

Ismael, J. S., & Vaillancourt, Y. (1988). Preface. In J. S. Ismael & Y. Vaillancourt (Eds.), *Privatization and provincial social services in Canada* (pp. vii-ix). Edmonton, Canada: The University of Alberta Press.

Jacobs, G. (1993). History, crisis, and social panic: Minority resistance to privatization of an urban school system. *The Urban Review, 25*(3), 175-198.

Jaeger, R. M. (1992, October). Weak measurement serving presumptive policy. *Phi Delta Kappan, 74*(2), 118-128.

Jamer, T. M. (1961). *School volunteers.* New York: Public Education Association.

James, T. (1983). Questions about educational choice: An argument from history. In T. James & H. M. Levin (Eds.), *Public dollars for private schools: The case of tuition tax credits* (pp. 55-70). Philadelphia: Temple University Press.

Janowitz, G. (1965). *Helping hands: Volunteer work in education.* Chicago: University of Chicago Press.

Jeffrey v. O'Donnell, 702 F. Supp. 513 (1988) pp. 519, 521.

Jencks, C. (1966, Winter). Is the public school obsolete? *The Public Interest,* (2), 18-27.

Jenkins, K., & Houlihan, G. T. (1990). We're cutting through the red tape to real school reform. *The Executive Educator, 12*(2), 18-19, 27.

Jennings, J. M. (1992). Parent involvement strategies for inner-city schools. *NASSP Bulletin, 76*(548), 63-68.

Johanek, M. (1992). Private citizenship and school choice. In P. W. Cookson, Jr. (Ed.), *The choice controversy* (pp. 146-170). Newbury Park, CA: Corwin Press.

Johnson, K. C. (1991). Socialization practices of Christian homeschool educators in the state of Virginia. *Homeschool Researcher, 7*(1), 9–16.

Johnson, M. E. (1994). *Roles and responsibilities of principals in deregulated schools.* Unpublished doctoral dissertation, Vanderbilt University, Nashville, Tennessee.

Judson, C. (1995, December 7). For education company, a shift in vision. *The New York Times,* pp. 12–13.

Kaestle, C. F. (1973). Common schools before the common school revival: New York schooling in the 1790s. *History of Education Quarterly, 12*(4), 12.

Kaestle, C. F. (1983). *Pillars of the republic: Common schools and American society, 1780–1860.* New York: Hill & Wang.

Kaestle, C. F., & Smith, M. S. (1982). The federal role in elementary and secondary education, 1940–1980. *Harvard Educational Review, 52*(4), 384–408.

Kaestle, C. F., & Vinovskis, M. A. (1980). *Education and social change in nineteenth century Massachusetts.* Cambridge: Cambridge University Press.

Kagan, R. A. (1986). Regulating business, regulating schools: The problem of regulatory unreasonableness. In D. L. Kirp & D. N. Jensen (Eds.), *School days, rule days: The legalization and regulation of education* (pp. 64–90). Philadelphia: The Falmer Press.

Katz, D. S. (1983). Planning to use volunteers. *Voc Ed, 58*(3), 28–29.

Kearnes, D. L. (1988). An education recovery plan for America. *Phi Delta Kappan, 69*(8), 565–570.

Keller, M. (1994). *Regulating a new society: Public policy and social change in America, 1900–1933.* Cambridge, MA: Harvard University Press.

Kemp, R. L. (1991). Introduction. In R. L. Kemp (Ed.), *Privatization: The provision of public services by the private sector* (pp. 1–21). Jefferson, NC: McFarland.

Kent, J. D. (1987). A not too distant past: Echoes of the calls for reform. *The Educational Forum, 51*(2), 139.

Kirkpatrick, D. W. (1990). *Choice in schooling: A case for tuition vouchers.* Chicago: Loyola University Press.

Kirst, M. W., McLaughlin, M., & Massell, D. (1989). *Rethinking children's policy: Implications for educational administration.* Stanford, CA: Stanford University, Center for Educational Research.

Klicka, C. J. (1994). *Home schooling in the United States: A legal analysis.* Virginia: Home School Legal Defense Association.

Klicka, C. J. (1995). *The right to home school: A guide to the law on parents' rights in education.* Durham, NC: Carolina Academic Press.

Knight, E. W. (1951). *Education in the United States.* New York: Greenwood Press.

Kolderie, T. (1991). Two different concepts. In R. L. Kemp (Ed.), *Privatization: The provision of public services by the private sector* (pp. 250–261). Jefferson, NC: McFarland.

Kolderie, T., & Hauer, J. (1991). Contracting as an approach to public management. In R. L. Kemp (Ed.), *Privatization: The provision of public services by the private sector* (pp. 87–96). Jefferson, NC: McFarland.

Kotin, L., & Aikman, W. (1980). *Legal foundations of compulsory school attendance.* Port Washington, NY: Kennikat Press.

Kozol, J. (1992). I dislike the idea of choice and I want to tell you why…. *Educational Leadership, 50*(3), 27–30.

Kuttner, R. (1991). The private market can't always solve public problems. In R. L. Kemp

(Ed.), *Privatization: The provision of public services by the private sector* (pp. 311–313). Jefferson, NC: McFarland.

Lamdin, D. J. (1996). *The economics of education provision by for-profit contractors.* Unpublished manuscript, University of Maryland–Baltimore County, Department of Economics.

Lamdin, D. J., & Mintrom, M. (1996). *School choice in theory and practice: Taking stock and looking ahead.* Manuscript in preparation, University of Maryland, Baltimore County.

Larrabee, J. (1995, June 7). The business of school reform. *USA Today,* p. A3.

Lawton, M. (1995). Ax education agency, Okla. state employees urge. *Education Week, 15*(9), 18.

A lesson from private practitioners. (1991, December 24–January 7). *Insight,* pp. 34–35.

Levin, H. M. (1983). Educational choice and the pains of democracy. In T. James & H. M. Levin, *Public dollars for private schools: The case of tuition tax credits* (pp. 17–38). Philadelphia: Temple University Press.

Levin, H. M. (1987). Education as a public and private good. *Journal of Policy Analysis and Management, 6*(4), 628–641.

Levin, H. M. (1990). The theory of choice applied to education. In W. H. Clune & J. F. Witte (Eds.), *Choice and control in American education: Vol. 1. The theory of choice and control in education* (pp. 247–284). New York: The Falmer Press.

Lewis, D. A. (1993). Deinstitutionalization and school decentralization: Making the same mistake twice. In J. Hannaway & M. Carnoy (Eds.), *Decentralization and school improvement* (pp. 84–101). San Francisco: Jossey-Bass.

Lieberman, M. (1988) Efficiency issues in educational contracting. *Government Union Review, 9,* 1–24.

Lieberman, M. (1989). *Privatization and educational choice.* New York: St. Martin's Press.

Lieberman, M. (1995). *Restoring school board options on contracting out.* Sacramento, CA: The Claremont Institute, Golden State Center for Policy Studies.

Life Baptist Church v. Town of East Longmeadow, 666 F. Supp. 293 (D. Mass. 1987).

Lindelow, J. (1980). *Educational vouchers.* Reston, VA: National Association of Secondary School Principals. (ERIC/CEM Accession No. EA 011 439).

Lindsay, D. (1995a). States take aim at regulatory beast: School codes. *Education Week, 14*(20), 1, 17.

Lindsay, D. (1995b). Critics decry N.Y. governor's proposal to repeal foreign-language mandate. *Education Week, 14*(23), 19.

Lindsay, D. (1995c). N.C. poised to slash size, power of state education agency. *Education Week, 14*(24), 12.

Lindsay, D. (1995d). Pa. district vote to hire firm to run school assailed. *Education Week, 14*(27), 1.

Lindsay, D. (1995e). Decentralization plan seen sparking "education revolution" in N.C. *Education Week, 14*(36), 19.

Lindsay, D. (1996). Bill to ax tenure for Milwaukee teachers advances. *Education Week, 15*(12), 10.

Lipson, L. (1994). Senior citizens as school volunteers: New resources for the future. *ERIC Digest Series, 93*(4). (ERIC Document Reproduction Service No. ED 369 774).

Lyons, J. E. (1995). Contracting out for public school support services. *Education and Urban Review, 27*(2), 154–167.

Lyng v. Northwest Indian Cemetery Protection Association, 485 U.S. 439, 108 S. Ct. 1319, 99 L.E.D. 536 (1988).

Madsen, J. (1996). *Private and public school partnerships: Sharing lessons about decentralization.* London: Falmer Press.

Magnum, J. (1996, July 23). At Sylvan, it's reading, writing and revenue. *USA Today*, p. B4.

Mann, D. (1987a). Business involvement and public school improvement: Part 1. *Phi Delta Kappan, 69*(2), 123–28.

Mann, D. (1987b). Business involvement and public school improvement: Part 2. *Phi Delta Kappan, 69*(3), 228–232.

Mann, D. (1990). It's time to trade red tape for accountability in education. *The Executive Educator, 12*(1), 26, 28.

March, J. G., & Olson, J. P. (1983, June). What administrative reorganization tells us about governing. *The American Political Science Review, 77*(2), 281–296.

Martin, B. (1993). *In the public interest? Privatization and public sector reform.* London: Zed Books.

Martinez, V., Godwin, K., & Kemerer, F. R. (1995). Private vouchers in San Antonio: The CEO program. In T. M. Moe (Ed.), *Private vouchers* (pp. 74–99). Stanford, CA: Hoover Institution Press.

Maryland Regulations Code, Title 13A §§ 10.01–05.

Maxwell, J. A., & Aronson, J. R. (1977). *Financing state and local governments* (3rd ed.). Washington, DC: The Brookings Institution.

Mayberry, M. (1995). *Home schooling: Parents as educators.* Thousand Oaks, CA: Corwin Press.

McCarthy, M. M. (1995). Private investment in public education: Boon or boondoggle? *Journal of School Leadership, 5*(1), 4–21.

McGriff D. M. (1995). Lighting the way for systemic reform: The Edison Project launches its version of a public-private partnership. *Network News & Views, 14*(10), 74–77.

McLaughlin, J. M. (1995). Wilkinsburg, Pennsylvania: History in the making. *The Education Investor, 3*(3), 1–3.

Mecklenburger, J. A. (1972). *Performance contracting.* Worthington, OH: Charles A. Jones.

Meltzer, A. H., & Scott, R. F. (1978, Summer). Why government grows (and grows) in a democracy. *The Public Interest*, (52), 111–118.

Menge, J. (1994). The evaluation of the New Hampshire plan: An early voucher system. In S. Hakim, P. Seidenstat, & G. W. Bowman (Eds.), *Privatizing education and educational choice: Concepts, plans, and experiences* (pp. 163–182). Westport, CT: Praeger.

Mereman, R. M. (1990). Knowledge, educational organization and choice. In W. H. Clune & J. F. Witte (Eds.), *Choice and control in American education: Vol. 1. The theory of choice and control in education* (pp. 79–85). New York: The Falmer Press.

Merenda, D. W. (1989). Partners in education: An old tradition renewed. *Educational Leadership, 47*(2), pp. 4–7.

Meyer, A. E. (1967). *An American history of the American people.* New York: McGraw-Hill.

Michael, B. (Ed.). (1990). *Volunteers in public schools.* (Report prepared for the U.S. Department of Education, National Research Council, Commission on Behavioral and Social Sciences and Education, Committee on the Use of Volunteers in Schools). Washington, DC: National Academy Press.

Michigan v. DeJonge, 501 N.W.2d 127 (1993).

Middle Tennessee Home Education Association. (1995). *Middle Tennessee home education association handbook.* Nashville, TN: Author.

Mill, J. S. (1935). On liberty. In P. Wheelwright (Ed.), *Jeremy Bentham, James Mill, J. S. Mill: Selected writings* (pp. 301–386). Garden City, NY: Doubleday, Doran & Company.

Miller, B. L., & Wilmshurst, A. L. (1984). *Parents as volunteers in the classroom* (Rev. ed.). Saratoga, CA: R & E Publishers.

Miller, J. R., & Tufts, C. R. (1991). A means to achieve "more with less." In R. L. Kemp (Ed.), *Privatization: The provision of public services by the private sector* (pp. 97–109). Jefferson, NC: McFarland.

Miller, L. (1995) Elementary principals' survey finds slim support for standards, inclusion. *Education Week, 14*(30) 7.

Miller, L. (1995). Colo. bill would kill cmpulsory age for school. *Education Week, 15*(11), 1, 22.

Moe, T. M. (1995). Private vouchers. In T. M. Moe (Ed.), *Private vouchers* (pp. 1–40). Stanford, CA: Hoover Institution Press.

Molnar, A. (1994). Education for profit: A yellow brick road to nowhere. *Educational Leadership, 52*(1), 66–71.

Molnar, A. (1996, September). Focus: School choice. *Educational Issues Series, 3*(2), 1–8. (Madison, WI: Wisconsin Education Association Council).

Monroe, P. (1940). *Founding of the American public school system.* New York: Macmillan.

Montgomery, L. (1989). The effect of home schooling on the leadership skills of home schooled students. *Home School Researcher, 5*(1), 1–10.

Moore, D. (1986, January/February). God's leading: A review. *The Parent Educator and Family Report, 4*(1), 7.

Moore, R., & Moore, D. (1984). *Home style teaching.* Waco, TN: Word.

Moore, R., & Moore, D. (1994). *The successful homeschool family handbook.* Nashville, TN: Thomas Nelson.

Moore, R. S. (1984). The school at home. *Moody Monthly, 84*(7), 1, 19.

Moore, S. (1987). Contracting out: A painless alternative to the budget cutter's knife. In S. H. Hanke (Ed.), *Prospects for privatization. Proceedings of the Academy of Political Science* (Vol. 36, No. 3, pp. 60–70). Montpelier, VT: Capital City Press.

Mueller, D. C. (1989). *Public choice II.* New York: Cambridge University Press.

Murnane, R. J. (1990). Family choice. In W. H. Clune & J. F. Witte (Eds.), *Choice and control in American education: Vol. 1. The theory of choice and control in education* (pp. 332–336). New York: The Falmer Press.

Murphy, J. (1990). The educational reform movement of the 1980s: A comprehensive analysis. In J. Murphy (Ed.), *The reform of American public education in the 1980s: Perspectives and cases* (pp. 3–55). Berkeley, CA: McCutchan.

Murphy, J. (1991). *Restructuring schools: Capturing and assessing the phenomena.* New York: Teachers College Press.

Murphy, J. (1992a). School effectiveness and school restructuring: Contributions to educational improvement. *School Effectiveness and School Improvement, 3*(2), 90–109.

Murphy, J. (1992b). *The landscape of leadership preparation: Reframing the education of school administrators.* Newbury Park, CA: Corwin/Sage.

Murphy, J. (1993). Restructuring: In search of a movement. In J. Murphy & P. Hallinger (Eds.), *Restructuring schooling: Learning from ongoing efforts* (pp. 1–31). Newbury Park, CA: Corwin Press.

Murphy, J. (1996). *The privatization of schooling: Problems and possibilities.* Newbury Park, CA: Corwin Press.

Murphy, J. (forthcoming). New consumerism: The emergence of market-oriented governance structures for schools. In J. Murphy & K. S. Louis (Eds.). *The handbook of research on educational administration.* San Francisco: Jossey-Bass.

Murphy, J., & Beck, L. G. (1995). *School-based management as school reform: Taking stock.* Newbury Park, CA: Corwin.

Murphy, J., & Hallinger, P. (1989, March-April). Equity as access to learning: Curricular and instructional treatment differences. *Journal of Curriculum Studies, 21*(2), 129–149.

Murphy, J., & Hallinger, P. (1993). Restructuring schooling: Learning from ongoing efforts. In J. Murphy & P. Hallinger (Eds.), *Restructuring schooling: Learning from ongoing efforts* (pp. 251–271). Newbury Park, CA: Corwin Press.

Musgrave, R. A., & Musgrave, P. B. (1976). *Public finance in theory and practice* (2nd ed.). New York: McGraw-Hill.

Nankani, L. T. (1988). *Techniques of privatization of state-owned enterprises: Vol. 2. Selected country case studies.* Washington, DC: The World Bank.

Natale, J. A. (1990). The drive for deregulation gathers steam. *The Executive Educator, 12*(1), 27.

National Association of Partners in Education. (1997, January). *How many school/business partnerships are there in the United States?* (Available from the National Association of Partners in Education, Inc., 901 North Pitt Street, Suite 320, Alexandria, VA 22314–1536).

National Commission on Excellence in Education. (1983). *A nation at risk: The imperative of educational reform.* Washington, DC: U.S. Government Printing Office.

National Governors' Association. (1986). *Time for results: The governors' 1991 report on education.* Washington, DC: Author.

National Governors' Association. (1990). *State actions to restructure schools: First steps.* Washington, DC: Author.

National School Boards Association. (1995). *Private options for public schools: Ways public schools are exploring privatization.* Alexandria, VA: Author.

Nelson, J. L., Palonsky, S. B., & Carlson, K. (1990). *Critical issues in education.* New York: McGraw-Hill.

Newark taps Sylvan. (1996). *Education Week, 15*(21), 4.

Nichols, W. B. (1961). Foreword. In T. M. Jamer (Ed.), *School volunteers* (pp. ix-xi). New York: Public Education Association.

Niskanen, W. A. (1971). *Bureaucracy and representative government.* Chicago: Aldine-Atherton.

Niskanen, W. A. (1994). *Bureaucracy and public economics.* Brookfield, VT: Edward Elgar Publishing.

Oates, W. E. (1972). *Fiscal federalism.* New York: Harcourt Brace Jovanovich.

O'Connell, C. (1985). *How to start a school/business partnership.* Bloomington, IN: Phi Delta Kappa Educational Foundation.

Ohio Education 2000 Commission. (1989). Game plan for national championship for Ohio's public schools: A report to Governor Richard F. Celeste. Columbus: Ohio State Office of the Governor. (ERIC Document Reproduction Service No. ED 315 875).

Okun, M. A. (1994). The relation between motives for organizational volunteering and frequency of volunteering by elders. *The Journal of Applied Gerontology, 13*(2), 115–126.

Olson, L. (1992). A matter of choice: Minnesota puts "charter schools" idea to test. *Education Week*, *12*(12), 1, 10–11.

Olson, L. (1994). N.S.B.A. endorses alternatives to traditional school governance. *Education Week*, *13*(29), 3.

Olson, L. (1996). New studies on private choice fan the flames. *Education Week*, *16*(1), 1, 20–21.

Olson, L. (1997). Math gains noted for students in voucher program. *Education Week*, *16*(21), 5.

Oregon Department of Education (1988). *Home school data report, March 1 (1988)*. Salem, OR: Author.

Pack, J. R. (1991). The opportunities and constraints of privatization. In W. T. Gormley (Ed.), *Privatization and its alternatives* (pp. 281–306). Madison: The University of Wisconsin Press.

Paine, T. (1791/1945). The rights of man. In P. S. Foner (Ed.). *The complete writings of Thomas Paine*. New York: The Citadel Press.

Pauly, E., Kopp, H., & Haimson, J. (1994). *Home-grown lessons: Innovative programs linking work and high school*. New York: Manpower Demonstration Research Corporation.

Payne, J. L. (1995). *Profiting from education: Incentive issues in contracting out*. Washington, DC: Education Policy Institute.

Peirce, W. S. (1981). *Bureaucratic failure and public expenditure*. New York: Academic Press.

Peters, T. (1991). Public services and the private sector. In R. L. Kemp (Ed.), *Privatization: The provision of public services by the private sector* (pp. 53–59). Jefferson, NC: McFarland.

Peterson, L. J., Rossmiller, R. A., & Volz, M. M. (1978). *The law and public school operation* (2nd ed.). New York: Harper & Row.

Phares, D. (1981). The fiscal status of the state-local sector: A look to the 1980s. In N. Walzer and D. L. Chicoine (Eds.), *Financing state and local governments in the 1980s: Issues and trends* (pp. 145–173). Cambridge, MA: Oelgeschlager, Gunn & Hain.

Pierce v. Society of Sisters, 268 U.S. 510 (1925).

Pines, B. Y. (1985). The conservative agenda. In S. M. Butler (Ed.), *The privatization option: A strategy to shrink the size of government* (p. v). Washington, DC: The Heritage Foundation.

Pirie, M. (1985). The British experience. In S. M. Butler (Ed.), *The privatization option: A strategy to shrink the size of government* (pp. 51–68). Washington, DC: The Heritage Foundation.

Pirie, M. (1988). *Privatization*. Hants, England: Wildwood House.

Pitsch, M. (1995). House Republicans unveil bill to ax E. D., create block grants. *Education Week*, *14*(36), 25.

Pitsch, M. (1996). Clinton position on private vouchers debate. *Education Week*, *16*(7), 19.

Plyer v. Doe, 457 U.S. 202 (1982).

Ponessa, J. (1996). Wilkinsburg should rehire teachers, arbitrator says. *Education Week*, *15*(18). p. 5.

Poole, R. (1985). The politics of privatization. In S. M. Butler (Ed.), *The privatization option: A strategy to shrink the size of government* (pp. 33–50). Washington, DC: The Heritage Foundation.

Potter, L. (1995). *How to improve teacher morale: Create a duty-free school*. Reston, VA: National Association of Secondary School Principals. (ERIC Document Reproduction Service No. ED 380 911).

Powell, B. (1986). Volunteers in the schools: A positive approach to schooling. *NASSP Bulletin, 70*(494), 32–34.

President's Commission on Privatization. (1988). *Privatization: Toward more effective government.* Washington, DC: U.S. Government.

Pulliam, J. D. (1991). *History of education in America.* New York: Macmillan.

Rakestraw, J. F. (1988). Home schooling in Alabama. *Home School Researcher, 4*(4), 1–6.

Ramsey, J. B. (1987). Selling the New York City subway: Wild-eyed radicalism or the only feasible solution. In S. H. Hanke (Ed.), *Prospects for privatization. Proceedings of the Academy of Political Science,* (Vol. 36, No. 3, pp. 93–103). Montpelier, VT: Capital City Press.

Ravitch, D. (1983). *The troubled crusade: American education 1945–1980.* New York: Basic Books.

Ravitch, D. (1985). *The schools we deserve: Reflections on the educational crises of our times.* New York: Basic Books.

Ray, B. D. (1986). *A comparison of home schooling and conventional schooling: With a focus on learner outcomes.* Corvallis, OR: Oregon State University, Science, Math, and Computer Science Education Department. (ERIC Document Reproduction Service No. ED 278 489).

Ray, B. D. (1990). *A nationwide study of home education: Family characteristics, legal matters, and student achievement.* (Available from the Home Education Research Institute, 5000 Deer Park Drive SE, Salem, OR 97301).

Ray, B. D. (1994). *1994 Iowa test of basic skills analysis.* Paeonian Springs, VA: National Center for Home Education.

Ray, B. D., & Wartes, J. (1991). The academic achievement and effective development of home schooled children. In J. Van Galen & M. A. Pittman (Eds.), *Home schooling: Political, historical, and pedagogical perspectives.* Norwood, NJ: Ablex.

Raywid, M. A. (1992). Choice orientations, discussions, and prospects. In P. W. Cookson, Jr. (Ed.), *The choice controversy* (pp. 3–23). Newbury Park, CA: Corwin Press.

Renner, T. (1989, November/December). Trends and issues in the use of intergovernmental agreements and privatization in local government. *Baseline Data Report, 21*(6). Washington, DC: International City Management Association.

Reynolds, P. L. (1985). *How home school families operate in a day-to-day basis: Three case studies.* Unpublished doctoral dissertation, Brigham Young University, Salt Lake City, Utah.

Richards, C. E., Shore, R., & Sawicky, M. B. (1996). *Risky business: Private management of public schools.* Washington, DC: Economic Policy Institute.

Richardson, J. (1993a). For-profit firm to run district in Minneapolis. *Education Week, 13*(10), 1, 14.

Richardson, J. (1993b). Private firm prompts suit in Baltimore. *Education Week, 13*(15), 1, 13.

Richardson, J. (1994). Superintendent for hire. *Education Week, 13*(20), 31–33.

Richardson, J. (1995). Minn. abolishes education department. Merges state services in new agency. *Education Week, 14*(37), 11.

Richardson, M. D., et al. (1993, March). *School deregulation: A second look at South Carolina.* A paper presented at the Annual Conference on Creating the Quality School, Oklahoma City, OK. (ERIC Document Reproduction Service No. ED 358 542).

Riemer, J. (1994, September). Perspectives from a home schooling educator. *Educational Leadership, 52*(1), 53–54.

Riley, K. (1996). *Changes in local governance–collaboration through networks: Post-16 a case study.* Unpublished manuscript, Rochampton Institute London, Centre for Educational Management, London, England.

Rippa, S. A. (1992). *Education in a free society: An American history* (7th ed.). New York: Longman.

Robertson, B. (1994, October). Is home schooling in a class of its own? *Insight Magazine,* 6–9.

Roehm, H. A., Castellano, J.F., & Karns, D. A. (1991). In R. L. Kemp (Ed.), *Privatization: The provision of public services by the private sector* (pp. 276–288). Jefferson, NC: McFarland.

Rogers, D. (1973). Foreword. In J. M. Cronin, *The control of urban schools: Perspectives on the power of educational reformers* (pp. xiii-xx). New York: The Free Press.

Rose, R. (1984). *Understanding big government: The programme approach.* London: Sage.

Ross, R. L. (1988). *Government and the private sector: Who should do what?* New York: Crane Russak.

Rossiter, C. (1956). *The first American revolution.* New York: Harcourt Brace & World.

Roth, G. (1987). Airport privatization. In S. H. Hanke (Ed.), *Prospects for privatization. Proceedings of the Academy of Political Science, 36*(3), 74–82. Montpelier, VT: Capital City Press.

Rowicki, M. A., & Martin, W. C. (1994). Fighting violence without violence. (ERIC Document Reproduction Service No. Ed 385 388).

Rubenstein, M. C., & Adelman, N. E. (1994). Public choice in Minnesota. In S. Hakim, P. Seidenstat, & G. W. Bowman (Eds.), *Privatizing education and educational choice: Concepts, plans, and experiences* (pp. 217–229). Westport, CT: Praeger.

Russo, C. J., Sandidge, R. F., Shapiro, R., & Harris, J. J. (1995). Legal issues in contracting out for public education services. *Education and Urban Review, 27*(2), 127–135.

Sanchez, R. (1995, October 29). School-privatization experiment getting bad grades. *Salt Lake City Tribune,* p. A15.

Savas, E. S. (1982). *Privatizing the public sector: How to shrink government.* Chatham, NJ: Chatham House.

Savas, E. S. (1985). The efficiency of the private sector. In S. M. Butler (Ed.), *The privatization option: A strategy to shrink the size of government* (pp. 15–31). Washington, DC: The Heritage Foundation.

Savas, E. S. (1987). *Privatization: The key to better government.* Chatham, NJ: Chatham House.

Schemmer, B. A. S. (1985). *Case studies of four families engaged in home education.* Unpublished doctoral dissertation, Ball State University, Muncie, Indiana.

Schlechty, P. C. (1990). *Schools for the 21st century: Leadership imperatives for educational reform.* San Francisco: Jossey-Bass.

Schmidt, B. C. (1994). The Edison project's plan to redefine public education. *Educational Leadership, 52*(1), 61–64.

Schmidt, P. (1992a). Employees protest firm's tactics at Baltimore schools. *Education Week, 12*(2), 1, 19.

Schmidt, P. (1992b). Management firm finds schools a tough sell. *Education Week, 12*(6), 1, 13–14.

Schmidt, P. (1994a). Mayor seeks deep cuts in N.Y.C. bureaucracy. *Education Week, 13*(21), 3.

Schmidt, P. (1994b). Baltimore's Amprey backs off plan to increase E.A.I. role. *Education Week, 13*(34), 14.

Schmidt, P. (1994c). Private enterprise. *Education Week, 13*(35), 27–30.

Schmidt, P. (1994d). Hartford hires E.A.I. to run entire district. *Education Week, 14*(6), 1, 14.

Schmidt, P. (1995a). Baltimore mayor seeks changes in E.A.I. contract. *Education Week, 14*(27), 3.

Schmidt, P. (1995b). Attacks mount against E.A.I.'s Hartford plans. *Education Week, 14*(35), 1, 10–11.

Schmidt, P. (1995c). L.A. breakup plans gather head of steam. *Education Week, 15*(8), 1, 20–21.

Schmidt. P. (1995d). EAI school contract pits candidates in Hartford races. *Education Week, 15*(9), 6.

Schmidt, P., & Lindsay, D. (1995). Privatization backers prevail in Hartford. *Education Week, 15*(11), 1, 15.

Schneider, B., Schiller, K. S., & Coleman, J. S. (1996, Spring). Some evidence from the National Education Longitudinal Study of 1988. *Educational Evaluation and Policy Analysis, 18*(1), 19–30.

Schreter, C. (1991). Older volunteers. *American School Board Journal, 178*(2), 35–36.

Scully, L. J., & Cole, L.A. (1991). Making the decision. In R. L. Kemp (Ed.), *Privatization: The provision of public services by the private sector* (pp. 110–121). Jefferson, NC: McFarland.

Seader, D. (1991). Privatization and America's cities. In R. L. Kemp (Ed.), *Privatization: The provision of public services by the private sector* (pp. 29–38). Jefferson, NC: McFarland.

The secret behind donated supplies. (1995, February/March). *The NAEIR Advantage, 6*(31), cover page.

Seeger v. United States, 380 U.S. 163 (1965).

Seldon, A. (1987). Public choice and the choices of the public. In C. K. Rowley (Ed.), *Democracy and public choice* (pp. 122–134). New York: Columbia University Press.

Serving difficult-to-educate students. (1996). *The Education Industry Report, 4*(9), 1–2.

Sewall, G. T. (1990). Volunteers are no cure-all, but they can nourish schools. *Education Week, 10*(14), 22.

Shanker, A. (1994). There is no free lunch. *Network News & Views, 13*(9), 58–59.

Shanker, A., & Rosenberg, B. (1992). Do private schools outperform public schools? In P. W. Cookson, Jr. (Ed.), *The choice controversy* (pp. 128–145). Newbury Park, CA: Corwin Press.

Shannon, J. (1981). The slowdown in the growth of state-local spending: Will it last? In N. Walzer & D. L. Chicoine (Eds.), *Financing state and local governments in the 1980s: Issues and trends* (pp. 223–245). Cambridge, MA: Delgeschlager, Gunn, & Hain.

Shannon, T. A. (1995). Privatization: An even-handed and informed approach needed. *Network News and Views, 14*(4), 75–76. (Reprinted from *School Board News*).

Shepherd, M. S. (1986). The home schooling movement: An emerging conflict in American education (Doctoral dissertation, East Texas State University). *Dissertation Abstracts International, 47*(4), 1216A.

Sherbert v. Verner, 374 U.S. 398 (1963).

Sheridan Road Baptist Church v. Department of Education, 396 N.W.2d 373 (1986).

Showdown in Wilkinsburg. (1995, August 29). *The Wall Street Journal* (unnumbered reprint).

Shyers, L. E. (1992). *The socialization of homeschool children: A communication approach.* Unpublished master's thesis, Radford University, Radford, VA.

Smedley, T. C. (1992). *The socialization of homeschool children: A communication approach.* Unpublished master's thesis, Radford University, Radford, VA.

Smith, A. (1776/1976). *An inquiry into the nature and causes of the wealth of nations.* In R. H. Campbell & A. S. Skinner (General Eds.) and W. B. Todd (Textual Ed.), *Adam Smith: An inquiry into the nature and causes of the wealth of nations.* Oxford, England: Clarendon Press.

Smith, F. L. (1987). Privatization at the federal level. In S. H. Hanke (Ed.), *Prospects for privatization. Proceedings of the Academy of Political Science* (Vol. 36, No. 3, pp. 179–189). Montpelier, VT: Capital City Press.

Smith, K. B., & Meier, K. J. (1995, December). School choice: Panacea or Pandora's Box? *Phi Delta Kappan, 77*(4), 312–316.

Sobis network to manage public school. (1995, June). *School Board News.* [National School Boards Association newsletter]

Sommerfeld, M. (1992). Survey charts rise in health problems among pupils. *Education Week, 12*(3), 8.

South Carolina State Department of Education. (1987). *State resource guide for school volunteer coordinators.* Columbia, SC: Author. (ERIC Document Reproduction Service No. ED 291 497).

Spring, J. (1982). The evolving political structure of American schooling. In R. B. Everhart (Ed.), *The public school monopoly: A critical analysis of education and the state in American society* (pp. 77–108). Cambridge, MA: Ballinger.

Starr, P. (1987). The limits of privatization. In S. H. Hanke (Ed.), *Prospects for privatization. Proceedings of the Academy of Political Science, 36*(3), 124–137.

Starr, P. (1991). The case for skepticism. In W. T. Gormley (Ed.), *Privatization and its alternatives* (pp. 25–36). Madison: The University of Wisconsin Press.

Stecklow, S. (1994). Fed up with schools, more parents turn to teaching at home. *Network News and Views, 13*(6), 32–33.

Stephens, R. D. (1996). The art of safe school planning. *The School Administrator, 53*(2), 14–20.

Stigler, G. J. (1971). The theory of economic regulation. *The Bell Journal of Economics and Management Science, 2*(1), 3–21.

Stiglitz, J. E. (1986). *Economics of the public sector* (2nd ed.). New York: W. W. Norton & Co.

Strom, R. D. & Strom, S. K. (1994). Grandparent volunteers in the school: Building a partnership. *Journal of Instructional Psychology, 21*(4), 329–339.

Swanson, A. D. (1989). Restructuring educational governance: A challenge of the 1990s. *Educational Administration Quarterly, 25*(3), 268–293.

Tanner, M. C., & Moe, M. T. (1996). *Lehman Brothers First Annual Education Industry Conference* [Brochure].

Taranto, S. E., & Johnson, S. O. (1984). *Educational volunteerism: A new look.* Springfield, IL: Charles C. Thomas.

Tax Foundation. (1993). *Facts and figures on government finance: 1993 edition.* Washington, DC: Author.

Taylor, J. W. (1986). *Self-concept in home schooling children.* Unpublished doctoral dissertation, Andrew University, Berrien Springs, MI.

Tennessee Code Annotated, § 49–6–3050.a.2.

Thayer, F. C. (1987). Privatization: Carnage, chaos, and corruption. In B. J. Carroll, R. W. Conant, & T. A. Easton (Eds.), *Private means, public ends: Private business in social service delivery* (pp. 146–170). New York: Praeger.

Thomas v. Review Board, 450 U.S. 707 (1981).

Thomas, W. B., Moran, K. J., & Resnick, J. (n.d.). *Intentional transformation in a small school district.* Unpublished manuscript, University of Pittsburgh.

Thomas, W. C. (1996, August 23). County privatizes hiring of substitute teachers. *The Tennessean*, B1–2.

Thompson, F. (1989). Privatization at the state and local level: Comment. In P. W. MacAvoy, W. T. Stanbury, G. Yarrow, & R. J. Zeckhauser (Eds.), *Privatization and state-owned enterprises* (pp. 202–207). Boston: Kluwer.

Thorne, G. F. (1983). Follow these policy guidelines to control school sports crowds. *American School Board Journal, 170*(3), 33–34.

Tierce, J. W., & Seelbach, W. C. (1987). Elders as school volunteers: An untapped resource. *Educational Gerontology, 13*(1), 33–41.

Timar, T. B., & Kirp, D. L. (1988). State efforts to reform schools: Treading between a regulatory swamp and an English garden. *Educational Evaluation and Policy Analysis, 10*(2), 75–88.

Tomlinson, J. (1986). Public education, public good. *Oxford Review of Education, 12*(3), 211–222.

Trachtman, R. (1988a). A focus on funding. In M. Levine & R. Trachtman (Eds.) *American business and the public school: Case studies of corporate involvement in public education* (pp. 155–174). New York: Columbia University, Teachers College.

Trachtman, R. (1988b). The policy arena. In M. Levine & R. Trachtman (Eds.) *American business and the public school: Case studies of corporate involvement in public education* (pp. 207–225). New York: Columbia University, Teachers College.

Trachtman, R. (1988c). Programmatic participation. In M. Levine & R. Trachtman (Eds.) *American business and the public school: Case studies of corporate involvement in public education* (pp. 175–206). New York: Columbia University, Teachers College.

Trotter, A. (1996, October 9). As states sign on, NetDay movement spreads. *Education Week, 16*(6), p. 5.

Tullock, G. (1965). *The politics of bureaucracy.* Washington, DC: Public Affairs Press.

Tullock, G. (1988). *Wealth, poverty, and politics.* New York: Basil Blackwell.

Tullock, G. (1994a). Public choice: The new science of politics. In G. L. Brady & R. D. Tollison (Eds.), *On the trail of homo economicus* (pp. 87–100). Fairfax, VA: George Mason Press.

Tullock, G. (1994b). Social cost and government policy. In G. L. Brady & R. D. Tollison (Eds.), *On the trail of homo economicus* (pp. 65–85). Fairfax, VA: George Mason Press.

Twentieth Century Fund. (1983). *Making the grade.* New York: Author.

Tyack, D. B. (1967). *Turning points in American educational history.* Waltham, MA: Blaisdell.

Tyack, D. B. (1974). *The one best system: A history of American urban education.* Cambridge, MA: Harvard University Press.

Tyack, D. B. (1986). Toward a social history of law and public education. In D. L. Kirp & D. N. Jensen (Eds.), *School days, rule days: The legalization and regulation of education* (pp. 212–237). Philadelphia: The Falmer Press.

Tyack, D. B. (1990). The public schools: A monopoly or a contested public domain. In W. H. Clune & J. F. Witte (Eds.), *Choice and control in American education: Vol. 1. The theory of choice and control in education* (pp. 86–90). New York: The Falmer Press.

Tyack, D. (1993). School governance in the United States: Historical puzzles and anomalies. In J. Hannaway & M. Carnoy (Eds.), *Decentralization and school improvement* (pp. 1–32). San Francisco: Jossey-Bass.

Tyack, D., & Cuban, L. (1995). *Tinkering toward utopia: A century of public school reform*. Cambridge, MA: Harvard University Press.

Tyack, D., James, T., & Benavot, A. (1987). *Law and the shaping of public education, 1785–1954*. Madison: The University of Wisconsin Press.

United States v. Lee, 445 U.S. 252 (1982).

Urschel, J. (1995, May 16). Fear, distrust, suspicion of the government. *USA Today*, pp. 1–2.

U.S. Department of Education. (1997, March 19). *President announces education as "number one priority," issues 10–point education plan in State of the Union* [Online]. Available: http://www.ed.gov/edplan.html [1997, May 7].

Utah State Office of Education. (1988). *Master plan for implementing a statewide volunteer system*. Salt Lake City: Author. (ERIC Document Reproduction Service No. ED 321 408).

Van Horn, C. E. (1991). The myths and realities of privatization. In W. T. Gormley (Ed.), *Privatization and its alternatives* (pp. 261–280). Madison: The University of Wisconsin Press.

Vermont Statutes Annotated, Title 16 § 166b.j.

Viadero, D. (1993). Majority of education workforce found to be non-teachers. *Education Week, 13*(14), 3.

Vickers, J., & Yarrow, G. (1988). *Privatization: An economic analysis*. Cambridge, MA: MIT Press.

Virginia Code, 22.1–257.A.2.

Voylsteke, C. (1988). *Techniques of privatization of state-owned enterprises: Vol. 1. Methods and implementation*. Washington, DC: The World Bank.

Wagstaff, L. H., & Gallagher, K. S. (1990). Schools, families, and communities: Idealized images and new realities. In B. Mitchell & L. L. Cunningham (Eds.), *Educational leadership and changing contexts of families, communities, and schools* (pp. 91–117). Chicago: University of Chicago Press.

Walsh, M. (1992) Yale President's move is touted as a 'coup' for the Edison Project. *Education Week, 11*(37), 1.18.

Walsh, M. (1993a). Behind closed doors, Edison Project tackles design task. *Education Week, 12*(18), 1, 28, 30–31.

Walsh, M. (1993b). Scaled-back Edison plan focuses on managing schools. *Education Week, 13*(1), 8.

Walsh, M. (1993c). Slow pace of school reform worries business leaders. *Education Week, 13*(6), 8.

Walsh, M. (1993d). Mass. officials endorse idea of Whittle-run schools. *Education Week, 13*(7), 16.

Walsh, M. (1994a). Details of Edison blueprint emerge in Mass. designs. *Education Week, 13*(23), 1, 13.

Walsh, M. (1994b). Beginning in 1995, Edison Project to manage two schools in Wichita. *Education Week, 13*(34), 9.

Walsh, M. (1994c). Even as Whittle falls on hard times, Edison model leaves Wichita hopeful. *Education Week, 14*(11), 1, 12.

Walsh, M. (1995a). Edison Project announces $30 million in investments. *Education Week, 14*(26), 6.

Walsh, M. (1995b). International group to take over Mass. school this fall. *Education Week*, *14*(37), 3.

Walsh, M. (1995c). The lights come up on first four Edison Project schools. *Education Week*, *15*(6), 14–15.

Walsh, M. (1995d). Despite election win, EAI's business picture is still far from clear. *Education Week*, *15*(11), 14.

Walsh, M. (1995e). Baltimore to terminate EAI schools contract. *Education Week*, *15*(13), 1, 12.

Walsh, M. (1995f). Sylvan makes quiet inroads into public schools. *Education Week*, *15*(13), 3, 12.

Walsh, M. (1995g). Baltimore vote ends city's contract with EAI. *Education Week*, *15*(14), 6.

Walsh, M. (1996a). Hartford outs EAI in dispute over finances. *Education Week*, *15*(19), 1, 9.

Walsh, M. (1996b). Brokers pitch education as hot investment. *Education Week*, *15*(22), 1, 15.

Walsh, M. (1996c). EAI gets contract to develop N.Y. district budget. *Education Week*, *15*(22), 14.

Walsh, M. (1996d). Edison posts high marks in inaugural year. *Education Week*, *15*(36), 1, 10–11.

Walsh, M. (1996e). Court clears Cleveland's voucher pilot: Law dodges first church-state test. *Education Week*, *15*(41), 1, 20.

Walsh, M. (1996f). For the first time, students use vouchers for religious schools. *Education Week*, *16*(1), 18.

Walsh, N. J. (1995). Public Schools, Inc.: Baltimore's risky enterprise. *Education and Urban Society*, *27*(2), 195–205.

Walters, A. A. (1987). Ownership and efficiency in urban buses. In S. H. Hanke (Ed.), *Prospects for privatization. Proceedings of the Academy of Political Science* (Vol. 36, No. 3, pp. 83–92). Montpelier, VT: Capital City Press.

Warren, D. (1990). Passage of rites: On the history of educational reform in the United States. In J. Murphy (Ed.). *The educational reform movement of the 1980s* (pp. 57–81). Berkeley, CA: McCutchan.

Wartes, J. (1987). *Report from the 1986 homeschool testing and other descriptive information about Washington's homeschoolers.* (Available from Washington Homeschool Research Project, 16109 NE 169PL, Woodinville, WA. 98702).

Wartes, J. (1988, April). *Homeschooler outcomes.* Paper presented at the annual meeting of the American Educational Research Association, New Orleans, LA.

Wartes, J. (1989). *Report from the 1988 Washington homeschool testing.* (Available from the Washington Homeschool Research Project, 16109 NE 169 PL., Woodinville, WA. 98702).

Wartes, J. (1990). *Report from the 1986 through 1989 Washington homeschool testing.* (Available from the Washington Homeschool Research Project, 16109 NE 169 PL., Woodinville, WA. 98702).

Washington Governor's Council on Educational Reform. (1992). *Putting children first: Improving student performance in Washington State.* Olympia: Author. (ERIC Document Reproduction Service No. ED 362 988).

Weise, R., & Murphy, J. (1995). SBM in historical perspective, 1900–1950. In J. Murphy & L. G. Beck, *School-based management as school reform: Taking stock.* Thousand Oaks, CA: Corwin Press.

Welch, S. (1991). *Home school questions and answers* (Rev.) [Pamphlet]. Portland, OR: Teaching Home Magazine.

Wenger, D. A. (1994). The idea of private practice. In D. A. Wenger (Ed.), *Enterprising educators as school partners: A manual for educator entrepreneurs and school officials.* Watertown, WI: American Association of Educators in Private Practice.

West, P. (1996). Thousands turn out to wire Calif. schools for the internet. *Education Week, 15*(36), 8–9.

Weston, M. (1996). Reformers should take a look at home schools. *Education Week, 15*(28), 34.

Whitehead, J. W., & Crow, A. I. (1993). *Home education: Rights and reasons.* Wheaton, IL: Crossway.

Whitty, G. (1984). The "privatization of education." *Educational Leadership, 41*(7), 51–54.

Wichita State University. (1996). *An independent program evaluation for the Dodge-Edison Partnership School: First year interim report* (Prepared for Wichita United School District #259). Wichita, KS: Author.

Wildavsky, A. (1985). Equality, spending limits, and the growth of government. In C. L. Harriss (Ed.), *Control of federal spending. Proceeding of the Academy of Political Science* (Vol. 35, No. 4, pp. 59–71). Montpelier, VT: Capital City Press.

Williams, L. C., & Leak, L. F. (1995). *The UMBC evaluation of the Tesseract program in Baltimore City.* Baltimore: University of Maryland - Baltimore County, Center for Educational Research.

Williams, S., & Buechler, M. (1993). Charter schools. In *Policy Bulletin* (PB-B16). (ERIC Document Reproduction Service No. ED 356 540).

Wilson, L. A. (1990). Rescuing politics from the economists: Privatizing the public sector. In R. C. Hula (Ed.), *Market-based public policy* (pp. 59–68). New York: St. Martin's Press.

Wisconsin v. Yoder, 406 U.S. 205 (1972).

Wise, A. E. (1978, February). The hyper-rationalization of American education. *Educational Leadership, 35*(5), 354–361.

Wise, A. E. (1979). *Legislated learning: The bureaucratization of the American classroom.* Berkeley: University of California Press.

Wise, A. E. (1989). Professional teaching: A new paradigm for the management of education. In T. J. Sergiovanni & J. H. Moore (Eds.), *Schooling for tomorrow: Directing reforms to issues that count* (pp. 301–310). Boston: Allyn & Bacon.

Witte, J. F. (1990a). Introduction. In W. H. Clune & J. F. Witte (Eds.), *Choice and control in American education: Vol. 1. The theory of choice and control in education* (pp. 1–10). New York: The Falmer Press.

Witte, J. F. (1990b). Choice and control: An analytic overview. In W. H. Clune & J. F. Witte (Eds.), *Choice and control in American education: Vol. 1. The theory of choice and control in education* (pp. 11–46). New York: The Falmer Press.

Witte, J. F. (1993). The Milwaukee Parental Choice Program. In E. Rasell & R. Rothstein (Eds.), *School choice* (pp. 69–110). Washington, DC: Economic Policy Institute.

Witte, J. F. (1997). *Achievement effects of the Milwaukee voucher program* (Paper presented at the annual meeting of the American Economics Association, New Orleans, LA) [Online]. Available: http://dpls.dacc.wisc.edu./choice/aera97.html [1997, June 10].

Witte, J. F., Sterr, T. D., & Thorn, C. A. (1995). *Fifth-year report: Milwaukee parental choice program.* Madison: University of Wisconsin-Madison, Department of Political Science and The Robert La Follette Institute of Public Affairs.

Witte, J. F., Thorn, C. A., & Pritchard, K. A. (1995). *LaFollette issues: Private and public education in Wisconsin: Implications for the choice debate* [Online]. Available: http://dpls.dacc.wisc.edu/choice/choice_implications.html [1997, June 10].

Worsnop, R. L. (1992, November). Privatization. *Congressional Quarterly Researcher, 2*(42), 977–1000.

Wright, L. B. (1957). *The cultural life of the American colonies.* New York: Harper & Row.

Yelich, C. (1994). A private practice option for teachers? The time has come! In D. A. Wenger (Ed.), *Enterprising educators as school partners: A manual for educator entrepreneurs and school officials.* Watertown, WI: American Association of Educators for Private Practice.

Yelich, C. (n.d.). *EDVentures '96 Conference: Teacher entrepreneurs* [News release].

Young, T. W., & Clinchy, E. (1992). *Choice in public education.* New York: Teachers College Press.

Zlatos, B. (1995, September). Pros, cons of privatization have one school system astir. *The Tennessean.*

Author Index